MW00975051

Sherlock Holmes
Reports from the Dark Side

Tom Cavenagh

iUniverse, Inc.
New York   Bloomington

Copyright © 2009 by Tom Cavenagh

All rights reserved. No part of this book may be used
or reproduced by any means, graphic, electronic, or
mechanical, including photocopying, recording, taping or
by any information storage retrieval system without the
written permission of the publisher except in the case of brief
quotations embodied in critical articles and reviews.
This is a work of fiction. All of the characters, names, incidents,
organizations, and dialogue in this novel are either the products
of the author's imagination or are used fictitiously.

iUniverse books may be ordered through booksellers or by contacting:

iUniverse
1663 Liberty Drive
Bloomington, IN 47403
www.iuniverse.com
1-800-Authors (1-800-288-4677)

Because of the dynamic nature of the Internet, any Web addresses or
links contained in this book may have changed since publication and
may no longer be valid. The views expressed in this work are solely those
of the author and do not necessarily reflect the views of the publisher,
and the publisher hereby disclaims any responsibility for them.

ISBN: 978-1-4401-2045-9 (sc)
ISBN: 978-1-4401-2046-6 (ebook)

Printed in the United States of America

iUniverse rev. date: 02/02/2009

CHAPTER 1

AS Holmes and I savored the last two cups of tea to be coaxed from Mrs. Hudson's teapot, including the squeezing of the bags to ensure that not a drop was lost, our landlady knocked and entered. So engrossed was I in my newspaper, that I didn't even look up, assuming that she was here to collect the breakfast trays and tidy up a bit around us.

"Yes, Mrs. Hudson," Holmes said, having noticed that she sought our attention, rather than our crockery.

"Excuse me gentlemen, but a Mister Nevin Wainwright from the Strand Magazine is here asking to be shown in immediately."

"Ah, Wainwright, of course," I said, jumping to my feet, "please bring him up immediately."

"Yes Doctor, but he is not here to see you, sir. He specifically said that he must see Mister Holmes immediately."

"Holmes? What the devil for?" Turning to my associate, I asked, "Holmes, have you ever met Wainwright?"

"No," came the simple reply.

"I wonder what he wants with you," I mused.

Holmes laid his paper aside and reproached me, I have concluded in retrospect, by saying, "Watson, you know it is not my way to conjecture on anything when there is factual data to be collected. Conjecture is on facts. We will know in a few minutes what Mister Wainwright wants."

"Yes...umph...of course."

With that Holmes nodded to Mrs. Hudson, who scurried down the stairs to fetch Wainwright. I knew with certainty that this unusual visit by the Strand's Managing Director was his first to our rooms in tidy little Baker Street, which I had recently learned was named after a Mister William Baker, who had planned out the road over a century ago, about 1755, but I digress. What the devil could Wainwright want with Holmes?

As we shook hands with our guest, one could not miss the look on his face. It was not the dread or fear that has marred numerous countenances entering these chambers, but confusion or consternation.

Wainwright is a tall, wiry man, with grayish, barely controllable hair. He often gives the appearance of being edgy and hurried

"Doctor Watson," he began, "*The Adventure of the Engineer's Thumb* has been extremely well received by our readership. I commend your journalism once again." The words seemed not the least insincere, but merely perfunctory and most certainly prefatory. He quickly got to the point of his visit before I could even offer a word of thanks for his kind words.

"But," he said, turning to my associate, "I am here to see Mister Holmes today, to discuss a startling development in our office."

Holmes nodded interest, but did not speak, motioning for Wainwright to be seated and present an explanation for his visit.

"Mister Holmes, if Doctor Watson has never mentioned my name, I'll take a moment and identify myself. I am with the Strand Magazine, Managing Director and Director of the Editorial Department. As such, I am in charge of reviewing and accepting or rejecting articles or stories that are submitted for publication. In other words, I more or less decide what goes into the edition that we publish."

Wainwright smiled rather sheepishly. "I must credit you and the doctor for my good reputation as an editor. In the issues when we have one of your adventures to publish, we sell every copy we print. In fact, we receive letters urging you, Doctor, to be a bit more prolific so that we could have one in every issue."

He continued to smile, but seemed ever more uncomfortable, wanting to get the preliminaries out of the way, so as to unburden himself of the worrisome message that he bore.

"Mister Holmes, I am here today because I received the most remarkable letter in today's post. It came by courier and was marked 'To Be Delivered only to Mr. Nevin Wainwright.' My interest was piqued, of course, but I was a bit annoyed to find that the envelope contained a story that the sender wanted to submit for publication, along with a letter of transmittal.

"My first reaction was, uncharitably, I suppose, to assume that the writer had attempted to circumvent our screening process by sending it directly to me and making it look like a more important document. I was tempted not to read it out of spite. We do have well-published procedures, you know. But I noticed that the letter was from Scotland, Aberdeen, actually, and thought that he may not have known our rules. Therefore, I thought I would accord him the benefit of any doubt, and decided to at least read the letter.

"Frankly, sir, I was shocked by the letter and didn't really know what to make of it. Before I proceed further, I would entreat you, sir, to read this letter. I promise you that I am not here to waste your time or mine."

"Of course you're not, Mister Wainwright. I will be happy to read the letter. Frankly, my own curiosity is piqued by a letter that could drive you out of your office and into our rooms on such short notice."

For my benefit, I'm sure, Holmes read the letter aloud.

"My Dear Wainwright,
  I have been reading the Strand Magazine for several years now and have become appalled by the one-sidedness of your reporting. You continue to publish claptrap by Doctor John Watson and others lauding the abilities of men like Sherlock Holmes and some of those French detectives as though they were the only ones working in

the field of crime and accomplishing their objectives.

I'm sure that many of the stories are true, but some, particularly the most bizarre of those Sherlock Holmes things, stretch credulity. I would say that they are either contrived or embellished so egregiously that they may as well have been.

But even if we concede that they are true, my point is still to be made. There are some, if not many, persons of equal or greater intelligence operating very successfully on the other side of the law, persons whose significant accomplishments are never recognized.

They plan crimes that are such works of art that the local authorities do not even know that a crime has been committed, much less have any ability whatsoever to solve them. I myself have planned and executed several such crimes.

I submit one to you and suggest that you print it to let your readership know that, as brilliant as Sherlock Holmes may be if the stories are all true, there is nonetheless a greater intellect abroad in the land, operating on the other side of the law. If this one is published, I'll give some thought to publishing others.

With Warmest Regards,

Norma Bainsteas

"Norma Bainsteas," Holmes mumbled... "a woman"...do you know that name, Mister Wainwright?"

"I've never heard it before in my life."

"Bainsteas..." Holmes repeated, "I haven't heard it either, but it has a Scottish ring to it. The letter, of course, is from Aberdeen."

"Yes, Mister Holmes. It could well be a Scottish name, but there's more. The letter was so outrageous, purporting to be about a perfect crime, that I read the story. It's not particularly well written, but it has a rather unusual story line. Allow me to read you the opening paragraph. It's actually listed as a prologue."

Wainwright pulled spectacles from his pocket, shook the paper into place, and read.

"The murder of Carlton MacKenzie was absolutely essential to my plan. But it was also necessary that the murder never be uncovered or the body found; therefore the planning must be meticulous, the timing precise, and the disposition of the body permanent.'

"That's the opening paragraph, Mister Holmes, a frame of reference, so to speak. The writer then starts the story from the beginning, and tells it over about sixty pages. Much too long for the Strand...I'd have to run it in about four issues. But it's not too bad a story. It doesn't have the complexity, drama, or suspense of Doctor Watson's stories, but it could be published."

Holmes nodded. "I'm sure you aren't here to critique it, Mister Wainwright. What aspects of the story line are interesting?"

"Well, it turns out that this MacKenzie in the story, is the keeper of accounts for a large coal exporter in

Aberdeen. He gets himself involved in a business transaction with a rather powerful, but disreputable, character in the city of Aberdeen, and the venture flops. MacKenzie loses a fortune that he doesn't possess. Being pressed now for the money, almost ninety thousand pounds, and even threatened with a lot of publicity, possibly even violence, he comes up with this convoluted scheme to bilk his company out of the money.

"Through a series of draughts that are cashed and accumulated, he amasses the money. One day, while his wife is at the home of a relative in Braemar, MacKenzie brings home the last of the money, but comes to suspect that he couldn't really have fared that poorly in the business deal, and that he is being swindled. He confronts the man who he believes is cheating him and is brutally murdered.

"The killer takes the ninety thousand pounds, has his henchmen pack up MacKenzie's luggage and disposes of the body and the luggage. I trust it's clear so far, Mister Holmes?"

"Completely, Mister Wainwright, please continue."

"Yes, sir. Now, according to the story, the ninety thousand pounds is way too much to be permanently overlooked. The company finds that it's missing after Wainwright stops coming to work. The wife reports her husband missing, and he is now suspected of embezzling that huge sum and then decamping, leaving the company in financial peril and his wife in the lurch.

"The final paragraphs written by this Norma Bainsteas seem to portray the author of the story as the one who killed MacKenzie and ultimately wound up with the money. The police in Aberdeen, according to the story, never find MacKenzie and are still seeking him for the embezzlement of the funds. Since the author is never involved with the police, she claims that she has committed the perfect crime, and wants me to publish it."

Holmes looked genuinely perplexed. "Is there more to this story, Mister Wainwright? I mean, I still don't understand why you are here. No matter how interesting the story, you can't really think that I have any interest in an unpublished manuscript."

"Of course not, sir, but I *am* befuddled by the whole thing. I have a story that I could probably publish because it did have at least the requisite amount of suspense and uncertainty, Mister Holmes, but I also have a cover letter indicating that the story is true. So I didn't know what to do with it.

"I decided that I would do a little investigating if I could, but there would be no point to investigating if I wasn't going to publish it. So, I called in Ian McDonough, one of my editors, to go over it for believability, syntax, spelling, all the things that good editors do. Since there were some descriptive scenes about the highlands, I chose McDonough because he was born there.

"So this is why I am here. McDonough was back in half an hour saying that the story is not only true, but that he remembers the case very well. He lived in Aberdeen at the time it was happening and is sure that it is still in the books as an embezzlement and an escape with the money, but just that. He says there was no mention whatever of a possible murder. As far as he knew the only person being sought was Mackenzie himself.

"The police aren't working on the case anymore, he says. It's been twelve years...but they would certainly like to solve it."

Holmes smiled, it seemed, briefly.

"This is indeed a very interesting development, Mister Wainwright. If there is anything to it, I'm sure it will go a long way toward dispelling the occasional boredom that grips London. I would like to read the entire manuscript and examine the envelope, as well.

"*If* this is a true story, and I am *not* at this point inclined to believe that it is, by careful reading, we might be able to glean some information on the supposed disposition of the body."

Wainwright raised his eyebrows. "*Glean some information*, Mister Holmes? Norma tells us on page fifty-four precisely what she did with the body."

Holmes snatched the manuscript from the Editorial Director and read page fifty-four quickly, but thoroughly, before looking back to Wainwright.

"How many people have read this?"

"In my office...only McDonough and I. You make the third on the small portion that you have read, sir."

"Can McDonough be trusted to be discreet in your absence?"

"No sir, he can not."

Holmes was forced to chuckle at such a forthright admission. "You shouldn't have left him alone in the office," he chided gently.

"I didn't, Mister Holmes. He's sitting in the cab downstairs with instructions not to engage the driver or anyone else in conversation until I come down. I did promise him that he would get to meet you, sir, however briefly."

"He'll meet me sooner than he thinks. Get a bag packed, Watson. We're on our way to Scotland."

Chapter 2

IN less than an hour, we were steaming north out of Charing Cross station, comfortably ensconced in a roomy dark paneled compartment with thick, plush seats and, for at least a short while, clean windows. If one has to travel the better part of five hundred miles, two thirds the length of the whole island, what more pleasing way to do it than in a modern English compartment car. If I were a man of less congenial bent, I could use my Strand articles to excoriate the rudeness of the French conductors and the eternal tardiness of the whole Italian train system.

But for today, the glory of modern British rail travel put me in so relaxed a humor that I almost loosened my tie. Holmes and I sat facing the young McDonough and Nevin Wainwright, with a teacart nestled comfortably between us. Holmes was clearly reluctant to discuss any aspect of our journey because there were no facts worth discussing. The story was very specific, especially about the corpse of poor old MacKenzie, which is described as "lying there to this day."

As Holmes said, "If we find a body and it can be identified, through other articles present, to be the missing keeper of accounts, then we have a case. If not, we have been duped, but would be none the worse for a leisurely trip north."

I must have fallen asleep, and rather quickly at that, because I had no recollection of steaming through the East Midlands. We were well into the trip, I gathered, as Wainwright commented that the road we had just crossed was the Leeds to York axis. This meant that we would soon be passing through the Yorkshire Dales, which I have always felt should be shown to those bumptious Irish to quash their ill-mannered trumpeting of their Glens of Antrim as the most beautiful spot in the empire.

Before long we were into Scotland and slowing to enter the cavernous station in Edinburgh, where we were to change trains. As Holmes studied the story, he realized that even though the main action all took place in the seaside town of Aberdeen, the body was actually said to be buried just south of Grantown-on-Spey. That meant, of course, that we would pass through Perth, rather than Dundee, and up into the vast highland Glen More Forest, probably lodging in Braemar for the night.

It would be quite late when we arrived and, if I knew Holmes, quite early when we departed in the morning; all of this to be compounded by an unsatisfying evening meal. Such were the travails of an adult life spent in observing and chronicling crime.

All that I had feared, did indeed happen, but at least I was able to coax time for a civilized breakfast out of Holmes in the morning. Promptly at half past eight, the carriage pulled away from our inn and we began the last leg of our journey, the forty or so kilometer ride to a rocky hillside southwest of Grantown-On-Spey. There was no train service between Braemar and the little Scottish village, so carriage was our only possible means of access.

I found that the discomfort of the carriage ride was more than compensated for by the loveliness of the terrain and our closeness to it. The world seen through the closed window of a speeding train does not have the freshness or immediacy of a view out an open carriage window. The temperature can be felt, the moisture sensed, the noises of nature experienced.

The sunshine of London, rare as it was, had given way to scattered clouds in the Midlands, to heavy mist in the Dales, and finally to rain in Edinburgh. This day and this place were gray and dry, at least as we started out, but the threat of rain was constant.

The terrain rose and dipped as we headed northwest and brought back to my mind times spent with a great Aunt Ellen, who told of travels through Scotland in her youth. The skies were now a panorama of dark, sullen, slightly swirling clouds. They glowered and threatened imminent inundation, but, at least so far, did not beset the anxious traveler.

The loveliness of the heather-graced hillsides sweeping gently upward to green, then suddenly rocky, barefaced mountains that formed the deep valleys we traversed, was awe-inspiring. Great Aunt Ellen spoke of the harsh breezes out of the twisted glens carrying echoes of ancient chants and war cries of fierce clans defending their independence. The great drums of the past could also be heard and the clash of steel, all mixed with the wailing cries of the wounded and dying.

I tried to imagine the sounds borne to my ears still carrying the lingering remnants of clan warfare, as well as the glory of the march of Bonnie Prince Charlie to the gates of London in the "forty-five". But the leaden skies seemed only to remind one of the somber retreat before the inexorable march of Cumberland.

Nevertheless, sensing of the past was strong in me, causing me to link my middle name, Hamish, of Scottish origin, with another pronouncement of great Aunt Ellen. "Only those with some Scottish blood can hear the echoes in the winds. Blood flows from the heart and carries the pain of the historical injustices meted to the Scottish".

The logic of reason, as well as anatomical correctness, may have suffered somewhat in her narrations, but her passion was eloquent and undeniable.

I was shaken out of my reverie by an abrupt turn on the road and brought back to the present. Throughout the trip, Nevin Wainright and young McDonough had waited patiently every step of the way, but one could sense an excitement in the Senior Editor. As someone close to, but on the other side of the publishing industry, I could understand the impact on magazine sales of a bizarre murder, narrated by the killer, and investigated alongside the fabled Sherlock Holmes.

Wainright could easily plan on a double printing, at the very least. If the body were found here, and verified, they would be cabling from all over Europe for copies of the Strand. For that reason, Wainwright had been willing to go right from Baker Street to the Charing Cross Station, without toiletries or change of clothes. He would not pass up such an opportunity for any worldly gain. Young McDonough also seemed to sense the awesome potential for his own career just by being a part of this.

Holmes unfolded a paper he had worked on during the train ride. Looking over his shoulder, I observed that he had drawn the roads and towns onto a crude map, adding all of the landmarks cited in the story. We were in a rather desolate area, with no manmade dwelling visible in any direction, so all of the additions to the map were of natural objects. There were arrows pointing to rock formations, stands of trees, and low points in the terrain.

The largest marking was an X on the north part of the sheet at one of the highest points of land visible. Holmes calmly looked from the map to the mountainside a few times, then pointed at a naturally arched rock about two thirds of the way up the slope.

"There is our destination, gentlemen, about six feet beyond the large arched rock. I estimate that it will take a good twenty minutes and a pint of perspiration to get there, so we'd best be about it.

"With your permission, I'll take the lead and ask that you follow at a safe distance, at least twenty meters. One can never be sure what is in the mind of someone who would do a letter and story like the one that brings us here. We may find some kind of trap laid up there that could cause serious injury."

I hadn't thought of such a possibility until Holmes mentioned it, but now found the climb apprehensive for more reasons than the exertion. Nevertheless, I considered it my place to lead Wainwright and McDonough, so with them safely behind me I began to follow the exact path that Holmes had taken.

The air was thinner and less sustaining than the air of London, causing me to tire in an embarrassingly short time. I was able to convince Wainwright that our frequent rest stops were intended for his comfort alone. Young McDonough seemed as though he could scamper up and down the mountain without a forced breath.

It was fully a half-hour before the four of us had passed through the arch and stood before a gathering of rocks that seemed not to have been moved in a millennium.

"Gentlemen," Holmes said, "If we have not been mischievously misled, the body should be under those two rocks in the back of that heap."

Holmes climbed up the side of the hill and examined the rocks and those behind them to make sure that moving one did not cause a cascade of them to bury us. After shaking several and feeling between them, Holmes seemed satisfied that it was safe to search further.

Motioning us to move a good ten meters to the left, Holmes positioned himself with his back to the largest boulder and his feet against the one he wanted to move.

He began applying pressure and relaxing, causing the rock to sway back and forth. The distances of the sway gradually increased until with a strenuous effort, Holmes dislodged the rock, causing it to roll free and smash into the side of the arch. It was firmly wedged, presenting no further danger.

Looking from the rock to Holmes, I found him staring intently into the small chasm created by its removal. He looked to us somberly and nodded, a gesture which I took to mean that he had made a grim discovery. The master detective carefully lowered himself into the pit until only his head was visible. Soon that disappeared as well, as he either stooped or squatted.

In only a few moments, he emerged with two objects clasped in his hand, which were quickly identified as a watch and billfold. Holmes seated himself on a bench-like flat rock and laid the items side by side. It turned out that there was also a crumpled cigarette package, obviously very old, and retrieved from the pit, as well.

Holmes said soberly, "Any thought of this story being a prank is now past. There is the fully dressed skeleton of a man under those rocks, and I am confident it will turn out to be our Carlton MacKenzie."

Looking closely, I could identify the package as being French Gaulois cigarettes, not rare exactly, but certainly not common in Scotland. Holmes rifled through the billfold and unfolded papers which seemed to confirm that the skeleton in the hole was indeed Carlton MacKenzie.

"Everything seems in order," Holmes said. He then turned the watch over and pointed to the initials "C.M." on the back. "We won't disturb the skeleton any further today. The remains in the hole are the responsibility of the local police. We shall go up to Grantown-on-Spey and give them the map and these few objects."

Before rising, though, Holmes drew something from his pockets and laid it beside the old ragged cigarette package. The object was another package, quite similar, but seemingly new. The print was larger than on the old container and very clearly said "Gaulois".

"I say, Holmes, where did you get the new cigarette package?"

"I found it halfway up the mountain. You'll notice that it is in excellent condition, so it can't have had a lengthy exposure to the elements."

"I see," I responded, "and you are drawing a connection between it and the package you found near the body?"

Holmes pursed his lips and studied them before saying, "This isn't a well-known cigarette brand in Scotland. Does it not make sense that the writer of the letter, assuming she actually killed MacKenzie, would take the time to re-inspect the burial site? She would certainly expect us to learn that there really was a Carlton MacKenzie, and armed with that knowledge, to verify her story. If she returned to the site and dropped a cigarette pack, it could verify a second visit here."

"Of course, Mister Holmes, but couldn't it just be a coincidence?" asked Wainwright.

"It certainly could, Mister Wainwright, and I'm not placing any great reliance upon it, but I collect all details. Now supposing we go to Aberdeen which, incidentally, is our next stop after we visit the local police, and find a woman named Norma Bainsteas living there. In conversation we learn that she actually knew Carlton

MacKenzie, perhaps well. Would you not ask her if she smokes cigarettes, and if so, what brand?"

"I suppose I would," he answered tentatively.

"And if she said 'Gaulois', would you not find that fact to be...intriguing?"

"Yes, I'm sure I would. I certainly see your point, but..."

"So, "Holmes recapped, "we have verified that at least part of the story is true, that relating to the final resting place of poor MacKenzie. Now we must seek to prove the rest of it. The only additional clues that we have to this point are a lady's name, and a curiosity regarding Gaulois cigarettes. We'll get the local police onto this, gentlemen, and we'll be off to Aberdeen."

The local police, it turned out, had no interest in the location of any dead bodies because the area in question was unincorporated. That made it a concern of the Scottish National Police, who had a regional office in Aberdeen.

Having arrived in Aberdeen late in the day, we were unable to arrange an appointment with anyone of stature in the National Police Office. Therefore, we secured lodging and presented ourselves to Mister Harrison Samuels, Executive Director, on the following morning.

Holmes began by giving Samuels a complete recitation of the initial visit by Nevin Wainwright that had brought us to this point. Samuels seemed moderately interested as soon as Carlton MacKenzie's name came up. His level of interest rose dramatically when Holmes talked about a location of the body being revealed in the story. He was on the edge of his seat as Holmes described moving the large rock,, and standing by the time Holmes revealed the discovery of the body.

Samuels asked how he could possibly identify a skeleton, and Holmes presented the wallet, the watch, and the two Gaulois cigarette packages. The police official snatched up the wallet and rifled through the papers, finding MacKenzie's name on several of them.

At Holmes' suggestion he turned the watch over and acknowledged the "C.M." on the back. The cigarette packages held his interest for less than ten seconds.

Samuels suggested a first course of action to be undertaken while they spoke, and Holmes agreed. Samuels' assistant was dispatched to the tax recorder's office to get the names and addresses of any listees named Bainsteas. "First names as well as last," he directed.

Samuels' next steps were to dispatch a clerk to fetch the twelve-year-old file on the unsolved embezzlement and flight of Mister Carlton MacKenzie, and a secretary to fetch tea. The tea arrived first, and by the time it was poured, the file was laid before Director Samuels.

His suggestion was that Holmes read the file while he, Samuels, took the time to read the story and letter from this Norma Bainsteas. This suited Holmes, so Wainwright, McDonough and I were left to drink tea, chat about the few true facts in evidence thus far, and wait patiently for the reading to be concluded.

Young Ian McDonough, Wainwright's editor, was the closest to Holmes and, to my surprise, the brash young scamp picked up the loose papers from the file and read them after Holmes had. No one seemed to mind, so I slid my chair over and did the same. As expected, the file contained little about Mackenzie after the theft. The conclusion was reached that he had stolen the money and left, adding optimistically that he would be apprehended soon.

There were lengthy statements from the Directors of the coal exporter that employed MacKenzie prior to his disappearance, all of which expressed shock and characterized his previous work record as exemplary. At least six pages were filled with fraudulent account entries and misappropriated company checks that constituted the individual acts of theft that MacKenzie had arranged. In summary, more than ninety-one thousand pounds had been stolen.

Holmes finished with the file before Samuels completed his reading of the story, so he refreshed his teacup and waited patiently. When Director Samuels was done, he set the story before himself and shook his head. "Incredible," was all he mumbled. Looking at Holmes he said, not asked, "And after reading the incredible story you went right to the spot and found the body."

Holmes simply nodded.

"We'll add the story to the evidence file," said Samuels, "and we'll..."

Wainwright came off of his chair as though stung by a bee. "You'll do no such thing," he said heatedly, as he snatched the story and cradled it to his breast. "This story is my property and it will not be appropriated by you or anyone else."

Samuels was taken aback by the vehemence of Wainwright's statement and stared wide-eyed at him.

"Mister Wainwright, those papers could constitute important evidence in this case."

"I don't care what you think this story constitutes. It is the property of the Strand magazine and will remain such." In a somewhat mollifying gesture, he offered to have the letter and manuscript transcribed and forwarded to Samuels, but the originals would remain in his possession.

I, used to dealing with the publishing industry, completely understood the fervor with which an editor would protect potentially explosive material, especially something as sensational as this. Holmes seemed to, as well. I noted an amused smile playing about the corners of his mouth.

"But surely you don't plan to publish this story?" Samuels asked.

"In the very next edition," Wainwright said firmly.

Holmes stepped in quickly to prevent any further escalation of this conflict by suggesting that they all discuss other matters for awhile and leave decisions regarding the manuscript for another time. Although they both nodded reluctantly, neither seemed any less resolute in his position.

Holmes addressed Samuels, "What do we know of the whereabouts of Mrs. MacKenzie?"

"To the best of my knowledge, Mister Holmes, she still lives in the same home she shared with her husband prior to his disappearance. We watched her intently for a year, on the assumption that Carlton would contact her and she might be able to lead us to him, but nothing developed."

"We watched her less intently for another year, kept loose track of her for a third year, and seeing nothing amiss, we closed the file on Mrs. MacKenzie. By that time, I must admit, we unofficially closed the file on Carlton as well. We had exhausted every avenue of investigation and needed some new development to bring it back to active attention."

Holmes nodded, "So this address on Carlyle Street is her current residence, to the best of your knowledge?"

When Samuels answered affirmatively, Holmes moved to a new subject. "Who is Garret Dickinson?" I had noticed the name in the file as well, but didn't think enough of it to ask. Obviously Holmes did.

"Dickinson was a bit of an oddity," Samuels said pensively. "He also worked at the coal company, but there was no known connection between he and MacKenzie. The only reason his name is in the file, is that he resigned the day after MacKenzie disappeared, and was never seen or heard from again."

"You checked his home?"

"He lived alone in a flat just north of the docks. His landlady said that he was a quiet, well-mannered chap, who said he had taken a job in another town..."

"Did she know where?"

"He apparently never mentioned it and she never asked. He announced he was leaving, paid her through the end of the month, and was gone. We were never able to uncover a man by that name again."

Holmes persisted a bit more on Dickinson. "Did you consider him a suspect, perhaps having complicity in this matter?"

"We never had any reason to suspect him of anything. We could not uncover an employee at the company who had ever seen Dickinson and MacKenzie speak to each other. If he had left the company a month earlier or a month later, we would never have given him a thought.

"But leaving so suddenly, and not being seen again naturally aroused some curiosity. But I'll say this, Holmes, if he showed up tomorrow, all we'd do is ask a few questions about MacKenzie. We'd have nothing else to say to him."

Holmes nodded and looked to his left as the clerk arrived with a list of everyone named Bainsteas in the local tax rolls. Samuels placed the list at an angle between Holmes and himself in a position where both could read it. I walked around behind them to read it as well. There were eleven names on it, nine saying "Mr. and Mrs." followed by a man's Christian name. Only two had female first names, a Helen and a Chastity.

Seven of the names had Aberdeen addresses, while four listed other town names. Holmes spoke of that first. "The towns listed here other than Aberdeen, Mister Samuels. I assume they are close by?"

"Very. They all abut the city borders...farming communities, I believe."

Holmes next asked, "Do you know any of the names?"

"No," Samuels replied, "I can't say for sure that I've ever even heard the name Bainsteas before."

With the conversation concluding, Holmes said, "This is your jurisdiction, Mister Samuels, so I'll give you the wallet, the watch, the cigarette packages, and my little map. You should have no trouble whatever locating the body with it."

Samuels took the items. "I'm sure we won't have any trouble, but tell me once again, Holmes, what is the significance of the Gaulois packages?"

"I'm not sure there is any significance. One was in the pit where the body lies, the other, of recent vintage, was less than fifty meters from the burial site. It could mean nothing, sir, but such details are important to me."

"Yes, yes, of course, details are important to me as well."

Holmes continued, "I'll leave the burial scene investigation in your hands, Mister Samuels, but I'm sure you won't mind if I poke around a bit here in Aberdeen. I'd like to speak with Mrs. MacKenzie and interview some of the Bainsteas families."

"It would be a privilege to have you here, Mister Holmes. I'm sure that you will apprise me of any developments. I would accompany you, but I would like to direct the recovery of MacKenzie's body and search the area myself. Perhaps we could dine together upon my return tomorrow evening and report on our activities. Let's say at Carrington's, at eight?"

"Carrington's at eight," Holmes repeated. He had slid the list of Bainsteas addresses to young McDonough earlier with a gesture to copy it. The master detective now compared the two lists for errors, folded our copy into his pocket, and shook hands with Director Samuels as we left.

CHAPTER 3

ENID MacKenzie was a timid, forlorn figure, who looked quite a bit older than her late fifties, an age we had estimated from knowing Carlton's age at the time of his disappearance. She seemed confused to have four men present themselves at her front door, and a little frightened. Holmes was able to give her adequate assurance of our good intentions, and she allowed us into the parlor.

To my surprise, he did not mention finding the body of Carlton, only that he believed that Carlton was not a thief and would like to ask a few questions. I realized that it was probably a wise course. Even after all of those years, she would be too upset by confirmation of her husband's death to be of any use in recalling the years before his disappearance.

I noticed a picture of a young man in a navy uniform on the table beside her chair. He was standing beside a smiling, strikingly pretty young lady, who I suddenly realized was Enid MacKenzie. Although the facial structure could be discerned upon close examination, she was almost unrecognizable now as the same person in a photo from a happier time. The ravages of fear and loneliness seemed to have sapped the vitality from her completely.

Holmes prodded her recollections from the period prior to the disappearance. She was slow to answer, but seemed forthright in all things nonetheless. No, she had no idea where Carlton was.

No, they were not in financial difficulty at the time.

No, Carlton did not seem depressed or upset before he disappeared.

No, he had not contacted her since.

No, she had never heard the name Garret Dickinson.

No, she did not know anyone named Bainsteas.

No, she had not been approached by anyone but the police in the time after Carlton's disappearance

No, she knew nothing more that she thought might help in finding her husband.

The conversation was into the second hour and clearly turning up no new information. Enid was rambling on about the loneliness of life alone when I happened to look away from her and over to Holmes. I was startled to see the intensity of his gaze at something beyond the pitiful Mrs. MacKenzie.

I followed his line of sight to the mantle and saw it as well. An opened package of Gaulois cigarettes.

Holmes waited for a stopping point in her narrative, then quickly asked, "Mrs. MacKenzie, do you smoke cigarettes?"

She seemed surprised by such a sudden change of subject, but answered quickly, "Yes I do, sir, would you like one?"

"No, no, thank you. What brand do you smoke?"

"Gaulois...they're French," she said, then added somewhat defensively, "There are few enough pleasures in life for a lonely widow."

Holmes eyes narrowed a bit. "Why do you refer to yourself as a widow? There is no reason to suspect that your husband is dead, is there?"

She looked defiantly into Holmes' eyes. "My husband is dead," she said firmly. "I know that the police think he stole that money, and maybe he did, but if he was alive he would have contacted me. Carlton loved me, and I loved him. All of you may think differently, but I don't care. There are things that a wife just knows... for sure. Carlton would have sent for me."

Holmes looked at her very sympathetically, "I don't doubt your feelings, ma'am. You may be right. May I ask one final question, and then we'll abuse your hospitality no longer?"

She nodded.

"How do you happen to smoke Gaulois cigarettes?"

"Carlton smoked them for years. I just picked the habit up from him and never had a reason to change. In a small, probably pitiful, way, they are a connection to him. It's something we did together."

Leaving the MacKenzie home, we went to a hotel to have tea and study a map. Holmes had procured a detailed layout of the city, and made little notations of the location of all of the Bainsteas' from the list.

Finally, he was finished and young McDonough asked a question that I'm sure was in everyone's mind.

"I'm a bit puzzled, Mister Holmes. What does it mean that you found a new Gaulois pack outside of the grave, if the package inside belonged to MacKenzie himself?"

Holmes' look acknowledged McDonough's confusion, but his answer shed no further light. "We don't know yet, Ian, but it is intriguing to say the least. One could come up with endless speculations, but it is too early for that. Our mission at this point is to continue gathering information. When we have all the facts that we can collect, we'll make rational judgments from them. To propound any theories at this point would be unwise. They would undoubtedly be wrong."

Holmes was of the opinion that four men was too large a group to present to the various Bainsteas families of Aberdeen. Accordingly, he dispatched Wainwright and McDonough back to the hotel with a firm promise that nothing that we learned would be withheld from them. Reluctantly, they acceded in a debate that they knew they could not win. It was now almost four in the afternoon, so we agreed to be back at the hotel by eight to share dinner.

The first three Bainsteas' that we visited were the three closest to where we parted company with our publishing associates. They lived within a six square mile area and seemed, for all the world, to be average citizens of Scotland. None of them knew anyone else named Bainsteas, except the third. He stated that the Henry Bainsteas at the bottom of the list was a reclusive farmer in his seventies, whose wife had died of heart failure many years earlier. He also happened to be his older brother.

None of them could recall the name or case of Carlton MacKenzie. Neither did they know a Garret Dickinson, nor smoke Gaulois cigarettes. They all seemed to have stern Scottish dispositions, but were pleasant enough for all that, and seemed sincere and forthright.

The fourth Bainsteas that we visited was one of those with a female name, Chastity. She was in her mid-sixties, a teacher who had never married, and viewed the world, especially Holmes and I, with great suspicion. Her given name had led me to form a picture of a prudish, gentle little woman, who would answer questions cheerfully. In person, Chastity had the bearing of the howling, dirk-wielding, ferocious clan warriors of yore. I would best characterize her as formidable.

She also answered all of Holmes' questions negatively, and like the previous Bainsteas families, did not smoke Gaulois cigarettes.

We returned to the hotel after encountering the formidable Chastity Bainsteas. Wainwright and McDonough were disappointed with our meager progress in the last few hours, but Holmes asserted that eliminating potential suspects from the list is only a few rungs down the ladder from adding them. These interviews had to happen and did, so we were now down to six Bainsteas'.

Dinner was a seemingly interminable rehashing and speculating on the part of Wainwright and McDonough, which Holmes bore with graceful patience.

The following morning found us back on the trail of the elusive Scottish name. It had occurred to me countless times that we might never find Norma Bainsteas because she would not be foolish enough to confess to a murder and sign it with her own name. Holmes agreed, readily enough, but said such things didn't matter. All of the Bainsteas' had to be checked out, and it was idle to waste one's time thinking of anything else.

Things as seemingly illogical as the scenario I had outlined could take on a completely different look when all circumstances were revealed.

The first few visits of the new day were very much like those of the previous day in that they added nothing to our scant storehouse of knowledge. I had to admire Holmes' patience in moving onto the next prospect in no less hopeful a mood than that with which we had started the day.

William Bainsteas was a farmer and, by far, the most pleasing personality of all those we had met thus far. He seemed a prosperous, well-educated landowner who actually enjoyed unexpected callers. Ruddy-faced, short yet robust, and possessed of a booming voice, William poured tea for us before asking if we wanted any.

He apparently had read most, if not all, of the Strand articles that I had written and was enthralled at the prospect of having tea and conversation with the famous Sherlock Holmes. He must have had an extraordinarily clear conscience, because he never asked what we wanted, but launched right into a discussion of the case of the Blue Carbuncle. Holmes tried to interject a question, but William would have none of it until

Holmes had signed, with a salutation, four different issues of the Strand.

Holmes finally insisted upon asking a few questions, and our ebullient host relented. Unfortunately, he had no answers of interest and didn't smoke at all, so the Gaulois cigarettes were never mentioned.

"Your wife, William, is she at home?"

"No, you just missed her. She took the wagon into town to do her marketing."

"Would her name be Norma, by any chance?"

"No, no, not at all. Her name is Martha. You must have misunderstood whoever sent you here. Norma's my *sister*, not my wife. They're nothing alike at all."

I am frequently amazed at how casually a stunning revelation can be introduced into a conversation. Our quest for a Norma Bainsteas was about to burst into blossom, and our revealer sloughed it off as a mere misunderstanding.

Holmes did not react with great excitement, fearing the possibility of alarming our host, and causing him to be less forthcoming.

"Ah, your sister, of course," Holmes said. "My misunderstanding. Actually it is Norma that I am trying to contact. Does she live nearby?"

"My goodness, Mister Holmes, don't tell me Norma has gotten herself involved in something illegal."

"Oh, no," Holmes answered reassuringly. "I have been engaged by a London attorney to find her and deliver a document to her. As I understand it, the document is for her benefit, not her distress."

"Well, that's a relief, Mister Holmes, but I'm afraid you've gotten closer to her, but still a long ways away."

"Oh?"

"The truth is, we don't know where she is, *exactly* where she is, I mean. She lives in France, married to some vagabond Frenchman that none of us cared for."

"There was conflict in the family over the wedding?" Holmes asked.

"Nothing overt, more snide than anything else. But Norma perceived it and resented it. Rather than stay here in Scotland, as this Denis seemed willing to do, she insisted that they move to France. I got a letter from her asking that I send a few things that she had forgotten. The address was in Aix-en-Provence. I wrote her again later, but the letter was returned, saying she did not live there any longer. To the best of my knowledge, no one in the family has heard from her since."

Holmes then went through the litany of questions he had asked the others, but William knew nothing about Garret Dickinson, Carlton MacKenzie, or the coal company. He also said he had no recollection of the story about the embezzlement and, therefore, nothing regarding its aftermath.

Holmes took down the last name of this Denis, whom Norma had married, expecting that one of his resources in France would be able to track him down. We left shortly thereafter.

In the cab on the way to the next Bainsteas, I asked Holmes if there was something faintly connective between the Gaulois cigarettes being French and the emergence of a Frenchman married to a Norma Bainsteas.

"If there is," Holmes replied, "it is a very faint connection, but it is the kind of detail to bear in mind.

One must not connect things or rule them out until sufficient data has been collected."

The remainder of the Bainsteas addresses on our list yielded nothing and we were soon back at Carrington's dining with Ian McDonough, Nevin Wainwright, and Director Samuels. Samuels had successfully completed the recovery of the body and ascertained, at least to his satisfaction, that it was Carlton MacKenzie.

"There were many items that clearly belonged to him and were identified by his wife. It was a distressing experience, but she confirmed a wedding ring, belt buckle, pocket watch, and shoes as belonging to her husband."

"Or", Holmes mused, "someone exactly the same size."

Samuels was lifting his teacup to his lips as Holmes made the comment, but stopped and left it suspended in air. He looked at Holmes, who blithely continued with his meal, and asked, "Holmes, do you have any reason to suspect it might not be Mackenzie that we have found?"

"No," Holmes replied, "but early in an investigation, we must be careful not to rule out anything. Making firm assumptions, such as the body definitely being MacKenzie, makes one's thinking rigid and prevents travel down roads of thought that may lead to the solution. My experience tells me that each complicated solution has only one road that leads to it. My mind is open to every possibility."

"That point is incontrovertible, Holmes, but I've read all of the stories about your cases that the gentlemen at this table have published. There are numerous examples of you noticing a detail so fine as to be almost invisible upon which the solution turns. You are also known to be secretive until such solutions are achieved. Therefore, I repeat my question. Do you have any solid reason to believe that the body we have found is not Carlton MacKenzie?"

Holmes answered simply, "No."

"What is the next step?"

"That is up to Norma Bainsteas, if that is her, or his, correct name."

"Do you expect further contact, Holmes?" I asked.

"Of course there will be further contact, old fellow. We have been served an hors d'oeuvre, a canapé, which is virtually meaningless on a stand-alone basis. We appear to be dealing with a very clever...lady, we'll call her for now. There is most certainly an as yet undisclosed point to all of this."

"But," I said, "the letter said that she wanted to show that there are brilliant people operating on the wrong side of the law as well as the right side."

"That was not the undisclosed point," Holmes replied simply.

CHAPTER 4

HOLMES' prognostications, as I have come to expect, were right on the mark. We had been home only two days, discussing our brief, but bizarre, trip to Scotland, when Mrs. Hudson announced the arrival of Mister Nevin Wainwright. Holmes had spent considerable time in pondering the letter and story that had been submitted, the events of the trip, and the motivation of this Norma Bainsteas. He had also gotten at least four letters off to various contacts in France, relative to Denis La Mauret and his wife, the former Norma Bainsteas.

"Mister Holmes, Doctor Watson!" Wainwright boomed, "There's another story in today's post. I came as soon as I received it."

"Come, come, Wainwright. Take your coat off and get comfortable. Tea will be up directly. Now, is this story also from our Miss or Mrs. Bainsteas?"

"Not exactly, Mister Holmes. It's a bit unusual. Actually I received a letter from Norma Bainsteas saying that she had prevailed upon a dear friend to submit another story, but gloating a bit about her success in the MacKenzie affair. Here I'll let you read it."

Holmes snatched the letter and read aloud.

> "Dear Mister Wainwright,
>
> "I've asked a dear friend, Rene LaDier, to write in story form about the most marvelous adventure. It is a story about brilliant accomplishments in the field of advanced mischief that you will find stunning.
>
> "I will not give you any details in this missive, so as not to detract from your reading pleasure, but you will note that the crime that was made public in my last communication was never solved, and the crime that will be revealed in the next story not only was never solved, it was never known about, even by the authorities."
>
> "I must assume that, by now, you have disinterred that pathetic little Carlton MacKenzie and have ascertained how cleverly the entire plot was conceived and executed. It will be a treat for your readership.
>
> "A word of warning; If that story is not published forthwith, you will lose your exclusive status. I will send copies of my story, as well as Rene's, to other publications. Please also see that Mister Sherlock Holmes and Doctor John Watson receive copies. They'll be interested in

knowing that their brilliance is dwarfed by some of us on the other side of the law."

With Warmest Regards,

Norma Bainsteas

Holmes handed the letter back to Wainwright and smiled. "Our Norma Bainsteas certainly sounds very confident of her ability to avoid capture and prosecution. And she now introduces a compatriot in crime. Do I observe the promised package from this Rene LaDier sitting on your lap?"

"You do, Mister Holmes. This package and Norma's letter arrived in the same batch of mail. I didn't even take the time to open it, feeling sure that you would like to see it as quickly as possible."

"I thank you for your consideration, Mister Wainwright. I am indeed anxious to look at it."

He studied the package before opening it and then said, "No return address, just like Norma's letter. But both of them posted from Paris."

Holmes went to his room and came out wearing thin leather gloves. He took a letter opener from the desk and slit the top of the package, speaking as he withdrew the sheaf of papers. "It's not likely that Miss Bainsteas or this Rene LaDier would leave fingerprints on these papers, but we must be thorough and check for them. Even if we find them, it's not likely that we will have a matching set until we catch her, but one never knows."

Removing the sheaf of handwritten papers, Holmes took his seat, lit his pipe and settled in to read. "Gentlemen," he said, "we have no choice but to read this story in its entirety and let what ensues from it determine our course of action.

"The first bit of evidence that I have observed is that the letter from Norma is written by the same hand, as would be expected, and the story by Rene LaDier has completely different handwriting, as we should also be able to expect. We can take no element of these letters or stories for granted, but at least those few elementary observations are consistent with the story as she tells it.

"The other point is that the story by Rene is clearly a feminine hand, while the letters signed by Norma are less certain. For what it is worth, and perhaps I'm looking too deeply for complexity, we have a letter signed with a woman's name that could have been written by either a man or a woman. We also have a story signed by Rene, a name that could be either a man or woman, but in a clearly feminine handwriting. I don't know if any of that means anything yet, or not".

Holmes slid deeper into his chair, crossed his long slender legs, and began to read. He was soon enshrouded in a thin cloud of smoke from the shag cut tobacco that I found the most offensive among the several varieties he fancied.

As he read a page, he laid it on the couch within my reach. I read the story and passed it page by page to Nevin Wainwright. Holmes was an extremely fast reader, as one would expect of a man of his intellectual gifts. Occasionally he would snatch one of the sheets back and compare it with the one he was reading.

I was nine pages behind, out of forty-eight, by the time Holmes finished. Without a word, apparently waiting for us to finish, he repacked his pipe and stood staring out the window, feet spread apart, arms folded across his chest.

The story was about complicated financial dealings that resulted in Rene La Dier apparently bilking a major Swiss bank out of almost three million Swiss Francs. While I didn't completely understand all of the machinations, the story went approximately as follows; Rene LaDier presented herself as a business woman, unusual for Switzerland, but not unheard of, in need of financing to erect a multi-level store in the center of Zurich, selling expensive French clothing and jewelry to only the wealthiest clientele. The project was simply entitled "Chez Francoise".

The loan was to finance not only the building but the merchandise needed to stock the shelves and cases. As collateral, she produced a deed for the land, supported by a signed contract with the construction company. The deed covered only a portion of the value of the loan, with the balance covered by shares of ownership in an Italian locomotive manufacturer, well known to the bank officer.

Moreover, the bank officer was given three-percent ownership in the new venture as "consideration" for rushing the loan through quickly, quietly, and at the lowest reasonable rate of interest. Rene had selected a man in the line of direct progression to the Managing Director's position, but a man of venal propensity nonetheless.

Shortly after the money was deposited in a numbered account, a small amount of money was given to the contractor, who began work. The bank officer spent more than one afternoon watching with satisfaction as the excavation was completed and materials piled up in the building area.

The bank officer, Karl Mundt, realized one day that little progress was being made and was stunned to read in the financial news, a few days later, that the contractor had not been paid since the beginning of the job. He stopped work when the down payment was exhausted, and reported that he hadn't seen Miss LaDier in weeks.

Immediately checking the numbered account, he found all of the money diverted to various other banks, who reported that it had been cleared out of their control as well. The deed for the property under construction turned out to be already mortgaged by a French bank and the ownership certificate in the Italian locomotive firm were forgeries.

Because of Swiss banking secrecy, the legality, if not the morality, of which had been questioned on occasion, there was no connection between the bank and the construction project. Rene had paid what little of the three million Francs she expended with draughts from another bank.

Therefore, the only way that the bank could be connected to the failed project, which would be an enormous embarrassment, was if the bank identified itself as a victim.

But the bank's embarrassment was the least of Karl Mundt's fears. The bank would survive the loss of three million Francs, not a staggering sum, but Mundt would not. He would be forced to resign in disgrace, and would never secure an important banking position again. His career would be over.

As the story was unfolding, Mundt received a letter marked "personal and confidential" from Rene LaDier. In it she enclosed a copy of the stock certificates issued to Karl Mundt verifying ownership of three-percent of the new company. An accompanying affidavit showed that he had paid nothing for his stock. Mundt knew that the bribe he had accepted might not get him fired, but would certainly impede his progress toward the leadership of the bank.

Also enclosed was a copy of a letter addressed to the Managing Director of the bank, the Minister of Justice, and the editors of the three leading newspapers in Zurich. The letter not only spelled out Karl Mundt's part in the debacle, but slanted and exaggerated it to make him appear to be a co-conspirator.

On the bottom of the note, Rene informed Mundt that she had not sent these letters, but they were in stamped envelopes ready to be posted. Any unpleasantness that Mundt might wish to cause her over the incident would trigger delivery of the letters.

Therefore, six years had passed, Mundt ascended to the Managing Directorship, and the three million Franc loan stayed on the books with collateral of questionable value pledged against it. It required little manipulation to give the impression that interest was being paid on the loan.

The last paragraph of the story not only presented the account number into which the funds had gone but more or less challenged the reader to confront Herr Karl Mundt with the entire story. Rene closed the story by describing it as the best kind of crime, one in which the victim is as interested in keeping it from the police as the perpetrator. A work of art, she called it, vastly superior to the accomplishments of Sherlock Holmes in sniffing out a few mistakes by inept amateurs and apprehending them.

Holmes read the last paragraph aloud and chuckled a bit as he passed it on.

"We must give the devil her due," he said. "It is an exceedingly clever twist to manipulate your victim into complicity, thereby assuring his silence. In these six years her trail would have grown so cold, it would be silly to even consider trying to track her down.

"So gentlemen, here we sit with two undetected crimes from the past. Virtually perfect crimes, in that they were never made public, and no effective attempt was ever made to bring the criminal to justice.

"There is a similarity in that in both cases, the victims were enlisted as accomplices, more or less, and then left holding the bag. In Carlton MacKenzie's case, he wound up murdered while Karl Mundt has to live every day of his life with a significant bad loan on his books, the discovery of which could end his career. In this case, the absolute secrecy of the Swiss banking system serves to assist in keeping the fraud under cover.

"Well, gentlemen, it's off to Zurich. Even though I'm sure it is true, the whole matter must be checked out. I'm sure Karl Mundt will not enjoy our visit."

⚜

After a rough channel crossing and a tedious train ride through France and into, around, and tunneling through the mountains, our train chugged into the Hauptbahnhof.

We exited the central railroad station and headed down the Bahnhofstrasse to the business and banking center of the great city of Zurich.

It was just Holmes and myself, because the master detective told Wainwright that a matter as delicate as this required a much smaller assemblage. Karl Mundt would be difficult to open up even with two inquisitors, impossible with more. Wainwright was downcast, but saw the logic of Holmes' pronouncement. He was mollified by our assurances that nothing would be kept from him upon our return. Holmes bolstered the publisher's confidence by pointing out how key he was to the investigation. Without the material submitted to him by our mysterious Norma Bainsteas, we would not have anything to investigate and no conduit for future communications from her

Perhaps I read too much into it, but the expression on Wainwright's face seemed one of epiphany. He had felt like a hanger-on, but Holmes had given rise to the notion that Wainwright could withhold further correspondence if he felt left out. We would have no further angst from him, I felt sure.

Not necessarily so from Ian McDonough, the young editor in Wainwright's employ. He had seemed like a school child at a circus through out the entire affair, starting with his introduction to Holmes. He was a study in unbounded exuberance at the news that he would be included in the trip up to the Aberdeen area to seek the burial place of the hapless Carlton Mackenzie.

I was quietly glad that he did not understand that he was brought along only because Wainwright did not trust him to hold the whole situation in confidence in his absence.

He was a sturdily built young man, with blue eyes, sandy colored hair, and a ready smile. I was amused to see the fastidiousness with which he dressed, a good habit for an aspiring young businessman.

Even as we prepared to go to Zurich, the young lad pleaded to go along, if only to carry luggage, find taxicabs, and make hotel arrangements. Holmes politely declined the offer and extracted a promise from Wainwright that, despite his indignant pronouncement to Harrison Samuels in Aberdeen, he would not publish the first story from Norma Bainsteas until we had returned and discussed our progress. Wainwright agreed, albeit reluctantly.

❦

My mind had been on such delights of the city as the Lindenhof for the past twenty-four hours and I realized I had overlooked the practicalities of our mission.

"Holmes, I know that it's a bit late to mention this, since we are already in Zurich, but what if this Mundt will not receive us?"

Holmes smiled patiently. "He will receive us, Watson, I assure you."

"I don't see how you can offer such assurances, Holmes, your celebrity status notwithstanding. These Swiss bankers are like troglodytes as I understand it, and do not like to discuss banking affairs even with their wives, much less complete strangers."

"My dear Watson, as you refreshed yourself in the rest room in the London train station, I sent Mundt a telegram announcing our arrival. To be sure that he would not even consider avoiding us, I mentioned the name of Rene Ladier. Believe me, old fellow, while he views our interview with understandable dread, he will receive us promptly. Of that there is no doubt."

I accepted that and moved on to another subject. "Holmes, I believe that I will not accompany you back to London after the interview. Not having been here in several years and being enamored of the Lindenhof area, I have decided to spend the afternoon and evening there and return home late tomorrow. There is a small hotel near the Predigerkirche..."

"My dear Watson, you are as transparent as a pane of glass. What you are doing is suggesting that we stay over, and couching it in terms that you think will be more convincing. Say no more. I am perfectly amenable to staying on. In fact, I think it a necessity. We have to track down the construction company that started work on Miss LaDier's hole in the ground."

We approached the bank building and, even though I had seen it before, found it very impressive. Built of massive grey stone blocks, with six huge Doric pillars guarding the entrance, it gave the impression of an impregnable fortress rather than a financial institution. The vast lobby, with its marble floors, would not have seemed inappropriate in a palace.

We were shown immediately into an uncommonly large conference room, served tea and a tray of assorted pastries, and informed that Herr Mundt would arrive directly. In the event, he entered the room before his secretary left, informing her that we were not to be disturbed under any circumstances.

Mundt was quite a bit taller than I had expected him to be, although I had no reason to have expectations other than from experiences with other bankers. He was wide-shouldered, with black hair combed straight back, and possessed of a handshake like a blacksmith.

Eschewing the straight-backed chairs around the table, Mundt poured himself a cup of tea and motioned us to a group of overstuffed chairs near a window on the far side of the room. It occurred to me that he was meeting with us at the point of the room furthest from the door, to be certain that we could not be heard by any possible eavesdroppers.

Taking a seat, setting his tea aside, and crossing his legs, Mundt spent a moment peering into our eyes before speaking, perhaps attempting to give the impression that he would be the lead figure in the conversation. That would not last long.

"I assume that you gentlemen arrived in Zurich just today?"

Holmes nodded and answered tersely, "We did."

"And how long do you plan to stay in our fair city?"

"Today and tomorrow, perhaps another day." Holmes seemed content to allow him his small talk for now. Mundt, apparently seeing that Holmes was not going to offer anything but brief, curt answers to inane questions, shifted his approach and got to the point.

"Gentlemen, how can I be of service to you?"

"Approximately six years ago, you entered into a financial arrangement with a Miss Rene Ladier. We would like to..."

"I've never heard that name before in my life. I hope you have not come so far today for nothing."

Holmes smiled. "Not for nothing, sir, and I'm sure that your memory will improve dramatically in the next few minutes."

"Mister Holmes..."

Holmes held a hand up to hold off further denials from our understandably recalcitrant host. "Please, Herr Mundt, hear me out. Let me restart the conversation. I should have begun by saying that we are not here bearing any ill will or any intention to embarrass you or cause you any harm.

"The three million Francs that she bilked you out of, and the three percent equity in "Chez Francois" that she used as an inducement are of no interest to us."

Mundt looked momentarily shocked, though he rolled with it well. A man does not rise to the top of as venerable an institution as this bank without the ability to retain his composure in times of crisis.

"I know nothing of the things you have mentioned, Mister Holmes, but if *you* have no interest in them, as you just said, why have you come this considerable distance to mention them to me?"

"An eminently reasonable question, sir. Our interest is in Miss LaDier herself, not her activities that involve this bank. We seek to find her in regard to matters far more serious than cheating a bank and a construction company."

Mundt turned to the exquisitely inlaid table to his right, opened a small silver cigarette box and offered it to each of us. We both declined. He then took one, lit it in deliberate fashion and inhaled deeply, obviously taking time to ponder his next response.

"Well, gentlemen, as I said, I know nothing of these things. I would like to help a man with as distinguished a reputation as yourself, Mister Holmes, but I'm afraid your trip has been in vain."

Holmes did not lose his patience. "Herr Mundt, we appreciate your willingness to help, as you so generously offered, but we *do* think that you can. Moreover, we think that you *will.* Let me change the subject briefly." Mundt said nothing, just looked at us with narrowed eyes through a thin blue haze of smoke.

Holmes continued. "I wonder, Herr Mundt, if you have ever read any of the articles Doctor Watson here has published in the Strand magazine regarding criminal cases that he and I have worked together on."

Mundt seemed delighted that the conversation had taken a turn away from the quicksand he feared Holmes was leading him to. "As a matter of fact, I believe that I have read *most* of them. The Strand is published here in Zurich in German, French, and English. I'm sure you know that large portions of our population speak in each of those languages, depending, of course, on where they live."

Holmes nodded and Mundt continued, affably. "I've enjoyed the stories immensely and look forward to the next. But why do you ask?"

Holmes detonated a cannon shell into Mundt's face. "Since you know nothing of these things, you will have no trouble defending yourself when the whole story, with far more detail than I have revealed to this point, is published in the next issue of the Strand."

Mundt was stunned, but held on, in fact took the offensive. "Published in the Strand, sir? How dare you make such a shallow threat to me? You have no such story and if any such fiction is ever printed I will sue every person even remotely connected with the Strand, including yourselves."

Holmes smiled cordially and rose to his feet. "That being the case, I'm sure you have nothing to fear. I'll autograph your copy of the Strand article and mail it to you next month. I'm sure the three million Franc problem is no longer hidden in your accounts, so you have no fear of an audit, and I'm sure the construction company that lost money in the transaction will not be able to sue you. Come, Watson, we've taken enough of Herr Mundt's time."

As I started to rise, Mundt waved us back down. "Please, gentlemen, wait a moment, let's not part company in such a manner. I don't know how I can help, but let me try. What exactly do you want?"

"First of all, we want to see the original application that Miss LaDier made when she took out the loan."

"Why?"

"Only to verify the handwriting," Holmes assured him, "and to see if there is any other information that could help in locating her. Nothing you show me will be revealed outside of this room."

"What about the Strand article?"

"Unfortunately, there is very little I can do about that, other than to promise you at least a month's respite and give you the name of the managing editor of the magazine. If you are able to plead, threaten, coerce, cajole, or bribe him, it is not my concern. I repeat, Doctor Watson and I are interested only in finding Miss LaDier, not causing you any discomfort."

Mundt pondered it at length, then rose, saying, "if such a document were to exist, it could not be taken from the bank, under any circumstances."

"Agreed. If you set such a document before me, I will not even lift it from the table."

Mundt was back in five minutes with a single sheet of paper, which he laid before Holmes. I assumed, from the speed of his return, that he kept the file locked in his desk, not in a distant, dusty records cabinet.

Holmes took a sheet of paper from his breast pocket, flattened it out, and set it beside the application. I recognized it as being from the story Norma Bainsteas had sent to Nevin Wainwright.

In seconds, Holmes said, "A perfect match. Both of these documents were written by the same hand." He made no attempt to prevent Mundt from looking over his shoulder, as he scanned the rest of the sheet.

After just a few minutes, he slid it across to me. "Nothing else of value in the application. We know that her financial representations were all false,"

I saw nothing more in the sheet either and gave it back to Mundt. "Herr Mundt," Holmes said, "from all appearances, it would seem that she is right-handed. Can you confirm that from your memory?"

Mundt looked out the window, squinting slightly, as though picturing the lady in question, and nodded firmly. "I can definitely confirm that she is right-handed, but I would like to know what the document you have is."

Holmes grimaced sympathetically. "It is, perhaps, your biggest problem in life. It is one page of a forty-eight page story submitted by a Miss Norma Bainsteas for publication in the Strand magazine."

The blood seemed to drain from Mundt's face. He took on the appearance of a man tied to a railroad track at night and hearing a locomotive's steam whistle. "Who is Norma Bainsteas?" he asked softly.

"We don't know. Perhaps she and Rene LaDier are one and the same, perhaps not. If not, they are certainly in league with each other, but we are just beginning our investigation, so I repeat, we don't know."

"If she is Rene," Mundt asked, "why in the name of all that is holy would she want to publish a story that clearly implicates her in the commission of a felony? Actually several felonies tied into this one case."

"We don't know that either, but we do know that you are not the one she is seeking to embarrass, even though that is an inevitable consequence. The object of her ridicule is...me"

"I don't understand."

"Unfortunately, there is nothing more that I am free to tell you. I can only add that our reasons for seeking her are far more serious than bank fraud."

The next hour was spent in getting as detailed a physical description of Rene LaDier as Mundt could manage. Holmes must have asked seventy-five different questions, gleaning that and information about speech patterns, mannerisms, and other things that I would never have thought to ask. He made a few notes on small slips of paper, organized them in some way that was not apparent to me, and slid them into a pocket.

Under the intense pressure of Holmes' gaze, Mundt was adamant in insisting that he had not had any communication whatever from Rene since the final letter. He also said that no organization or person other than the bank had been seriously harmed in the loan transaction. If Rene had cheated the construction company, that was a separate matter and not a concern of the bank.

Holmes nodded and gave Mundt the name and address of Nevin Wainwright and reiterated his promise that the story would not be published for at least a month "Beyond that, it is up to you and Wainwright. Perhaps you could persuade him to publish the story in an altered form, such as changing names and locations. Set it in France," he said with a smile, "Brits are not terribly fond of the French."

It was a long, invigorating walk up to the crest of the hill, to the Lindenhof, a lovely esplanade of robust shade trees. From a particularly picturesque overlook, one could see most of the sprawling city of Zurich, with the Limmat below us flowing swiftly down to the eponymous lake, known world wide to travelers.

We stood on the site of ancient Celtic and Roman settlements from which evolved the modern city we now viewed. I have long considered it one of the most touching vantage points in Europe.

Mindful of the time, we strode quickly down to Schneller's elegant little hotel, engaged rooms, and dressed for dinner, having reserved a table at Braun's café across the street.

Over a repast of schnitzel, kraut, boiled red potatoes, and strudel, we discussed the case. The schnitzel was accompanied by a bottle of chilled Gewurtztraminer and the strudel washed down with rich black coffee.

"So, Holmes, what have we accomplished today?" I asked in commencing analysis of the conundrum facing us.

"First of all, we have confirmed that the story submitted is true, down to the last detail. Although having found Carlton Mackenzie's body from the previous story, that comes as no great surprise. The handwriting confirms that Norma Bainsteas, whoever that actually is, was the central figure in both crimes. I am a bit disappointed in what we have garnered in the way of physical descriptions."

Holmes compared two small slips of paper, taken from a side pocket "The physical description of his sister that William Bainsteas provided seems, at first glance, to differ markedly from the description that Mundt gave us of Rene LaDier. "Let's see," he mused, muttering to himself, but loud enough for me to hear, "black hair versus brown hair. Hair color can be easily masked or changed. Plumpish versus thinnish could be explained over time, but these occurrences happened in a short time frame, so that could be a problem.

"Both stated the eyes were brown, but most Caucasians have brown eyes. Very little help there, but at least not a problem. Average height, they both said.

That is such a relative term, that it is of no value. Mundt is a good four inches taller than William Bainsteas, so average to him could be a couple of inches taller than for Bainsteas.

"Probably the biggest problem is their description of the voice. Norma's was described as "soft, almost velvety," while Mundt described Rene's as "somewhat harsh, occasionally raspy." At this point, I would have to conclude, tentatively, that we are talking about two different women, which complicates things a bit. But then, we are so early into our investigation, even two dead-on descriptions would not have advanced us significantly."

We discussed other aspects of the case after dinner and again the next night after interviewing the building contractor, the architect, and another bank that Rene LaDier had involved in the transaction. We learned nothing more of great import.

Nevertheless, Holmes was in a buoyant mood as we headed back to London. In too many of his cases, he had determined the culprit within the first twenty-four hours and found it difficult to maintain his enthusiasm.

We were now two trips into the case and could see only the very tip of the iceberg. We hadn't a clue as to the whereabouts of our villain, and barely an understanding of who she was. Although he didn't say it, I believe that part of Holmes' buoyancy could be attributed to the fact that our prey was a woman and one so supremely audacious as to confess to serious crimes and dare the master detective to try to catch her,

We had never been faced with a diabolical plot of this magnitude that was engineered by a woman. Irene

Adler was indeed a formidable intellect, but a bewitching woman nonetheless. She had passed through our lives briefly in *A Scandal in Bohemia* and was never seen again by either of us.

Being closely attuned to at least some of Holmes' habits, I realize that he does not like oral or verbal references to that mysterious lady so I will respect his wishes and keep secret some of his most intimate comments about her.

All other avenues of inquiry being exhausted, we returned to London, expecting the pace of the case to accelerate. We would not be disappointed.

As was his wont, Holmes dispatched several telegrams from the train station in Calais before boarding the ship back to England. One of them was to Nevin Wainwright, inviting him and young Ian McDonough to join us at Simpson's-in-the-Strand, locally noted for its roast beef, for supper and a revelation of what we had uncovered in Zurich.

"Any new communications from the dark side?" Holmes asked Wainwright to shift the conversation away from the brisket with horseradish.

"Nothing yet, Mister Holmes, but I've decided that I have to proceed with publishing the story about our unfortunate Mister Mackenzie in Scotland. Norma has warned me that if I do not, she will send it to another magazine, which would take me out of the picture, probably for good. I think that any other magazine in London would have a special edition in the shops already."

Holmes gave an understanding nod. "I personally don't see any harm in doing that. Normally, the reason a story like this is kept under wraps is to keep the perpetrator in the dark as to what we are up to. Norma doesn't seem to care. She has gone out of her way to draw attention to herself. I assume that you have informed the police in Aberdeen of your intentions."

"I have, Mister Holmes. I sent a wire to Director Samuels and he responded saying he had no objection. The case has been dormant for so long, with everyone thinking that it was a simple embezzlement. He's hoping that since it has now taken on the sinister character of murder, some publicity might get people to take it seriously and report anything that may not have seemed important in the past."

Holmes shrugged, giving the impression that he wasn't optimistic about such a development.

"I suppose it's possible," was all he said. He then launched into a detailed summary of our trip to Zurich, concluding with notice to Wainwright to expect a communication from Karl Mundt, our quite nervous banker.

Wainwright smiled. "I already have. He will be here tomorrow to discuss my publishing plans."

Holmes smiled broadly. "You may expect bluster, then threats, and all of that failing, heartfelt importuning."

The night ended with mutual promises to keep each other informed of developments, and a gentle warning to Ian McDonough. "Mister Wainwright informs me that you do not always exercise discretion in your daily activities, young man. We've allowed you to be a part of all of this, since you were there at the outset, but that is subject to change at the first instance of your discussing these matters with anyone,"

McDonough was leaning forward as though he could not wait for Holmes to finish so he could respond. "Mister Homes,... gentlemen...I swear that I have not said a word to a soul and that I will not in the future. This has been the most exciting period of my life...I live a boring life. I would never do a thing to harm your investigation. Please believe that."

The words came so rapidly and his face registered such urgency and sincerity, that we were all forced to smile. "Very good answer, Ian, we'll expect you to live up to it."

It was such a pleasant evening that Holmes and I decided to walk home rather seek a cab. We found a surprising telegram awaiting us.

CHAPTER 5

NOT being as early a riser as Holmes, I am never surprised to find him gone when I make my first appearance of the day. I rested at night in the certain knowledge that the master detective, with whom I shared the simple, but comfortable rooms on Baker Street, would not hesitate to jolt me awake in the event of an important development. For that matter, he wouldn't hesitate on an unimportant matter. Actually, not even on a whim.

He had very early in life concluded that the notion of sleeping eight hours every night was an abominable waste of a significant portion of one's life. To spend a third of one's earthly existence unconscious was no less absurd than spending two or three thirds in a comatose state. As a medical doctor, I could not condone his practice of sleeping a mere four hours a night, five on selected weekends, but I was forced to concede that no one in my experience exhibited such boundless energy or mental acuity as Holmes. Therefore, I had long since refrained from chiding him about it.

Holmes, in fact, had taken to frequently chiding me about not training my mind to get by with the same amount of sleep he allowed himself. Over time, we both accepted the impasse we were at on this issue.

As I poured tea and waited for Mrs. Hudson to deliver my breakfast, I reread the startling telegram that Holmes had received last night, which was undoubtedly the cause of his early departure this morning.

It read;

> *"Mister Holmes, while passing through Aberdeen, I learned that you have been seeking to find me. I can't imagine why, unless you are intruding yourself into the communication I have carried on with Mister Nevin Wainwright of the Strand magazine.*
>
> *Please be advised that your intrusion is not only unwelcome, but futile. There is nothing that you can do to solve any of the delectable puzzles I have presented, so please do not bore me with a vain pursuit.*
>
> *Let me also assure you that in arranging the order of the stories that I would present, I began with the most mundane, not the most dramatic. You will find future developments stunning.*
>
> *With warmest regards,*
>
> *Norma Bainsteas"*

Holmes had smiled as he read it, before handing it over to me. "Cheeky little tart, isn't she Watson? She throws down a gauntlet before me in the form of a request to mind my own business."

He pondered in silence for a moment, then added, "I wonder if she realizes what a blunder it is to engage me directly. Carrying on with Wainwright, clearly not her equal, necessitating his recitals to me, leaves room for any small errors she might make that he is too obtuse to recognize. Engaging in this arrogant repartee with me gives me a first hand look at whatever she does. We shall pounce upon her missteps like a panther, Watson. She has managed to pique my interest to such an extent that I look forward to conversing with her as she sits in police chains."

I was forced to chuckle myself as I responded to Holmes. "If I were to play a bit of devil's advocate and approach this from her point of view, I could make the case that *you* are being a bit arrogant. You seem to regard it as a foregone conclusion that you will, in fact, see her in chains."

"I *do* regard it as a foregone conclusion, old fellow. Don't you, considering that I always get my man?"

"Well, there was the time that..."

"Watson, the boat sank, drowning the culprits before I had a chance to apprehend them," he said, referring to an incident I had chronicled called *"The Five Orange Pips"*

"And there was the time that..."

"That was a photograph to be retrieved, Watson. There was no true culprit to apprehend." He was referring, of course, to *The Scandal in Bohemia.*

"I hope, Watson, that you will get those two cases out of your mind. Your frequent mention of them is becoming rather tedious."

I smiled graciously and promised never to bring them up again, but then I had made that promise frequently in the past. When debates like this one arose, they were the only two cases I could point to.

⛥

Breakfast was another chapter in the culinary legend that Mrs. Hudson was becoming, at least in my mind, and was followed by a few hours needed to complete an intriguing case called *The Adventure of the Golden Pince-Nez.* I would present it to Nevin Wainwright at the next opportunity, which I did not expect to arise as quickly as it did.

At about two-thirty, I heard footsteps rapidly ascending to the second level and assumed it was Holmes. I was not surprised to see the door opening without a knock, but was very surprised to see Wainwright burst through it.

"I say, Wainwright..."

"Doctor Watson! I must see Holmes." He looked around desperately. "Where is he?"

"I have no idea. He's been gone all day, but what brings you here in such an obviously high state of agitation?"

"This situation that this monstrous Norma Bainsteas has visited upon me is going to be the ruin of me. It has already begun." He plopped into an overstuffed chair and buried his face in his hands.

"Great Scott, Wainwright, gather a hold of yourself and take a seat. I'd ask Mr. Hudson for tea, but I think you need something a bit more bracing, perhaps a Port, or even a brandy."

"A brandy would be the thing, Doctor, a stiff one at that."

The first one disappeared before I could even get a peek out the window to see if Holmes might be approaching. By the time I had the second one poured, I heard Holmes in the foyer greeting Mrs. Hudson. He bounded up the stairs like a youth.

He did not seem surprised to find Wainwright there, but then very few things truly surprised the master detective.

He nodded affirmatively as I held up the brandy bottle and turned to face our guest as I began to pour.

"So, Wainwright, you are beset with some serious problem."

"Then you know," Wainwright blurted out.

Holmes took the glass I offered and settled into his seat. "I have no idea what your problem is, old fellow, only that you have one."

"But how..."

"You'd be able to see it yourself with a quick glance in the mirror. Your hair is windblown and you are perspiring, as though you have been running. Your coat is buttoned off kilter, as though in your haste to get here you paid no attention to getting the top button aligned with the top buttonhole, and you are missing a cuff link. Being a normally fastidious dresser, you would never leave home or office in such personal disarray unless you were dealing with something more important than your appearance.

"Add to that the significant dent that has been put in the bottle of brandy which was unopened when I left this morning, we have all the trappings of a perilous situation."

Before Wainwright could answer I said to Holmes, "He was starting to tell me that this situation with Norma Bainsteas is hurtling him toward ruination, when you arrived. I waited for you to come up before having him begin his explanation."

"Excellent, old fellow," Holmes said, turning to our visitor. "Be at ease, Mister Wainwright. I'm sure that the resources in this room are sufficient to deal with the problem. I would venture a guess that you have been visited by Herr Karl Mundt and that that is the provenance of your undeniable angst."

"Mundt." He spit the word out venomously. "He didn't come right away. Instead, he had a courier deliver me a letter from the sole owner of what was once the limited partnership that owned the Strand. He now owns the entire magazine and is my employer. The message said that I am to treat Herr Mundt like royalty because he has entered into negotiations, on behalf of his bank, to purchase the Strand at a price considerably above its assumed value.

"I was stunned. Then as I sat in my office, paralyzed with indecision, Mundt arrived. The first word out of his mouth was 'hello.' The second words were, if I dare to print the story, he would complete the transaction and I would be sacked before the ink on the contract was dry.

"Moreover, he would find, or create, evidence of financial improprieties perpetrated under my stewardship of the Strand. Even if they were later proven to be unfounded, my reputation would be destroyed in the publishing industry. I'd be on the corner *selling* magazines, instead of upstairs publishing them."

Holmes was sympathetic to the poor man's plight.

"Wainwright," he said, "All is not lost. We'll ponder this problem together and find a way to rescue you. I'm sure it can be done."

There was no relieving the anxiety that was so grievously oppressing the pathetic Wainwright.

"That is not the whole problem, sir. I have also received a threatening letter from the vile Norma Bainsteas. She was sure that we would put out a special edition devoted entirely to the story of the Aberdeen murder and embezzlement. She says that if she does not see it on the stand in ten days, she will send it to another magazine, one that she is certain will publish it forthwith.

"So, gentlemen, I am doomed. If I attempt to publish the Zurich story, the desperate Mundt will have the magazine owner stop me. Then he will buy the company and sack and ruin me.

"If I do *not* publish it, Norma will find someone who will and announce to the world that I let it slip through my fingers. Then my owner will sack me for letting such a sensational story go to the competition. I will have to throw myself into the Thames to avoid the humiliation that will be heaped upon me."

Holmes smiled benevolently. "Watson, please pour another brandy for our distraught compatriot. Then we will reason something out."

In all my years of association with Wainwright and the Strand Magazine, I had never seen him take a drink. I was now handing him his third in a ten minute period. He merely sipped this one, though, and set it down, looking somewhat like a Basset hound in the mournful way he looked at Holmes. "Have you any ideas, sir?"

"Yes, of course. My first thought is that we should set aside any anxiety and conduct ourselves here in a logical manner. First of all, we do have some time. I'm sure our devilish Norma Bainsteas will wait for the publication of the Zurich adventure until the completion of the Aberdeen case. You agree with that, I assume."

"Of course, sir."

"Then I'd suggest you make it the cover story and..."

"I'm definitely planning to do that," Wainwright interjected.

"And then serialize it. That will not only boost your sales dramatically, and please Norma to see it in the news for a longer period of time, it will extend the time we have to catch her before either she or Mundt carries out their threat. In the meantime, Doctor Watson and I have some business to attend to before we meet again."

CHAPTER 6

F IVE days after our meeting, a courier delivered a copy of the new Strand magazine that would be issued to shops and news stands the following day.

It reached the pinnacle of the hyperbole of which Nevin Wainwright was capable.

"Shocking revelations of embezzlement and murder in Scotland!" read the banner in very bold type. Below it, "See page five for the astounding details."

Turning to page five, the reader found an introductory letter from the Managing Editor, couched in serious tones to assure the reader that he must not miss a word of it.

"Never before in my long career in publishing have I been handed a story like the one that will follow shortly," it began. "The Strand magazine has obtained not only the solution to a crime that has baffled the Scottish police for six long years, but the means of verification of the crime, and amazingly, a confession from the perpetrator.

"The Managing editor of the Strand, Nevin Wainwright, along with the world famous detective, Mister Sherlock Holmes, viewed the remains of Mister Carlton Mackenzie in a rocky grave on a desolate mountainside near Grantown-on-Spey, several miles west of Aberdeen."

Having gotten his name prominently into the early paragraphs, Wainwright then went on to describe the conferences with Harrison Samuels of the Scottish police force, and the beginning interviews of the various Bainsteas families of Aberdeen.

Backtracking, he described, in unnecessary detail, the arrival of the story and the letter from Norma Bainsteas that accompanied it. It was clear to me, as it might be to any sophisticated reader of Wainwright's bloated prose that this would be a long, drawn-out presentation.

After his lengthy and self-aggrandizing introduction, Wainwright published approximately one fifth of the text of the story. Good. He would stretch it out for well over a month with publication of the story itself, supplemented by analysis and ongoing progress reports from the Scottish police, not to mention whatever he could gather from Sherlock Holmes that Holmes would allow him to reveal.

⛥

The following day, the Aberdeen newspapers jumped on the story as though Atlantis had been found. Other papers gradually picked up the story until even the stately London Times printed a lengthy article along the lines of, "will wonders never cease."

"No law enforcement officer that we interviewed," it said, "has ever heard of a crime being filed away as virtually unsolvable, only to be resurrected by, of all people, the perpetrator.

"One must be drawn to the question of why? Why would she do that? Is it random chance that this Norma Bainsteas sent the story exclusively to the Strand, the publisher of the Sherlock Holmes heroics, as chronicled by his close associate, Doctor John Watson, or are we to speculate that she is throwing a gauntlet down before the master detective? We shall see in coming installments.

"The only police official known to have read the entire text, Executive Director of the Scottish force Harrison Samuels, steadfastly refused to reveal any details not already published in the Strand. He claims his reasons are to protect the integrity of the investigation, and not to show any favoritism for the magazine.

"Sherlock Holmes was not available for comment, but then, he rarely is,"

❧❦

Three days after the Times article, with shops and stands around the country clamoring for more copies of the Strand, a second printing was run. It would soon be followed by a third and a fourth. By the time the figures were all tallied, it would be the largest single issue in the publishing company's history.

Orders for the next edition, which would carry the second installment of the story, had already broken company records. Nevin Wainwright was now sleeping more comfortably than he had since his visit from the threatening Karl Mundt.

෨෬

After the Times article, as Holmes and I sat reading the morning papers, Mrs. Hudson brought a note to Holmes that had been delivered by a courier.

Holmes tore it open and announced that we had been summoned, not invited, to lunch at the Diogenes club by his brother, Mycroft.

Mycroft"s position in Her Majesty's government has never been publicly confirmed, but insiders knew that the first man summoned to 10 Downing Street in times of crisis was the formidable Mycroft Holmes. Moreover, he was the only man in the empire who could show up at the Prime Minister's office unannounced and expect to be shown in forthwith.

Sherlock and Mycroft Holmes shared two major aspects of life; common parentage and brilliant intellects. Other than that, very little that met the eye linked them. Sherlock was tall and thin as a rail. Mycroft could most generously be described as rotund. The less kindly disposed would refer to him as obese.

Sherlock was possessed of boundless energy and would bolt out of our Baker Street rooms at the drop of a clue related to any new challenge. Mycroft found distasteful a journey across the room to refill his teacup.

While Sherlock spent a great deal of time on trains around the United Kingdom and frequently journeyed to the continent, Mycroft spent virtually one hundred percent of his time in one of three places; His flat in Pall Mall, his office at Whitehall, or the Diogenes Club. All were situated within walking distance for a person of normal energy, but Mycroft had last walked from one to another three Prime Ministers ago. For the foreseeable future, Mycroft had no further ambulatory ambitions.

Today's summons was to the Diogenes Club, the only place that Mycroft trusted for important events like his daily luncheon. If the Prime Minister's needs kept him in his office, a courier was dispatched to the Club to return with a heaping tray.

Many would prefer the relative ambient din in an undiscovered tomb to the total silence in the Diogenes Club. No one was allowed to speak in a common area, other than to cry for help in the event of a heart attack. No one could receive visitors except in the Stranger's room or a private dining room

Members had been known to be subjected to reproving glances if their shoes squeaked when walking through a common area or if their handling of their newspaper caused an offensive rustling.

Arthur, the ancient butler, led Holmes and Watson through the Stranger's room and into an elegantly appointed private dining room. It was empty when they arrived, but the table had been set for three in the finest silver, china, and crystal that could be found in the empire.

Small sterling silver domes in the center of each place setting covered what would undoubtedly turn out to be lobster bisque, Mycroft's favorite starter.

Arthur said that Mycroft would join us directly and asked if he could pour us a Port or some other libation. We both took the Port.

From past encounters, I knew that Mycroft could be both irascible and charming in the same sentence, depending on to whom he was addressing himself. Today was no exception. He plodded heavily into the room and shook my hand with vigor and a warm smile, saying, "It is always a pleasure to see you, Doctor. With the same breath, he said, "Good day, Sherlock," in a tone that could best be describes as churlish.

Sherlock gave him an amused smile and said cheerfully, "Good day to yourself, Mycroft, and to what do we owe today's truculence."

"Truculence, indeed. I'm appalled at the disrespect that you have visited upon me." His gruff manner in opening dialog with Sherlock was not unknown to me. Nor was a quick change of attitude within a matter of minutes.

"My dear Mycroft," Holmes said without a waver in his smile, "please identify the specific disrespect that I have visited upon you so that I can couch my abject apology in the most appropriate terms." He gave me an unobtrusive wink of the eye.

"Specific, indeed," Mycroft said, taking his seat, shaking his napkin loose with a flourish, and removing the silver cover from his soup. "The Prime Minister came into my office this morning-where the devil is the Sherry?-carrying a copy of the Strand." Sherlock handed his rotund brother a crystal cruet brimming with Sherry. Mycroft poured a generous amount into his soup and handed the cruet to me.

"The Prime Minister asked me what I knew about it and I hadn't seen the magazine and knew *nothing* about it."

"I see," Holmes said gravely, "and your lack of knowledge of an obscure murder in Northern Scotland has placed the empire in peril?"

"Do not be snide, Sherlock, it ill becomes you. When the Prime Minister asks me a question, he expects me to know the answer. Here is a story in which my own brother turns out to be hip deep and I know nothing about it. I find that very vexing. Anyone in the British Isles who has read the Strand today could answer the P.M.'s question, but his most trusted advisor could not."

"Then my apology is not only sincere but profuse. I will endeavor to see that you are the first to be informed of my activities."

Mycroft shot Sherlock a glance, trying to detect any sarcasm in the reply, but if intended, it was well masked.

"Tell me the story." Mycroft said grumpily.

Holmes went through it in great detail, pointing out, as he did so, any facts that had not been made public. Mycroft nodded, but said nothing through the salad and into the entrée, a delicate Dover sole.

"The Gaulois cigarettes?"

"Too early to determine anything about them yet."

Mycroft nodded, "A red herring?"

"Certainly possible. As we wrap it up we'll learn for sure."

"Garret Dickinson?"

"The only mysterious thing about him is that we can't find him," Holmes said. "There is nothing to connect him to Mackenzie or anything illegal. We just don't know, but Harrison Samuels is widening his search area. We may find him working somewhere in Scotland with nothing to link him to anything, and drop him from our lists. I would say only that if we cannot locate him, that would be a curiosity."

"Anything else?"

Holmes smiled and said, "There has been another story delivered from this Norma Bainsteas."

It had the effect Holmes thought it would. Mycroft snapped his head up from his teacup to face his brother. "Another story? Another perfect crime?"

"Exactly."

"Mother of Heaven, tell me about it!"

Holmes started into a description of our Zurich adventure in the same painstaking detail as the one in Aberdeen.

Mycroft smiled at the first mention of Karl Mundt's name, but listened in silence. As his brother concluded with the dire threat that had reduced the hapless Wainwright to jelly, Mycroft smiled knowingly.

"I've met Herr Mundt, Sherlock. He can be a tough old goat. Scotland Yard was looking into some transactions his bank, directed by Mundt personally, was into. There was a faint whiff of skullduggery, but no apparent victim, at least none willing to pursue it in court."

"So, Mycroft, it's refreshing to see him getting a little comeuppance from this Rene Ladier."

"Indeed. So let's recap this business. We have an unsolved crime in Scotland and an uncovered crime in Switzerland, both reaping substantial amounts of money for the perpetrators, and both several years dormant.

"Now comes Miss Bainsteas to reveal the crimes, but to also confess to them."

"Correct."

"Tell me, Sherlock, do we know how many people are involved in all of this? I mean we seem to have two women, at least two women's names, LaDier and Bainsteas and at least one unnamed man mentioned in the Aberdeen story. Depending on how big a man Carlton Mackenzie was, it could have been very difficult to kill him, transport him to Grantown-on-Spey and lug him up the mountain."

"Exceedingly difficult, Mycroft. It's an effort to walk up that mountain empty-handed, but to carry a man...?" Holmes shook his head. "Mackenzie was a good-sized man, over six feet tall and a good fifteen stone in weight."

"So it would seem that at least two men were involved," Mycroft speculated.

Holmes nodded as Mycroft continued. "'This is unprecedented in my experience. I'm sure we both expect culprits to be denying everything but their names. It leads one to wonder what the motivation could possibly be. I think it is insufficient to say that she just wants to boast and ask that recognition be given to those operating on the dark side."

"Agreed, Mycroft, but at this point we don't have enough to even speculate about. You will recall the Antique Weapons Murders, which seemed so pointless until we tracked down our half sibling, Linville, and the whole insidious plot was revealed. We had no idea where that one was going at the outset."

Mycroft nodded agreement. "Yes, yes, you're correct, of course. As we've always said, find the motive and you'll find the criminal." Mycroft gave a gesture of finality. "We'll set this aside for now since I must return to Whitehall, but about that note you sent me a few days ago...about this Norma Bainsteas. Although you didn't give me any idea what it was about..."

Sherlock Holmes turned to me to explain. "You'll recall, Watson, that I received a telegram from our Norma a few days ago telling me that she was passing through Aberdeen and learned that I was looking for her. She then told me not to intrude in the ongoing dialog she had with Wainwright."

"Of course I recall it."

"Well, when I was out, I sent a telegram to Harrison Samuels regarding it. He verified that it was sent from Aberdeen but the telegrapher could not recall anything about the sender...only that it was a woman. He claims he gets so many requests, he doesn't pay any attention to the senders."

I shrugged and Holmes continued.

"We don't know if it's the same person, but we do know that we found a William Bainsteas there who had a sister named Norma, so there's a possible logic to it."

I nodded understanding.

"Since the one Norma that we could possibly be pursuing married and moved to France, I also sent a wire to Mycroft, asking him to contact customs to see when she may have returned to the United Kingdom, and what her point of entry was. That information could be helpful in tracking her down."

"Yes, of course," I answered.

Holmes turned back to Mycroft. "Were you able to learn anything?"

Mycroft shook his head negatively. "Nothing. As of this morning, they had traced back six months and determined that no Norma Bainsteas or Norma LaMauret had either entered or left the U.K. In fact, the only two Normas with any surname who entered were an eighty-eight year old who returned home from Belgium in a casket, and an American who entered from Paris, spent a few days in London, and returned to America."

Holmes nodded, "No real surprise there. Anyone clever enough to commit the two crimes she has told us about, and undoubtedly countless others, could easily obtain a passport under any name she wanted."

"Undoubtedly so," Mycroft said. "Incidentally, Sherlock, if this Mundt gets too overbearing with your man Wainwright, let me know. The Prime Minister is not very fond of the machinations of Swiss banks with British currency and I'm sure we can put some effective counter pressure on someone threatening one of her majesty's citizens."

Mycroft laboriously rose. "I must leave, gentlemen. What is your next step, Sherlock?"

"I'm heading back to Aberdeen. Whoever sent this telegram was physically in that city. We have to attempt to find her, difficult as that will be. I'll have to try to convince my associate, John Hamish Watson, to accompany me. That will cost me a meal at some outrageously expensive restaurant up there, but it will be worth it."

I merely smiled and nodded. As though he could keep me from going.

"One final request, Sherlock. Please see that the Prime Minister does not hear anything more of this case before I do."

⚜

We hurried back to Baker Street to pack and found a small package included in our mail. Holmes opened it and smiled wryly. It had no note and no return address, just a fresh package of Gaulois cigarettes.

CHAPTER 7

THE train ride up to Aberdeen was relatively uneventful, atrocious tea and nothing on the menu that would appeal to a man not in the final stages of death by starvation.

Of interest was the observation Holmes made on his two walks from one end of the train to the other, resulting from his inability to stay seated for the six hour trip. I was perfectly content to snuggle into my seat, pen in hand, and fill in my journal with facts regarding the case at hand. The Strand would print the stories from Norma's point of view, but I would write it from Holmes.' If Wainwright tried to do that, I'd threaten to allow the rival Gazette to publish future episodes in the career of Sherlock Holmes.

"I've made two observations, Watson, as I strolled back and forth on the train. One is that the national estimate of approximately ten percent of the population being left-handed is probably true, at least on this train ride."

I looked at all of the people within my limited sight and none of them were doing anything with their hands, which led me to challenge his assertion. Such byplay was one of the reasons Holmes enjoyed my company. His inquisitive nature required him to make sense of every visual reality he encountered. Anything out of place caught his attention but would be missed by almost everyone in the empire because so few truly observed their surroundings as Holmes did.

I had once strolled down Regent Parkway with Holmes when he took my elbow and led me into an apothecary. When I asked the reason, he said, "I need to observe something, Watson. Please amuse yourself for a few minutes."

Approximately three minutes later, he pulled a Bobby in from the sidewalk and said to him, "Please observe that gentleman standing beside the hansom cab, speaking to the cabbie."

"I see him, sir, what about him?"

"In a very few minutes, he is going to rob the jewelry store two shops down and flee with the help of the cabdriver, who will turn out to have stolen the hansom. In fact, he is not a cabbie at all."

Incredibly, it happened exactly as Holmes had predicted. When asked how he knew, he vexed the police officer no end by telling him he should be more observant.

That was early in his career, and taught me to never question his observations. Unfortunately, I haven't learned that lesson as well as I should have. Today, for example.

"I say, Holmes, my observation is that you have drawn a conclusion on woefully inadequate facts. None of the passengers within my view is writing or holding his tea cup. You have undoubtedly made your observations from the very small percentage of passengers who were. While your observation may be correct, it was made from too small a sample."

"Correct as far as your observations go, Watson," Holmes said cheerfully, clearly delighted that I had chosen to engage him in the jousting of logic, "but they do not go far enough. There are numerous other indicators, but I will content myself with just three.

"Since you mention those writing, I certainly did count them, but you must also note that a left-handed writer that stops to use his hand for another purpose will always deposit his pencil behind his left ear, and vice-versa. No one would reach around to the other side of his head. A small sample also, but a clear indicator.

"Since you mentioned tea drinkers, I did count those holding cups with their left hands, but also used another indicator. Left handed persons will always orient the cup so that the handle faces the hand they use to lift it. Indicator number two.

"Indicator number three, which you did not mention, is the side of the head on which a man parts his hair. He will always reach across his head to comb it because it is entirely too cumbersome not to. Add to that, the gentleman serving tea, who carries the tray in his right hand, so as to be able to use his left, the one he prefers, to set the tea before us."

As the valet took our cups and set fresh ones before us, I thanked him and added, "I notice that you serve the tea with your left hand. Are you left-handed?"

"Yes, sir. Just like my father before me."

In surrendering the point, I asked Holmes, "What was your second observation?"

"That fully a third of the riders on this train are reading the Strand magazine. If we were to interpolate that fact to the general population, Norma Bainsteas has overnight become one of the most popular authors in The United Kingdom, a worthy rival to Doctor John H. Watson."

"Hmpph," I mumbled, "beginner's luck."

⚜

We pulled into Aberdeen and engaged a carriage to convey us to the office of Harrison Samuels. Aberdeen is a lovely old seaport on the East coast in the North of Scotland. It is always a delight to approach and cross the sturdy old Brig o' Balgownie over the river Don.

Aberdeen is called the City of Granite, owing to the profusion of pink or grey buildings made of the granite cut from the Rubislaw quarries.

I had actually spent more time in Aberdeen over the years than Holmes had, due to my career in medicine. The University of Aberdeen, like Oxford and Cambridge, is not a single college. Aberdeen consists of Marischal college, founded in 1593, and the even older King's college, from 1495.

King's college was founded by a Papal Bull, and has the oldest medical school in the British Isles. It had been my honor and privilege to serve as guest lecturer several times, although it had been eleven years since my last invitation. The passage of time has not weakened my esteem and affection for the venerable old institution.

∂§∂

Upon our arrival in Harrison Samuels' office, Holmes immediately produced the telegram from Norma Bainsteas for Samuels' inspection.

It took only a few seconds to read and Samuels dropped it on the desk. "Well, Mister Holmes, we've thoroughly interrogated the telegrapher. He claims he can't recall what this Norma Bainsteas looked like. He says she was just a woman and he hardly looked at her. But here was an interesting development, though it may not lead anywhere.

"Officer Crawford heard me talking about Norma and that you were coming up and all and he said he thinks he saw her."

"Is Officer Crawford available now?"

"Of course. I told him to stand by until we called for him." With that, Samuels walked to the door and waved a tall, plumpish, rosy-cheeked officer in.

After introductions, Crawford took a seat and told us the story, such as it was.

"I was making my normal rounds in the North End yesterday in the morning. There's a large outdoor market and across several stalls, I saw what I thought was a very familiar looking woman. I say familiar looking because I couldn't be certain about any part of her.

"Who I thought it was, was Norma Bainsteas." He looked a bit sheepish, smiling shyly. "I had gone to school with Norma when we were young and, in truth...I was kind of sweet on her. Of course, that was twenty years ago and I haven't seen her since.

"What came to my mind was that I had heard her name mentioned in the office earlier. I was passing Mister Samuels' office and he mentioned the name to someone seated in front of him. I'm not sure who it was, but it was none of my business, so I kept on going and didn't think of it again.

"But now I'm making my rounds and don't I think I see Norma herself standing there...big as life? So I walked over behind her and said, 'Hello, Norma.' She didn't react at all, just kept inspecting the lavender. So I stepped closer and said it again, a bit louder, 'Hello, Norma.'"

"She turns and looks right into my eyes and says, 'Are you speaking to me?'"

"I am, says I, and I ask if she ain't the Norma Bainsteas that I went to school with all these years ago. She says she's not. I said to her, 'You sure look like her.'

"She looks at me and says, 'I am not Norma anything and I've never heard of that surname you mentioned. You look like Quasimodo to me, but I'm sure you're not. We all make mistakes.' Right cheeky she was. With that she scoops up the lavender and goes to the cashier.

"I had no reason to pursue it further, so I just took me comeuppance and moved on. This morning I was in the station getting ready to start out again and I mentioned to Director Samuels that I had heard him mention the name and think I saw her yesterday. Don't he get all excited and tell me to stay around until you get here, after he asked me a hundred questions, of course."

Holmes waited until Officer Crawford was finished and began. "First of all, is that the end of your story? Or did you see her again."

"No sir, end of story."

"Now Officer Crawford, from a distance, you thought it was her. Did your impression change when you saw her up close? Were you more or less sure it was her?"

"*Sure* is not the right word, sir. I'm not sure it was her, at all. But as you say, my impression did change. Up close, I felt more strongly that it was her, but I just can't be sure."

Holmes nodded. "We'll come back to that in just a moment. Let me ask you this first. Was the Norma Bainsteas that you knew when you were in school the sister of a farmer named William Bainsteas, who lives outside of town?"

"She was. She is. A lovely man, that. Always time for a friendly word, even a drop of tea."

"Yes," Holmes said, "that was my impression of him, too. So Crawford, describe Miss Bainsteas in as much detail as you can recall, then we'll discuss how she has changed over the years."

"Yes, well to start with, she's a good stone and a half heavier than she was in her younger days. Not unpleasantly overweight, but not as trim as she once was. Her hair is lighter, browner. I remember it being black."

"Her voice, Crawford. How would you describe her voice?"

Crawford pursed his lips, pondering. "A lovely voice, actually. Soft, a bit melodic, even though she was being as unpleasant as she could be."

The questioning went on for another forty minutes or so before Holmes was satisfied he had gleaned from Crawford's memory all that could be gotten. As soon as the officer was excused, Holmes suggested that we hasten out to the farm of William Bainsteas, certainly the most logical course of action.

The driver kept the whip to the gray stallions pulling the carriage and got us to the farm's entrance as quickly as it could be done. Mister Bainsteas not being anywhere to be seen, it was necessary to walk to the back of the property, where we found him in his huge barn.

His greeting was as effusive as the last time and, seemingly, no less sincere. "Mister Holmes, Doctor Watson! A pleasure to see you both again." He looked at Police Director Samuels and Holmes quickly made the appropriate introductions.

Bainsteas' eyes grew wary, as one would expect. We had visited him earlier, Holmes giving as a reason that he had been engaged to find Norma to deliver a document. Now he was faced not only with a famous detective, but with a high ranking police official. He would be much harder to deceive now.

Bainsteas eyed all of us carefully. "Why are you here? I'm sure that you will not try to tell me again that you have a letter for Norma, certainly not with a police executive like Mister Samuels."

Holmes got right to the point. "We need to see your sister immediately. Perhaps you could ask her to join us."

Bainsteas didn't respond very quickly. When he did, the previous warmth and cooperativeness he had evinced earlier were noticeably absent. "Why do you want to see Norma?" he asked quietly.

Samuels stepped in. "I'm afraid that we will be asking the questions, Mister Bainsteas, and, at the moment, not answering any. Now where is your sister?"

Bainsteas folded his arms over his chest, struck an aggressive pose and said nothing, staring firmly into Samuels' eyes.

Samuels stepped closer to Bainsteas, saying, "I asked you where your sister is Mister Bainsteas and I demand an answer right now." Bainsteas continued to stare, saying nothing.

Holmes spoke in a more conciliatory voice. I had the clear impression that he thought that Samuels had taken too firm a tone too early.

"Mister Bainsteas, I hope that we can conduct this business as amicably as possible. I understand that you are concerned for your sister, but you do not serve your interests well by forcing Director Samuels to issue threats and I promise you, sir, they will be forthcoming shortly. Please tell us where your sister is."

"Is this about the Frenchman?" Bainsteas asked.

"Her husband?"

"Yes, her husband. Are you here because of something related to him?"

"No. our business concerns only Norma, as far as we know at the moment."

That seemed to surprise him. "What would you want with Norma if he isn't involved?"

Samuels had had about enough, "See here, Mister Bainsteas...," but Holmes laid a gently restraining hand on his arm and offered an explanation. "I have a letter that I believe that she wrote. It was addressed to the publisher of the Strand magazine. We would like her to verify that she wrote the letter and provide some clarification of certain passages in it."

"A letter to the Strand...?"

Holmes nodded affirmatively, having given an honest, non-threatening answer that he was sure would provide little usable information to Bainsteas. It should surely lessen his tension.

"I don't think I understand, Mister Holmes. Why should a letter to a magazine be a matter for the police."

"It's possible that she witnessed something that could be of value in a theft investigation." Another exercise in benevolent obfuscation. "Now, Mister Bainsteas, I've tried to answer your questions, but we really must insist that you tell us where Norma is. Time is a factor in the business at hand."

Bainsteas sighed deeply, "I do not know where Norma is."

"Mister Bainsteas..." a frustrated Samuels started to interject.

"I'm telling you, gentlemen, I do not know where she is," Bainsteas replied, at the same level of frustration. "She spent a few days with us, then last night announced that she was leaving this morning and she left. That's all I know."

"How did she leave?" Holmes asked.

"In Mister Wrightson's carriage. He came to collect her promptly at eleven."

"If that's the truth, then I'm sure that you will not mind if we take a look through your home." Samuels said.

"I certainly do mind. Setting aside the fact that you are essentially calling me a liar, you are asking to do something that you have no reason or right to do."

"I can easily obtain a warrant, Mister Bainsteas, and between Mister Holmes, Doctor Watson, my driver, and myself, we can easily surround the house to prevent anyone from leaving."

"There is no one in the house, so that is not a concern."

Holmes excused himself, spoke briefly to the officer who had driven us to the farm, and returned to the conversation. The driver once again laid the whip to the horses and was gone at great speed.

Holmes broke into the, by now, heated conversation about a search of the house. He smiled understandingly, "Is there possibly something else in the house that you do not want us to see? Or perhaps do not want Director Samuels to see?"

Bainsteas once again fell silent while he thought. It was a most disconcerting and rather vexing habit. Finally he said, "If I may speak hypothetically... supposing I had a case of something that had been left in my safekeeping, *temporarily,* and Director Samuels saw it."

"For the love of heaven," Samuels roared, "are you talking about Mooney's poteen?"

"Poteen is an Irish word and I..."

"Mooney *is* Irish, that's why he calls it poteen!"

"Nevertheless..."

"Mister Bainsteas, *I* have a case of Mooney's poteen in *my* home, so if that's what you are concerned about..."

"That *is* what I am concerned about."

❧

It took less than half an hour to walk through the home and to thoroughly examine the room that Norma had used during her visit. The only thing of interest that we found was a crumpled scrap of paper that simply said "Lange," followed by an address in Cornwall. Holmes put it in his pocket as we returned to the kitchen.

Perhaps Bainsteas had been overly concerned about the illegal potato whiskey in his cellar, but that not being an issue, he loosened up considerably. When we returned to the kitchen, he had prepared tea and set out a plate of scones.

The conversation flowed a bit more freely as we had our tea. In brief, Bainsteas' story was that Norma showed up unannounced, but apparently in good spirits, saying that she was in Scotland for a short time and was only visiting selected family members and a few friends. Bainsteas took this to mean that she was avoiding the family members who had voiced disapproval of her marriage to Denis LaMauret, the Frenchman of uncertain reputation.

"I was just coming to that," Holmes said, "why was he not traveling with her?"

Bainsteas seemed a bit more animated in answering this question. "That was the only curious thing that arose during her stay, Mister Holmes. I asked her why Denis was not with her and she simply said, 'Denis and I are not together right now.'

"I asked if she meant 'right now' as in today, or were they apart of a longer duration. She repeated that they were not together right now and asked about one of our neighbors. We never got her back on the subject."

Holmes pondered that and changed the subject briefly. "An Aberdeen police officer believes he had a brief conversation with Norma yesterday in the morning."

"Yes," Bainsteas replied with a firm nod. "She mentioned that. An Officer Crawford, I believe."

"Did she tell you that she denied being Norma Bainsteas and was abrupt to the point of rudeness with Officer Crawford?" Holmes asked.

Bainsteas didn't seem to take it too seriously. "She did. I'm afraid that, with Norma, you are going to get that occasionally. She wouldn't deny who she is if it was police business, but she was not looking for any personal conversation with old acquaintances, except for those of her choosing."

"Mister Bainsteas," Holmes asked, "how do you account for the fact that according to the Ministry of Immigration, no Norma Bainsteas or Norma LaMauret has entered or left the United Kingdom in the last six months?"

He seemed genuinely surprised. "I can't account for that at all. I have no idea. She has never used another name that I am aware of."

Although we spent another hour on questions, nothing that I perceived as important was revealed. Holmes did not mention that he had observed anything else of significance, but with this frequently reticent man one never knew.

We were in the carriage a matter of seconds and Holmes asked the driver what he had learned, explaining that he had asked him to go directly to the train station and attempt to learn what train, if any, Norma had taken.

"Nothing of value, sir. I began by interviewing Wrightson, the carriage driver, who said that he took Miss Bainsteas straight to the train station. He carried her bag inside, accepted his pay, and left her there. He said that she entered into no conversation with him the entire way to the depot. In fact, she had her eyes closed at least half the time.

The train station master says that he sold at least six one way tickets to single women and couldn't describe any of them. For that matter, a visitor to Aberdeen could have arrived with a round trip ticket, in which case he might not have even seen her."

Holmes simply nodded and thanked him for the effort. Turning to us, he said, "She would undoubtedly cover her trail effectively. I feared that we would learn nothing, but we must go through the effort on any possible leads."

Turning to Director Samuels, Holmes said, "I'm sure that you have considered the possibility that she has not really left Aberdeen, even though it is most likely that she has."

"I have considered it, Mister Holmes, and I plan to have all of my officers meet and hear Crawford describe her. I will put a high priority on finding her here in Aberdeen, but I also think it unlikely."

"Doctor Watson and I will be returning to London on the first train in the morning, but we will certainly keep you abreast of any developments as we uncover them, and we thank you for your hospitality and cooperation."

Dinner was a fairly dismal affair, but it made me appreciate Mrs. Hudson's culinary ministrations even more. It occurred to me to suggest to Holmes that we bring her with us on long trips, but I knew that it didn't matter to him what he ate, not to mention when or if.

The journey home was uneventful. As usual, Holmes spent the half hour prior to departure sending telegrams and would expect responses upon our arrival in London.

CHAPTER 8

WE arrived at Baker Street a few hours before supper time, giving me an opportunity for a long leisurely bath. Holmes immediately snatched the small stack of telegrams he'd received, packed his pipe, and sat back to read them.

By the time I had finished my quite pleasurable ablutions and dressed for dinner, Holmes was on his third pipeful. The disgusting cloud of blue/grey smoke that often lingered across the top of the room was even thicker than normal. I hurriedly opened the windows and rather ostentatiously fanned the air with a newspaper, but got no reaction from Holmes.

"I say, Holmes, that shag cut tobacco, or whatever you call it has the most noxious odor."

No response.

"Could poison the lungs of someone not even smoking it," I mumbled.

After what seemed like several minutes, Holmes looked over, as though surprised to see me and said, "Ah, Watson, glad to see you. If you're having a Port, I'll join you."

"I was just going to suggest it, Holmes," I said pleasantly. Churlishness was often lost on him.

The Port poured and each of us comfortably ensconced in our favorite chairs, I inquired about the telegrams.

"A few things of interest, but nothing that has moved us closer to finding the elusive Norma Bainsteas, or Rene LaDier.

"First of all, you will recall that we found a scrap of paper in the waste basket that Norma used. It held an address in a small town in Cornwall. I sent a telegram to a local constable asking him to check on the address and he sent me a reply.

"There is a young couple living there with two small children. The man has run a small toy shop for the last four years and they seem to be perfectly normal in every way. Community involvement, children in the local school, a pint and game of darts in the local pub several times a week, all that.

"He has not approached either of them at my request. I've asked him to keep an eye on the property and inform me of any visitors. The town is so small that there is only one carriage operating as a cab from the train station. Most of the time, the carriage is used to deliver groceries. So, we'll have to await further developments down there. If we don't get any activity related to our case soon, we may have to journey to

Cornwall to interview the Langes, as he calls them, ourselves.

"The next wire presents a puzzle. I've asked a member of the French Surete, with whom I've done a little work, to look into this Denis LaMauret, hoping that we can find the one that is married to Norma Bainsteas.

"Amazingly, there is no one living in Paris, in any registry, with that name and that exact spelling. He found one in Rouen, but he is a man of great age. But more mystery mixed into the stew Watson. A Denis LaMauret in his late thirties died early in the year in Honfleur. You recall Honfleur, Watson...on the coast..."

"Certainly. One of my favorite little towns in all of France. How did he die, if we know, and have we any way of knowing if it's the LaMauret we are seeking?"

Holmes shook his head briskly. "Nothing specific yet. All we know is that he died in Honfleur, and that he seems to be of the right age. My associate, DeLanne, will travel up there in the next few days and look into it. So, more waiting, Watson. Enough to try a man's patience."

I smiled, thinking that of all the possible emotional commodities men possess, patience is the one which Holmes has in smallest measure.

"Anything more?"

"A note from Mycroft informing us of no further progress in finding any Norma Bainsteas or LaMauret in the immigration records, *and...*" he said lightly, "another telegram from Norma."

I snapped my head around to face him and found him smiling. "Seriously, Holmes?"

"Seriously, old fellow, and her intentions are just a little clearer. She seems determined to tweak our noses at every opportunity. Listen to this. It reads, 'My dear Mister Holmes, I've learned from my brother that you are seeking to find me. I can't imagine why, but I do intend to be in London in a fortnight. Perhaps I will have a chance to look you up."

I chuckled. "She raises disingenuousness to new levels with every communication. Had she not committed such foul deeds, I could see myself feeling a bit of affection for her."

"Yes," Holmes agreed, "she does have a rascalous charm to her. We shall see how clever she is when she is in chains."

It seems that Mrs. Hudson excels most on the first meal after Holmes and I have traveled. A welcome home, perhaps. Tonight's lamb shank with vegetables and a heavy gravy was a tour de force. We complimented her profusely.

With Port and our pipes after dinner, I asked Holmes what our next move was. "Cogitation, Watson. I am feeling more and more that there is more here than meets the eye...that things are not exactly as they seem to be."

I viewed him curiously. "Could you be a little more specific, Holmes? I agree that we have a devil of a task before us in trying to track down these women, Norma Bainsteas and Rene LaDier, but the big picture seems clear enough."

Holmes nodded patiently. "How so, Watson?"

"Well, we have a young lady who pulled off a seemingly perfect crime, the murder of Mackenzie and the theft of his funds."

"That would be Norma Bainsteas?" Holmes asked.

"Of course, Norma. Then later, she, possibly in league with another woman, commits another perfect crime, the bilking of the bank in Zurich. They now have enough money to live comfortably for a long time, maybe the rest of their lives. But inevitably, they grow bored. They read about your exploits in the Strand and they feel that their own accomplishments are equal to yours, so they seek recognition, while keeping themselves in a perfectly safe place."

Holmes waited until he was sure that I was finished and said, "Is that the case as you see it, Watson?"

"It certainly is. I assume you see it the same way."

He nodded, "And where did you get your information?"

"Where? From the letters and stories, of course."

I didn't like it when Holmes played word games with me, but on the other hand I had never disagreed with him and turned out to be right.

"My point, Watson. Everything we know that is of significance, came from the other side. All that our investigation, including three long trips, has done is verify that what they, or she, told us is true. Now, why would we believe them?"

"But Holmes, you just said that we have verified everything they have done!"

"Everything they *have done*, Watson, not what they *are doing.* I am certain that there is much more afoot than they are saying."

"Why?" I demanded.

"Because it doesn't make sense. It is inane to believe that they would jeopardize past successes and their futures just to act in some snobbish superior way. What they have told us is what they *want us to know*. What they have *not* told us is what *we* really want to know.

CHAPTER 9

T HE new day began just as the onset of our current adventure had, with Holmes and I reading the papers after breakfast and Wainwright arriving to see Holmes. He and Ian McDonough were shown in and seated quickly, obviously in a state of high excitement.

"Another communication from Norma, Mister Holmes. She says things are going too slowly and she wants us to finish the Carlton Mackenzie story in the next two issues, then publish the Zurich story in only two or three issues because, now listen to this, these are mere trifles. She wants to get to the *big stories*.

"Imagine it, Mister Holmes. A vicious murder and embezzlement, followed by the bilking of a major Swiss bank out of three million francs, still a problem for the bank all these years later, and she calls them *trifles*. What could possibly have been worse than these?"

"What indeed?" Holmes mused.

"*Multiple* murders, maybe." Ian McDonough interjected. "Whitechapel...Mother of God, what if she is Jack the Ripper?"

All eyes fell upon Wainwright's young assistant, whose relative youth and enthusiasm had been a source of amusement to all of us from the outset of the investigation.

"*Jack the Ripper?*" said Wainwright in astonished tones, "She's a *woman* for heaven's sake. Jack the Ripper is a man." He was prepared to dismiss the notion as absurd.

"How do we know it's a man if the monster has never been caught?" McDonough demanded. "Isn't it possible, Mister Holmes?"

Holmes shrugged. "In the ebb and flow of man's inhumanity, there are precious few things that are truly impossible. It's a very interesting thought, Ian. I would tend to doubt that the horrors in Whitechapel were perpetrated by a woman, but I would never allow an unsolved problem to close my mind to any possibility. Jack the Ripper a woman. One could conjure up a number of psychological scenarios to support such a theory, I suppose."

Turning to me, he asked, "What do you think, Watson? Is young McDonough on to something?"

I was taken somewhat aback to have the question posed to me so suddenly, especially since I did not have a strong feeling about it. "My first reaction, Holmes, to be honest, was the same as Wainwright's. It's an absurd idea. But in chronicling your cases over the years, I have come to the position that you just stated, that there are few true impossibilities in life.

"What could be more absurd than the notion of sending a snake down a false bell-rope in a locked room to kill a pair of sisters and preserve an inheritance? And yet, we know that that very thing occurred."

"Ah yes, *The Speckled Band*," said Wainwright, "one of the most successful stories we ever printed. I still get orders for it all these years later."

Holmes seemed anxious now to drop the subject and get back to Norma. "Watson, I have a thought. Perhaps you could send a note to that chap Freud in Vienna and ask his opinion on whether Jack the Ripper could be a woman. His reply might be of interest.

"For now, though, we'll applaud young McDonough for his original thinking, and get back to the problem at hand." Turning quickly to Wainwright, he asked,

"What do you plan to do as a result of Norma's orders?"

"Exactly as she says we should do," Wainwright answered, as though he found the question fatuous. "I've already assigned Ian here to edit the story, find the place to split it that best increases the suspense and our readership's anxiety to purchase the next issue."

"Yes, excellent," Holmes replied, "exactly what you should do. Now, beyond that..."

We were suddenly jolted by a sharp rap on the door. Mrs. Hudson came in, saying, "Please excuse the interruption, Mister Holmes, but there is a most boorish man downstairs demanding to see you. I told him that you were in conference and could not be disturbed.

"He uttered a profanity and said that if I did not interrupt you, he would."

As my outrage boiled to the surface, I stood to go down and confront this insolence, but noticed that Holmes had an amused smile on his face. "And did this boorish man identify himself, Mrs, Hudson?" He asked.

"He did, sir. His name is Karl Mundt and he claims that he has just arrived from Zurich, Switzerland."

"Mundt, Mrs. Hudson? He certainly has arrived from Switzerland. Please show the gentleman up." Holmes seemed almost jolly to hear of this new development. Turning to the rest of us, he said, "Gentlemen, I believe that our plot is about to thicken."

Mundt blew into the room like a gale off the North Sea. "Holmes! Thank God you're in today." He turned to me and nodded, "Doctor Watson.

"Ah, Wainwright, I'm glad you are here." Looking to McDonough, his face registered something like surprise. He asked, gruffly, "Who are you?"

McDonough rose and said respectfully, "Ian McDonough, sir. I work at the Strand, also...for Mister Wainwright." Mundt looked at him for a moment, as though he might order him to leave, but then turned back to Holmes."

"Mister Holmes, after all these years...I've seen Rene LaDier!"

We were stunned. "You saw her?" I blurted out, even though I normally let Holmes do all the talking.

"Yes I saw her. If the devil has a wife, it is surely this monster." He plopped into a chair and buried his head in his hands, then looked up to Holmes.

"Watson, could I impose upon you to ask Mrs. Hudson to send up another pot of tea and pour Herr Mundt a stiff brandy. I think he could use a bracer.

"Now Herr Mundt, tell us about your encounter with this devilish lady."

"I had finished my day's work, but I had a civic meeting later in the evening, so I stayed downtown. I went to a quiet restaurant, ordered my dinner, and had my head down over the newspaper, when the chair across from me moved and someone sat down, without invitation. I snapped my head up and my eyes met Rene LaDier's.

"I gasped, my head felt like it was spinning. It must have been a minute before I could even speak. She said to me, "Herr Mundt, you seem so surprised to see me, and not too happy at that. I'm disappointed. I thought people were always happy to see old friends."

By then, I had collected myself and said to her, "I'm *not* happy to see you. What do you want?"

"Following, gentlemen, is how the conversation went. She said; "We'll get to that in a moment. You've been keeping company with some disreputable people, Herr Mundt."

"Disreputable..."

"Yes. You've been consorting with the likes of Sherlock Holmes and my new publisher Nevin Wainwright. They operate on the other side of the law, Herr Mundt, while you and I live on the dark side of the law."

"I do *not* live on the dark side. I made one mistake in my dealings with you..."

"A very serious mistake, sir. But do not be terribly upset with yourself. Many others have done the same. To discuss why I am here, I have ordered Mister Wainwright to conclude the story he is serializing within two weeks and to publish your story immediately after that."

"You're a monster. We had an agreement ..."

"You can have agreements with others on the dark side, sir, but do not expect them to keep their promises unless it is convenient for them. It is no longer convenient for me to abide by our agreement."

"What do you want, more money?"

"Not at the moment, Herr Mundt, at least not *your* money."

"What then?" I asked.

"She smiled as sweetly as she could, like a cobra trying to look harmless. She said, 'I need to use your banking services. I have given Mister Wainwright the story that he is currently publishing. I'm sure you are aware of it."

"Of course I'm aware of it."

"I haven't discussed with him the fee I will require for allowing him to publish my stories. I plan to do that shortly. He is making obscene amounts of money on my first story and will do even better when all of the evidence I am providing is published."

"You still haven't told me what you want from me, Rene."

"Just this. When I inform Mister Wainwright of the price for this story and several future stories, I will need a conduit to flow the money from The Strand to me, since I do not want to leave a trail. You will be that conduit. I will instruct him to transfer the money to a numbered account at your bank. Then I will instruct you how to deliver the payment, *in cash*, to me."

"What if he refuses to pay for the stories, especially since it sounds as though you are planning to charge him an outrageous amount?"

"I'm very sure that he *will* pay because he sees enormous profits from these stories. If he does not, then I will sell them to another magazine. Never underestimate man's avarice, Herr Mundt."

"Or woman's avarice," I said bitterly.

"Or woman's, to be sure."

"So I said to her, why should I help you? You've already ordered Wainwright to destroy me by printing that horrible story."

"Yes, but I can just as easily tell him not to. I have several stories I can send him. As of right now, your destruction is three weeks away. You have to decide whether you want to survive or not."

"Suppose I decide that I can not live this way and I decide to seize you by the neck and drag you right down to the police station. I am a wealthy man, so all I will have to live with is disgrace. You, on the other hand, will spend a lengthy time in prison."

"Two things. Number one, you could not stand the disgrace. And you can not be sure that the bank will not press charges against you. Secondly, you could not lay a hand on me, even if you wanted to."

"Why couldn't I?"

"Because I will give a quick signal before you could get to me and someone else in the restaurant will shoot you."

"She said it with this most pleasant smile Then she said, 'Then I will then leave safely and send the story to the newspapers. You will either be dead from the bullet or wish you were when the story comes out. So, Herr Mundt, don't try to bluff me. I will proceed on the assumption that you will comply with my instructions.

"With that, gentlemen, she rose from her chair and left."

Holmes shook his head, seemingly in admiration of the lady, or ladies, that were vexing so many lives. "I also assume that you will comply, Herr Mundt. You do not seem to have any choice, just as Mister Wainwright would seem to have no choice but to accede to her demands. She certainly has put everyone involved in untenable positions. Quite brilliantly done, so far."

Wainwright seemed to be suppressing anger, rather than staying focused on the problem with the rest of us. At the first break in the discussion, it became clear what he was mulling over in his head.

He spoke directly to Mundt. "I still harbor great resentment against you for the way you threatened me, Herr Mundt. Make no mistake about this. I am under orders to print this story in my next two editions and I am going to do it.

"She has then instructed me to begin serialization of your story and unless she stops me, I will print it."

Mundt snapped his head around to face Wainwright and growled, "Make no mistake about this, sir. You will *never* print that story. I will buy the magazine and sack you so fast that your head will spin. That story is the property of The Strand magazine and I will see that it is destroyed and never printed."

"Do not take comfort in that, sir," Wainwright answered harshly. When Norma sent the Zurich story in, she addressed it to me, not the magazine. I know what she was thinking, but it doesn't matter. She addressed it to me! Therefore, I consider it to be my property and I have removed it from the Strand premises. If you ever decide to sack me, I will take it to any publishing house in the empire and they will hire me at a greater salary than I now enjoy."

Mundt was apoplectic, his eyes bulging, face reddening, veins in his neck seeming to expand. He rose as though preparing to attack Wainwright physically. It was a frightening scene.

"You will never publish that story, if it means that you are in your grave! I'll see to it that...'

"How dare you threaten me?" Wainwright stormed to his feet and stepped toward Mundt.

We were all jolted back to our sense as Holmes slammed his hand down on the desk. He did not raise his voice, though, so striking the desk was apparently just to get everyone's attention. He spoke in a calm voice. "Gentleman, please take your seats. We do not want to fight among ourselves. We have to all understand what the others are doing to be sure we don't make any mistakes.

"As regards what gets printed, we have three weeks before we are at a crisis point, the next two, finishing the Aberdeen case and at least one week in which you can publish an introduction to the Zurich case. If we haven't run her to ground by then, you two can fight it out. If we have, I'm sure that we can edit the story in a fashion that will satisfy both the Strand and Herr Mundt's bank.

"I am confident that we will have a solution by then, so let us proceed together instead of against each other. Herr Mundt, is the purpose of your visit to inform us of Rene's demands or was there another reason?"

"Certainly to inform you, Mister Holmes, and to see if you have made any progress in catching her. But I had also planned to try again to seek some accommodation with this imbecile," nodding to Wainwright, "but I can see that that will be a vain hope."

Wainwright started to react, but Mundt shut him off, by abruptly rising and snatching his umbrella and hat. "Don't bother responding, Wainwright. Whatever you say will be puerile and ineffectual."

He turned to Holmes and said, "I can no longer afford to leave this in your hands, sir. I will not impede you in any way and I will cooperate in anything you ask, but my passive involvement is over. I am going to handle this in my own way, whatever is required."

Turning to Wainwright, he said, "If anything happens to you, sir, bear in mind that you brought it upon yourself." With that, he turned and stomped out of the room. The last sounds we heard were his heavy footsteps on the stairs and an angry slam of the front door.

Holmes showed no emotion, possibly thinking Mundt's words were bluster. I was not inclined to take them that lightly. He turned to the Strand editor.

"Do you plan to cooperate in the transfer of funds to Mundt's bank, Wainwright?"

He was visibly shaken and did not answer immediately. When he did, it was in a grave tone of voice. "I don't know. I haven't thought about it yet, obviously.

In the normal course of events, we do pay for material that we publish. Doctor Watson has accrued significant amounts of our money, and deservedly so. But this... this is profitable for us, but it is turning into a nightmare. I am now concerned for my physical wellbeing, Mister Holmes. I do not think that Herr Mundt is a stable man any more. I can't be sure what he will do."

Holmes nodded vigorously. "You would be very prudent to exercise caution. Mundt right now could best be compared to a cornered rat, fearful and desperate. He will not go down without a fight. I'd suggest that you keep young McDonough with you at all times. I would also suggest that, for the short term, you do your very best to cooperate with both Rene and Mundt. We want her to think that everything is going according to her plan. We do not want her to run and hide as she has for the last several years.'

CHAPTER 10

THE next several days were filled with long periods of meditation for Holmes, interspersed with brisk walks in Kensington Park and strolls along nearby avenues observing our fellow man and their consorts.

He studied the original copy of both the Zurich and Aberdeen manuscripts for hours, hoping that the writer would have inadvertently left some clues that would help unravel their whereabouts, their true identity, if they were not Norma Bainsteas and Rene LaDier, and their ultimate purpose. He remained convinced that we did not yet know why these stories were being sent in.

"Have you found anything, Holmes?" I asked.

"Not really, old fellow, other than to convince myself that the stories were written by the same person."

"Did you think that they might not be?"

"I had no reason to think that they were or weren't, but nothing in an investigation can be left to chance. If we are certain that they were written by the same person, and yet know that the first story was posted from Aberdeen and the second from Zurich, that might be of value if Mycroft can find anything in the travel records between England, France, and Switzerland.

"If the names of a few single ladies were to show up as traveling to Zurich from England right before the posting of the bank story and right before Rene's visit to Mundt, we may have a lead.

"We could attempt to track the ladies down and possibly ferret out our villain. Long odds against that one, but we can never be sure which line of inquiry will lead us to Norma and Rene."

"How do you know that the stories were written by the same person if the first was handwritten and the second typed?"

"By a close examination of the syntax, old fellow. People have ways of saying things that show up in both their patterns of speech and their patterns of composition. With enough written material to examine, I would wager that I could tell with almost perfect consistency whether a particular person had written a particular article.

"A few of the easier examples would be a particular word, or words, misspelled or misused in their contexts, the use of slang or of extremely uncommon words, perhaps medical terms or expressions particular to mathematicians, for instance."

I grunted approval, but had never run across this particular avenue of investigation in Holmes' cases. "So what do you find in these stories that proved anything," I asked.

"Many examples, but I'll mention just two to keep from boring you. The first is that in each story she describes a character exiting a building, either a restaurant or a depot and saying that "he came from out of." the building. That is extraordinarily clumsy syntax. Normally one would say 'came from' or even 'came out of', but 'came from out of' is a fairly unique turn of a phrase.

"There are two others like it. She also misspelled 'several' three times in the two stories, in each instance putting an 'A' in the middle."

I commented, knowing how much he enjoyed documenting various analyses of evidence, "It's a wonder you don't write a monograph on the subject."

"It's well under way, Watson. It is entitled *The Forensic Analysis of the Phraseology of Undetermined Writers.*"

<hr />

On a particular day, after a walk through Regent Park, luncheon at the Blackstone, and carriage ride back to Baker Street, I noticed Holmes surreptitiously looking out the window on several occasions. He would move the shade ever so slightly, keeping his body pressed against the wall and look up the street. He would then change position and look down the street,

"I say, Holmes, you look as though you are evading a bill collector. What the devil is so interesting out there?"

"Nothing that I can see, right now, old fellow, but you will be surprised to learn that I believe that we have been followed the last couple of days."

"Followed? Great Scott, by whom?"

"I have no idea."

"What did he look like?"

"A nondescript looking chap, dressed casually, and with no physical traits out of the ordinary. Not too tall, or too heavy or thin. No scars or tattoos that I could see, no limp or other anomaly in his gait, or brightly colored hair..."

"Why do you think he was following us?"

"Our eyes met on two consecutive days in two different geographical locations. In each instance he looked away quickly and pretended to be reading his newspaper. Such behavior and such reactions seem to me the work of a rank amateur. Moriarty could have shared a cab ride with you and remained unobtrusive."

"Well, why didn't we confront the rascal and demand to know what he is up to?"

"That would be as rankly amateurish as his actions. I'm waiting for him to...aha! Here he is."

I rushed to the window as Holmes cautioned me to be careful. He stepped back and gave me his place at the window and raced to the door of our room. I wanted to ask him which man it was, but I heard him yelling down the stairs to Mrs. Hudson to see if she could fetch Wiggins.

Wiggins was the leader of a small group of frequently unwashed miscreants that lived in the neighborhood and had been enlisted by Holmes for the purpose of following people, carrying messages, or hanging around on corners looking for people Holmes had delegated to them

I had earlier questioned the wisdom of using thirteen or fourteen year olds as spies or information gatherers, but had come to see the wisdom in it. Anyone up to no good, or thinking he may be followed, would hardly see children as a source of concern.

Mycroft had derisively referred to them as Holmes' 'runny nose brigade', but had also been startled at the amount of information they had unearthed.

This Wiggins had the canny sense of a veteran criminal, using some Holmes-type techniques before even getting to know my room mate. He could tell within thirty seconds when a policeman would turn into Baker Street from Regent Parkway because he had observed and timed their rounds. That information had been of value in the cretinous activities of his earlier youth.

Holmes returned to the window and glanced out. "Where is he, Watson?"

"I don't know who you mean, Holmes. You dashed out without saying."

"Really, Watson, you should be more observant of your surroundings...ah, there he is."

"Where?" I demanded.

"There, Watson, coming out of the apothecary. Grey suit, walking stick, dark bowler. At least the dolt had the good sense to wear different clothes. Yesterday, he was dressed as a workman."

The man took a seat on a bench in front of a barber shop down the street and sat eating something out of a bag. He was trying to appear nonchalant, but frequently looked up at our window. Holmes suggested we sit away from the window and just look out occasionally, to be sure he did not catch sight of one of us. Knowing Holmes' delicate manner of speech when making such suggestions, I knew he was afraid that I would be seen. He knew there was no possibility of him making such a mistake.

We heard heavy footsteps racing up the stairs, and in seconds Wiggins burst through the door. "Mister Holmes! I came as quickly as I could."

"Yes, Wiggins, that's fine. Come here to the window. Careful now, do you see the man in the dark bowler in front of Blair's barber shop?"

"Certainly, sir."

"He's your target for today, Wiggins. *From a distance*, you are to observe him and take some notes. I would like him followed, if possible, back to where he is staying. That would be very valuable information.

"Now, Wiggins, recall the drill I taught you. If he moves and you are able to follow, I want you to use at least five of your associates, each one following him for only a short distance. If, for any reason, one of the boys makes eye contact with the man, he is to turn at the next corner and go home. He is not to be used again with this man. Is all of that clear?"

Wiggins has adopted, to my amusement, some of Holmes' personal mannerisms, whether involuntarily or by design. He now gave his best impersonation of Holmes' overly patient sigh, specially reserved for when someone has stated the patently obvious.

"It's not as though I'm an amateur at this, Mister Holmes. You don't need to condamend."

"Condescend." Holmes said, with a smile.

"Condescend, right sir. But I do know what I'm doing."

Holmes put his hand on the boy's shoulder. "Of course you do, Wiggins. That's why I trust you with such important assignments. Please forgive my "condamension.""

Wiggins smiled. "Condescension, sir."

"Condescension, to be sure. Now, on your way. Here are some coins if you have to follow in a cab. Be sure to share them with any of the lads that you employ, if you do not have to spend them."

Wiggins' eyes lit up at the sight of the money. As usual, Holmes was overly generous with his runny nose brigade.

Holmes went back to his studies while I moved my chair so that with just the turn of my head, I could see through the narrow slit between the curtains. Reading my paper, I checked every few minutes.

"Great Scott, Holmes, one of your cretins is engaging the man in conversation. He's carrying something."

Holmes hurried to the window and gazed out, nodding his head in an amused fashion. "It's Claude, with his shoe shine kit. A very nice touch, Watson. Our lad Wiggins is very resourceful."

As we could see, the man listened to Claude, looked down to his shoes, and told him to go ahead. The boy chattered constantly and the man answered occasionally.

Finally, he finished and, apparently, asked the man to inspect his work. Claude got a nod, even a small smile, and a generous tip. He appeared to thank the man more than once. Covering his true mission effectively, he asked several more men if they wanted shoe shines, even getting another customer back on our side of the street. Half hour later, he disappeared around the corner and approximately ten minutes after that, Wiggins came bounding up the stairs again.

"I got some information, Mister Holmes."

"So we observed, Wiggins. Nicely done. What did you learn?"

"Bit of a toff he is, sir, but pleasant enough, Claude thought. Good tipper. Claude may go back into the shoe shine business."

"Wiggins..."

"Right, sir. I'm gettin' to it. First of all, he ain't English, sir. Some kind of European, maybe German. Claude says he speaks good English, but with an accent. You know what else?"

"What?"

"He's got a gun. Holster on his chest under his coat, Big one, says Claude, but he ain't seen many guns."

Holmes nodded. "Claude was sure it was a gun?"

"Sure as sunshine, sir. When he leaned forward to look down at his shoes, the handle popped right out between his lapels. Ain't nuthin' looks like a gun handle, sir."

"Indeed not," Holmes agreed, "anything else?"

"That's about it, Mister Holmes. I told Claude not to try anything fancy, like asking him anything personal. Just shine the shoes and keep his eyes open. That's what he did."

"And brilliantly, at that. Here, give Claude an extra pound and retire him from the job. Tell him to stay off the street for a while now."

As Wiggins left, Holmes commented to me, "I'm sure you can see once again that my confidence in Wiggins is well placed, Watson. We have learned a great deal this morning."

"I stopped needing convincing a long time ago, Holmes. The rascal is bright as a new shilling. But... what does it all mean?"

Holmes shrugged. "Most of it is quite clear, old fellow, but the 'why' is not. You can't have failed to connect the sudden appearance of Herr Karl Mundt in our rooms, followed by an angry departure, and the immediate emergence of a man with a 'European,' as Wiggins calls it, accent, following us."

"Of course not." I hadn't connected it at all, but it was not something that I was forced to admit. "The 'why' is what I was referring to, old fellow."

"Mundt must not trust us to keep him fully informed, so he wants another pair of eyes on us. I'm sure the man reports back to Mundt every evening regarding our daily activities. For that matter, we do not know whether Mundt has returned to Zurich or if he is still in London."

"Mundt certainly is a volatile personality," I observed.

"More than volatile, Watson. I would say that he is teetering on the brink of running amok, out of control. That is why I find the gun to be a very ominous portent. If his role is strictly to observe and report, he certainly does not need a weapon. While it is not always true, quite frequently, people with guns intend to use them.

"If you don't mind doing so, I'd like to ask you to send a note to Wainwright apprising him of this development and urge him to exercise extreme caution for the next little while. There is obvious animus between the two men and a man out of control is unpredictable."

"Of course, Holmes. I'll get right to it, but what are we going to do next?"

"I'd say that we might take another walk this afternoon, to test once again this tail's intent. In fact, we might want to walk over to the Strand office and deliver your note to Wainwright in person. We haven't heard from him in a few days and...hello, we seem to have a courier arriving."

Mrs. Hudson had the note up to us shortly and Holmes tore it open.

"It's from Mycroft." He read it quickly, and looked up, in deep thought already.

"What is it, Holmes?"

"As you know, Watson, I've had Mycroft combing the immigration ministry's records, trying to gather some data that could lead to finding Norma or Rene, assuming they are two different people. He has now extended his search to cover the whole past year."

"And..." I asked impatiently.

"Nothing. No Norma or Rene."

I found that to be a deflating revelation. "The way you were pondering it Holmes, I thought that something significant may have shown up."

"It may have old fellow. While nothing has shown up on the ladies we have been seeking, Mycroft found that a Garret Dickinson has taken four trips from Dover to Calais in the past year, and three the year before. There is no way to determine where he went once he got there, but that name could be significant."

"So you had him checking that name, as well as Norma and Rene?"

"Yes. I even had him looking for a Carlton Mackenzie, even though we are almost certain that he truly was the corpse buried in the rocks in Scotland. Just a matter of being thorough, old fellow."

I pondered it for a while before commenting, "This occurrence of Dickinson's name, Holmes. We don't know that it means anything, do we?"

"You're absolutely correct, Watson, it could mean nothing. All we know was that he worked for the same coal exporter in Aberdeen as Carlton Mackenzie and quit the day after Mackenzie disappeared. The fact that he has taken four trips to France in the last two years could mean that he now works for another coal exporter and travels in the normal course of business."

"That's what I feared, Holmes."

"*Or*... it could mean that Mister Garret Dickinson is the key to this whole mystery. We don't know yet that that is *not* true. Remember, Watson, that he seems to have completely disappeared. That normally means that the person does not *want* to be found.

"So, in addition to seeking Norma and Rene, we must now concentrate some effort on the shadowy Mister Dickinson. Let's get our coats and head for the offices of the Strand magazine. On the way, we can stop and send a telegram to Harrison Samuels in Aberdeen and ask him to redouble his efforts to learn something of Garret Dickinson's present location."

CHAPTER 11

THE walk to the Strand was brisk, apparently bracing to Holmes, but a bit edgy for me. Holmes determined in short order that our mysterious follower with the Germanic accent was behind us and keeping a safe distance away.

We stopped in the telegraph office and Holmes sent at least two messages, but didn't bother telling me to whom. One, of course, was to Samuels in Aberdeen regarding Garret Dickinson.

Having noticed on the way into the office that the glare from the sun on the window made it impossible to see in from the outside, I was able to stare out and see the man following us clearly. After checking the sign above the window, he looked at his watch and made some notes with his pencil. It seemed that he was keeping an hour by hour journal to use as a basis for reporting to Mundt, if Mundt indeed was his employer.

He did not seem to be a very frightening person, but with a gun, I suppose, anyone is frightening. Not having mentioned It to Holmes, I had slipped my revolver into my coat pocket and found great security in it's touch.

I was so engrossed in watching the rascal that I did not notice Holmes slip in beside me. "Anything unusual with him, Watson?"

"No, just making notes on a small pad. I wonder if we shouldn't separate and see what he does. Assuming that he follows you, I could follow him at a safe distance and keep track of him from behind,"

"An excellent suggestion, old fellow, but too fraught with risk. If he ever happened to see you, the game would be up. He'd retreat and we probably wouldn't see him again. He would undoubtedly be replaced by a fresh face who may have a better idea of what he is doing. I think we are better off with someone who is so easy to track as this one."

"You make sense, I suppose, but I'm not terribly keen on having a man with a gun behind me."

"Ah Watson, my friend," Holmes said jovially, "take comfort in the fact that if he wanted to shoot us in the back, we'd be dead already."

I took no comfort whatever in that fact and had the very devil of a time not looking back as we walked to the Strand offices.

❧

Wainwright seemed delighted to see us, but I would imagine that after the unseemly scene with Mundt, the presence of Sherlock Holmes would feel very reassuring.

"Ah, Holmes, Doctor Watson, a pleasure to see you both. Please come in and be seated. I'll fetch some tea."

We settled in and after exchanging pleasantries for a moment or two, began to tell Wainwright that his situation may have become more dangerous. We were interrupted by the arrival of Ian McDonough carrying a tray laden with cups, spoons, cream and sugar and a large China tea pot.

McDonough poured for everyone, including himself, and took a seat. He had a large journal and a supply of sharpened pencils at his side. As Holmes began to speak, McDonough began writing in the journal.

Holmes stopped and asked what he was writing and McDonough answered enthusiastically, "I'm keeping a journal on this entire investigation, starting with the arrival of the story about Mackenzie and our trip up to Scotland. It's the most exciting thing I've ever done. That's why I thank Mister Wainwright profusely every day for allowing me to be a part of it. Here, perhaps you'd like to look at it." He slid it across to Holmes.

Whether as a matter of courtesy or genuine interest, Holmes took a few minutes to peruse the journal. From my perspective, I could tell that every section began with a date and was followed by clear, perfectly formed letters in a narrative form.

When he was finished, he passed it to me and said, "This is an excellent idea, Ian, but what do you intend to do with it?"

He immediately began offering assurances. "I have no intention of trying to convince Mister Wainwright to let me publish it. I know that anything that The Strand publishes relating to your work comes from the pen of Doctor Watson and I enjoy his stories as much as anyone. I just want to keep a record of things. If this becomes a famous national story, I could consider trying my hand at a book about it. That would not conflict with Doctor Watson's work at all.

"Pay no heed to that, Ian," I assured him. "I have no objection whatever to any efforts you might make. To the contrary, I'd be more than happy to review it with you periodically and even offer some editing suggestions. I think that young writers should be encouraged, not discouraged. There aren't enough of them doing serious work."

McDonough seemed overjoyed. "Thank you, Doctor. You can be sure that I will take you up on your generous offer."

Holmes called the meeting back to order, in a sense. "That would be excellent, Ian, I'll enjoy reading the journal myself. But to get back to our purpose for coming, I'll fill you in on an ominous development."

He described our being followed right up to our arrival at the office. McDonough bolted from his chair and sped to the window.

"Careful, Ian," Holmes said sharply, "keep yourself hidden. We don't want to scare our man away."

"I understand, sir, but I don't see a man of the description you just mentioned." He returned to his seat.

Holmes continued, "So, Wainwright, our purpose is to warn you to be very cautious in all that you do. We do not know what this chap is up to, and we can not do a thing about him unless he does something illegal. We could not possibly prove that he is actually following us,"

Wainwright seemed a bit shaken by Holmes' revelation, as Holmes tried to offer reassurance. "Now bear in mind that the man is following us, not you. He may not even know who you are. The only reason I bring this to your attention is that I am convinced that he is in the employ of Herr Mundt, although we may get a surprise on that, and the fact that Mundt obviously bears you ill will."

Wainwright just nodded, but Ian spoke forcefully. "I will accompany Mister Wainwright home every night, Mister Holmes, and I'll carry a hammer or some kind of weapon."

Wainwright could scarcely believe what he had just heard. "Ian, you will do no such thing. How dare you even suggest it. I will certainly see to my own security."

McDonough was adamant. "I am much younger, stronger and more athletic than you, sir. No disrespect, but that's the truth. If you do not allow me to walk with you, I'll follow you at a safe distance."

Wainwright was balancing a rising anger with the realization that Ian was only trying to help. Holmes cut in, "We'll leave you two to work that out. For now, do you have any news for Doctor Watson and I?"

"Actually we do, sir," said Wainwright. "Ian and I were going to stop at Baker Street after hours and show it to you. We've received a telegram from Rene LaDier, representing both herself and Norma Bainsteas, asking us for money in payment for the stories. Naturally, the demand was accompanied by a threat to go to a new publisher if we did not comply."

"From where was the wire sent?" Holmes asked quickly. Wainwright turned to Ian, "What was the name of that town?"

"Kusnacht, sir. Kusnacht, Switzerland. I dug out an atlas and checked. It's not far from Zurich on the east side of the lake."

I made what I thought was a reasonable suggestion. "Should we have the police comb through this Kusnacht...maybe look for single young redheaded ladies staying at the local hotels?"

Holmes shook his head briefly. "I don't think so, Watson. I'm sure that Kusnacht is the *one* town in the Zurich area that she is not in. From the way she or they have accomplished these crimes, she would be much too smart for that. Perhaps if we were in Switzerland ourselves, there might be a few things to look at, but we are not."

Holmes turned to Wainwright, "May I see the telegram?" Ian took it from an envelope and slid it to him.

Holmes studied it, musing aloud as he did so. "It was sent yesterday and Mundt's visit from Rene was the day before, so that is in order. Kusnacht...not worth a trip there...but we've just said that...probably nothing more to learn from the telegram..."

Holmes turned to Wainwright, "I'm not sure of the economics of magazine publishing. Are her demands as outrageous as one would expect?"

Wainwright shook his head briskly. "Actually, they are not. She's asking for a little more than I would normally pay an author, with the exception of people like Doctor Watson, who guarantee large sales, but I can certainly survive and make money at her royalty level. Perhaps a few pence less profit per magazine, but significantly more magazines."

Holmes pondered that reply. "That's interesting. She could probably demand more, but she remains reasonable in order to ensure that her stories are published...So tell me, Wainwright, do you plan to comply with her monetary demands and her method of payment...by transfer of funds to Mundt's bank?"

Wainwright did not hesitate, saying, "I've pretty much decided what I will do as she requests, but first I'd like to seek your counsel. What do you think I should do?"

"My opinion and my hope," said Holmes, "is that you will agree and take immediate action."

Wainwright nodded, "That was my decision, assuming that you can assure me that I am doing nothing illegal. Even though she seems to have committed serious crimes, you yourself have insisted that we don't really know who we are dealing with. I would simply be paying an author for a highly salable product and transferring funds to a legitimate bank...and I am cooperating with law enforcement in any way I can..."

"You are doing nothing improper, sir. We would normally not want to do business with criminals, but everything you are doing is getting us closer to solving some serious crimes. I will vouch for your honorable intent when we involve Scotland Yard."

"Excellent, Mister Holmes, then I'll begin immediately. I will send a telegram to Herr Mundt agreeing to everything and I will arrange for the first transfer of funds tomorrow morning."

Holmes nodded. "I would like to suggest that in your telegram, you ask for immediate written acknowledgment from him that he understands and agrees,"

Wainwright turned to Ian, "Please see to it immediately."

Ian closed his journal, shook the hands of Holmes and myself, and darted out of the office.

Wainwright smiled, "I've given Ian a promotion. He will still edit stories part of the time, but I'm more or less making him my assistant in running the magazine. He has brought a lot of energy and enthusiasm to his tasks,"

Holmes agreed. "He's a very likable young man and seems intelligent and industrious. You are lucky to have him."

CHAPTER 12

THE next four days were uneventful as regards the
pursuit of Norma Bainsteas. I spent most of my
time finishing the writing of *The Adventure of the Reigate
Squires* for publication in The Strand, while Holmes
answered correspondence, mainly related to his other
work as a consulting detective.

Not made entirely clear in the stories that I write
for The Strand, but true nevertheless, is the fact that
Holmes, because of his international reputation,
receives requests for help every day. Only a fraction of
them wind up in The Strand because they lack the deep
drama that readers expect in a story of true crime and
because, frankly, they are too boring for me to bother
with.

Holmes does read every one of the letters, though,
and receives every desperate soul who arrives at Baker
Street in person. The latter are the ones that normally
wind up in the pages of The Strand.

When I am between stories, I frequently help Holmes with his correspondence. The agreed upon price for my help is a sumptuous repast at either Simpson's or the Blackstone hotel dining room.

Our system has evolved into pure simplicity. Holmes scratches a brief insightful response in the margin of the letters and deposits them at the bottom of a stack on the mantle. Whenever I have time to work on the stack, I take a letter from the top, thus assuring that responses go out in the same order as they arrived.

The excessive candor of Holmes' responses, coupled with the innate gentleness of spirit that I possess, frequently requires me to reword his responses. I often find messages such as the following; "What your business rival did was perfectly legal. Hard as it is to face, he's smarter than you are."

Also requiring gentler syntax was a response that said, "Though what your wife is up to is not right, it is not a crime. I'd suggest that you lose forty pounds, pay more attention to her, and stop being so miserly."

Many others had terse answers like "not a criminal matter', or "consult local police." One particularly interesting response saved a man's life.

Holmes handed me the letter and asked if I would deal with it immediately, by telegram. The message read, "Stop whatever you are doing, engage a cab with closed window shades, and come directly to my rooms at Baker Street."

Approximately two hours after the man arrived, his house blew up. The story, with many interesting elements, will not be available to The Strand for at least six months, but I have tentatively entitled it, *"The Adventure of the Demented Brother-in-law."*

A rap on the door and a word from Mrs, Hudson heralded the arrival of Nevin Wainwright and Ian McDonough, an increasingly frequent occurrence. In came an excited McDonough and a positively ebullient Wainwright.

"Ah, Mister Holmes, I can hardly contain my excitement. Herr Mundt and I have mended fences, so to speak. He sent me a telegram acknowledging our agreement and saying that the future looked reasonably comfortable for both of us. I took that to mean that he has secured assurance from this Rene LaDier and/or this Norma Bainsteas-we don't know whether that is one person or two-that she will continue to supply these true unsolved crime stories without using the one about him.

"That assures safety for him, huge sales for me, and a lessening of the tensions between the two of us."

"Yes, excellent, sir. I'm delighted to hear it."

As a long time associate and friend of Sherlock Holmes, I often hear things in his voice and see things in his eyes that others failed to catch. Even Holmes is not perfect at hiding his feelings at all times. I don't think he was angry, but, let's say, nettled. I made a note in my mind to ask him about it a little later.

Holmes moved forward, "What else have you to tell us?"

"Another wire from Rene telling us to shelve the story from Zurich and prepare for one even more sensational to arrive early next week. Apparently she and Mundt have worked out a mutually satisfactory arrangement."

Holmes stood and walked over to the window, looking up and down the street. He then returned, but did not sit. "Well gentlemen, I know that Doctor Watson and I can expect to hear from you as soon as the next story arrives. In the meantime, we will continue to proceed down other avenues of inquiry."

They were barely out the door when Holmes said quickly, "Get your revolver, Watson, while I get mine. I don't think we will need them, but it's possible."

I was startled, to say the least, but quickly snatched up the weapon and followed Holmes down the stairs.

"What is it, Holmes?" I asked, "The man that has been following us?"

"Exactly, he is sitting on the bench in front of Blair's again. If he is going to move on Wainwright, I have a strong feeling that it will be very soon, perhaps even today."

I felt the flow of adrenalin that comes with anticipation of action of this sort and was ready. We were protected from sight well enough that I could take a position next to Holmes to peer out of my own small pane of glass. The man still sat on the bench with a newspaper before him and watched Wainwright and McDonough approach and then pass.

I tensed up and noticed Holmes' hand on the door knob as the man reached into his pocket.

The tension dissipated as quickly as it arose. The man simply checked his watch, made notes on his pad and went back to his paper.

Holmes and I watched until Wainwright and McDonough were out of sight, took a final look at our follower, and went back up to our rooms.

"What was that all about, old fellow?" I asked. "Were you expecting an attack on Wainwright today?"

"Not really, merely exercising an abundance of caution, but also to see his reaction. You see, Watson, I can't quite figure out what his assignment is. If Mundt and Wainwright are at peace, then there is no reason for him to be tracking Wainwright and, of course, he isn't.

"But if the deal is done between Mundt and Rene, as he says it is, then he is safe, and should not need to have anyone followed. He seems merely to be tracking us, but that should not be necessary if our target is Norma Bainsteas. *And*...if he is merely a time keeper, why is he armed?"

"Do you have a working speculation on that?" I asked.

Holmes nodded his head solemnly. "I've had what I thought was an unlikely foreboding, but I'm afraid it is moving closer to the top of the list. I fear, Watson, that our ordinary looking man out there is an assassin. He has been retained by Mundt, on the assumption that we will find Norma and /or Rene, to kill her. That would rule out, from his point of view, the eventual possibility of the Zurich story being published.

"It would also eliminate a potential blackmail problem. Mundt is smart enough to realize that there are only so many of these stories and that once they are published, and all the money collected, he is the most likely source of huge amounts of money for Rene. The complications in this case seem to grow daily, Watson. I am getting anxious for Norma or Rene to make her first big mistake, so that we can conclude this ugly mess once and for all."

"I say, Holmes, on another subject, you did not seem to accept the rapprochement between Mundt and Wainwright with your normal equanimity. Was there something there that I missed?"

He was pensive for just a moment. "Your acute powers of observation have served you well again, old friend. I had hoped it wouldn't show, but I found Wainwright's unbridled glee a bit irritating. Have both he and Mundt lost sight of the big picture? We are dealing with a murderer, a thief, and heaven only knows what else and they find cooperation with her perfectly acceptable. Mundt, because it protects his unethical and illegal behavior from years past, and Wainwright because it will result in huge sales while Norma gloats over past sins.

"Are they deluding themselves that this will go on forever? Do they think that I will not catch Norma or that they can convince me to do it all quietly? We have to abide them for now because they are useful in keeping in contact with Norma, but they most certainly have a day of reckoning coming."

⊰§⊱

A few days later telegrams and letters began to arrive in the office in response to inquiries Holmes or I had made in the last week or so. They seemed not to be of any consequence, and for the most part, they were not. But some of them began to push back the curtain of darkness that had enshrouded the truths that we sought.

The first reply was a hand written letter from Sigmund Freud in Vienna. He was beginning to amass an international reputation for his work in the mind, much of which was unprecedented. The letter would grow more important to me as a memento in the years to come, as Herr Freud grew to legendary stature.

For the present time, it was simply a reaffirmation of what we already knew. He said that it was very unlikely that Jack the Ripper was a woman, or even that a woman was involved in any way. The savagery notwithstanding, the physical strength to do the gruesome things that had been done to these women would probably be reason enough.

But Freud's work was in the emotional and psychological makeup of the perpetrator and all of the speculations he could make from the admittedly limited information he had, screamed out man. Not just a man, but one who had suffered extreme rejection, perhaps humiliation, in his dealings with the opposite gender. There was evidence of uncontrollable rage in his actions.

One interesting comment Freud made was that there was a good chance that the crimes would never be solved because he felt strongly that the Ripper was dead. The nature and ferocity of the attacks indicated a rage that could not be suppressed for this length of time. If he was alive, he would be killing.

He closed with an invitation to visit him in Vienna if we were ever in that lovely city, and a promise that he would call on us if ever in London.

We had earlier gotten a telegram from a policeman in Cornwall, who had interviewed a Mrs. Lange at Holmes' request. Her name and address had been on a scrap of paper Holmes found in the room Norma Bainsteas had used while visiting her father's home.

The only information she could offer was that she had gone to college with Norma Bainsteas in Aberdeen so many years ago, and had had a letter from Norma saying that she may be in Cornwall later in the season and might stop to visit.

She had a few pictures from their college days that were close-ups and could help in identifying Norma if we ever met her.

We, of course, had gotten a telegram, supposedly from Norma, saying that she might be in London in the next two weeks and would try to find time to call on us. We had dismissed that as a "tweaking of our nose," as Holmes had called it, by the arrogant mastermind of this ongoing adventure.

The pictures did indeed arrive in this morning's mail and showed a bright, smiling, reasonably attractive girl of college age. Her face was clear enough in the pictures and distinctive enough of features that there was little doubt that we would recognize her if we ever met her. Holmes set them on the mantle and went to the next item.

The last telegram was a lengthy one, from Harrison Samuels in Aberdeen. Because Garret Dickinson's name had appeared on travel documents for those journeying to the continent and back in the last few years several times, Holmes had asked Samuels to look a little more deeply into his background.

The telegram had no new usable data, which I found a bit discouraging. The report reiterated that he had been employed for over a year, had done an acceptable job, but had resigned the day after Carlton Mackenzie had disappeared.

Samuels had interviewed, at length, the clerks that had occupied the desks on either side of Dickinson's. Neither of them could recall for sure, any contact that he may have had with Mackenzie. They, themselves, claimed not to have known Mackenzie very well. The telegram did conclude with a paragraph-long physical description of Garret Dickinson that both of his office mates agreed was accurate. Holmes commented acerbically that there were probably no less that two million men in England that could fit with that description.

Surprisingly, there was also another telegram from, of all people, Norma Bainsteas. It said that she would be in London sometime in the next few weeks and would like to be received in our rooms.

"That's odd, Holmes. She sent one earlier that said virtually the same thing."

"I agree, Watson. She is clearly poking fun at us, but why the lack of sarcasm in this one? One would almost think she really plans to visit us."

We both shook our heads and moved on

The last bit of news came in the form of a courier bearing an apologetic note from Mycroft Holmes. The note decried the mental capacity of one of the men assigned to pursue the immigration material. It turned out that this "dolt," Mycroft's characterization, had not mentioned that in each of Garret Dickinson's trips to the continent in the last two years, he had been accompanied by a Mrs. Dickinson, his wife.

We found that newsworthy, but trivial in the extreme compared to what was coming three days later, and again three days after that.

It began with another unexpected visit from Wainwright and Ian McDonough.

CHAPTER 13

IAN McDonough was the first into the room and followed by a puffing Nevin Wainwright. They both took seats, not trying to contain their excitement. Ian was fully relaxed, but waited for Wainwright to catch his breath and do the talking.

"Excuse me, gentlemen," Wainwright began, "we were not able find a cab, so we had to walk all the way. Ian here is difficult to keep up with when he is excited.

"My goodness, gentlemen. I had never been in these rooms in my life until this adventure began, and now it seems that I'm here so often I should be paying part of your rent."

We all smiled, but Holmes was clearly anxious to hear the news. "Do I correctly surmise that you have received the next story from Norma?"

"Yes you do, sir. And there is a significant difference from the others."

Holmes and I both leaned forward in anticipation. "How so?" he asked.

"The first two stories were quite old. Perfectly committed, the investigations fruitless, and dust gathering on them."

Holmes simply nodded.

"This one is apparently about a crime that *will* be committed sometime in the near future."

"Great Scott!" I blurted out, unable to contain myself.

"Give us the details, please," Holmes said tersely.

"First of all, it's not a complete story. That's another difference. In fact, it's just an introduction, very short. She says I will have the rest of it before I have fully published the Carlton Mackenzie story."

"Short...," Holmes said, "very well, but what does she say?"

"It starts out by saying; "following will be the remarkable story of the brazen theft of the largest known emerald in the world, The Green Fire of the Incas."

"Great Heaven, I've read about it recently...last few months." I said.

"You read about it three and a half months ago in the London Times." Holmes said quickly. "It was transferred here from Munich, its permanent home, and put on exhibit in the British Museum. Other than tidbits saying that it was drawing huge crowds, that was the last news story about it in the London newspapers."

"But Wainwright," I asked, "Does it say how the crime will be committed?"

"No, Doctor, that's why I called it an introduction. All it really says is that it will be stolen, then goes into quite a bit about it's past. She seems to have a fiendish sense of humor. She finishes by saying to wait until the next exciting installment."

Holmes jumped to his feet and went to the door. We could hear him speaking down the stairs to our housekeeper. "Mrs. Hudson, would you see if you can possibly find a cab out on Baker Street?"

He was all energy now, suggesting that I get my coat and hat and asking Wainwright and young McDonough if they would prefer to accompany us to the British Museum or return to their offices and await our report. They answered quickly that they wouldn't consider not coming along.

Ian McDonough was feverishly writing in his journal, hardly looking up to say that he would be right with us. We all smiled watching his single-minded focus.

The British Museum was about a twenty minute cab ride from Baker Street and held some fond and some unhappy memories for both Holmes and I.

In the early years, before Holmes had established his practice as a consulting detective, he had a short supply of funds, but an abundant supply of time. As I reported in an earlier story, *The Musgrave Ritual,* Holmes lived on Montague Street, just a short walk away and spent many hours in the British Museum studying numerous branches of science to increase his effectiveness as an investigator.

It would take too many pages of this story to adequately describe all of the fields of scientific study of which Holmes had acquired a working knowledge. I can't even recall how many of his solutions were facilitated by the education he acquired in those years.

Together, Holmes and I had visited the British Museum a few years back, in an investigation of the antique weapons murders that I reported in *The Insidious Succession*. Quite by happenstance, we were leaving the building at the time Roger Dalton, Director of the massive museum, discovered the missing Lord Balderston hanging in an exhibit storage room.

It was a shocking occurrence, but concluded the business for which we were there; to investigate the unfortunate Balderston's disappearance. That was part of perhaps the most complicated investigation in out career together.

The carriage veered into Montague Street and we quickly passed the now seedy rooming house which had sheltered my illustrious companion in those early years.

The next turn brought us face to face with the magnificent stone edifice that all Englishmen viewed with unabashed pride. The carriage drove through the center court up to the huge colonnaded entrance, the wings on either side seeming to welcome and embrace us. The eight massive stone columns with their Corinthian capitals supporting the lovely carved frieze, seemed like mute eternal sentinels guarding this edifice for the ages.

I had long thought that just the library of the museum, if it stood alone, should be considered a wonder of the modern world.

We made our way through the vast rotunda and to the administrative area, having not communicated to Dalton that we would be arriving. Holmes did indeed have a touch of impetuousness in him when, like some hunting dogs, he was coming to point. His energy, which burst like a cannon shell when new developments arose, often propelled him out of his chair and into action. Far more often than not, it turned out to be the right move,

We were quickly seated in Dalton's office, after Holmes identified himself, and were told that Roger was helping in the preparation of an upcoming exhibit on Tibetan antiquities, but that he would be fetched forthwith. The secretary withdrew to organize a tea service.

Dalton was a tall, slender man of elitist bearing, but a warm and friendly person nonetheless. Always impeccably dressed, he would be the very model of a museum, bank, or opera house director. He greeted us warmly and assured us that tea would be forthcoming shortly.

After a few minutes of the inevitable recounting of our last time together, the death of Lord Balderston, primarily for the benefit of Wainwright and McDonough, a brief lull in the conversation signaled that it was time to get to the business of the day. Tea had been poured when Dalton looked to Holmes expectantly.

"We are here, Roger, to discuss the security of the Green Fire of the Incas emerald. We have reason to believe that a very creative, well organized effort will be made to steal it in the very near future."

Dalton seemed a bit taken aback, but not greatly alarmed. "The emerald stolen, Mister Holmes? I think it is unlikely in the extreme that a regiment of soldiers could steal the Green Fire of the Incas. Our security, not to be immodest, is impenetrable."

Holmes smiled. "Your security is impressive, Roger, it is not impenetrable. If Moriarty were still alive, I'd wager that it would be in his possession by now. Not to be uncivil, of course, but smugness regarding security, can have disastrous results."

"Not smugness, Mister Holmes, confidence. We have the most modern security systems available anywhere in the world. I hope you noticed that I used the plural form, systems, meaning that we have more than one in place." He smiled. "We could never take a chance on anything happening to German property in our care. We'd have Teutons marching on London."

We all joined in the smile and Holmes said, "We are pleased to hear that the gem is so well-protected, Roger, but please be alerted to the fact that we consider this to be a very credible threat. Everything that has come to us in the way that this information came has proven to be correct and verifiable, even to the extent of finding a corpse where our source said it would be."

Dalton raised his eyebrows at this revelation, but was not shaken. "The corpse is scary, Mister Holmes, but there are no threats of murder here. I will take your warning seriously and will alert my staff to be doubly careful."

"I hope that that is sufficient, Roger, and that your confidence is warranted. Could you give us just a bit of information regarding your security, so that I may rest comfortably, as well?"

Dalton hesitated, glancing over to Wainwright and McDonough. "I'm afraid not, Mister Holmes. While I would not for a moment suspect any deliberate wrong doing from anyone in the publishing industry, if even the most basic steps in our system were ever published through misunderstanding, error, or any innocent reason, it would certainly weaken our security to some extent, and would reflect badly on me.

"Please understand, gentlemen," he said to Wainwright and McDonough, "that this policy does not differentiate among individuals. It is very broad and encompasses only those whose job performance requires that they have this information. The entire system is understood by only two people; The Director of Security, who has held that position for over nineteen years, and myself. Everyone else commands a discrete, limited, area of the whole plan."

To my surprise, Wainwright, at least, seemed to not only understand, but agree. "We take no offense, sir. We also have systems in place regarding upcoming publications. No one sees the completed issue until it is ready for printing."

Holmes asked, "I realize that by this hour, the museum is closed to the public. Would it be possible to see the emerald up close?"

Dalton drew his watch from the hip pocket that held it and winced, "I'm afraid not today, Mister Holmes. The emerald is already back in one of the vaults deep in the bowels of the museum. I suppose I can mention something that you would already have speculated upon. There are several such vaults and the resting place of the gem changes frequently and...randomly.

"Obviously, I would be pleased to arrange a private showing of the gem for your party during any daytime hour."

Holmes nodded agreement. "We may take you up on your generous offer, Roger. You may also rest assured that we will return and apprise you when the next installment of the story arrives."

CHAPTER 14

HOLMES and I were breakfasting a few days later and discussing, of course, nothing but the brilliant Norma Bainsteas and her ability to communicate with us at will, leaving no way for us to get back to her.

As I marmaladed my last scone and refilled both of our tea cups, Holmes continued looking out the window. "Our tail is back, Watson, using the same bench as yesterday and a suit of clothes that he has worn several times. Very sloppy work on his part. I also do not see Wainwright or Ian approaching, another disappointment. I thought that we would have the next installment by now."

He hardly had the words out of his mouth when he said excitedly, "Hello, what have we here?"

"What is it, Holmes?"

"A cab arriving and...excellent. It's our publishing tandem from The Strand, hopefully with something of interest."

By the way they bounded up the stairs, even old Wainwright, I could sense a pulsating excitement building. Little did I suspect that the events of the next few days would be exciting beyond my wildest dreams. It began when they arrived in the room.

Holmes, normally the very paragon of courtesy and consideration to arriving guests, could not wait until all were seated with tea before them. As soon as they entered the room, he asked, "The next installment, you have it?"

"Indeed we do, sir," Wainwright answered, with the same level of excitement, "and it is very puzzling."

"How so?" Holmes demanded.

Both Wainwright and Ian stood with coats still buttoned and hats in hand, barely inside the room.

"We thought that she had changed the pattern of things by writing about a crime *to be* committed, rather than one that *has* been committed."

"Yes?"

"It seems from this that she is saying that she has *already* stolen the emerald, but we know that that is not true. We know that it sets in the British Museum at this very moment."

He handed a small sheaf of papers to Holmes, who immediately started into it. As he read, I took their coats, poured tea, and asked Mrs. Hudson to bring up another pot.

Holmes set the papers in his lap and looked up to the ceiling.

"Holmes," I began, "May I see..."

"Of course, old fellow, forgive me. It's another very short installment and the first few sentences probably are all that is necessary to read. The rest is self-serving claptrap on the part of the author. But there is a shock in those first sentences. Let me read them to all of us.

"At this point in the story, the reader's mind has undoubtedly turned to the Herculean task it would be to steal this fabulous gem from such a security-conscious citadel as the British Museum. While I would not shy away from such a challenge, and in fact remain confident that I *could* do it, the reality is that I did not.

"Choosing ease over adventure, I stole the emerald before it ever left the city of Munich. What traveled to London is not The Green Fire of the Incas."

"Great Heaven," I exclaimed, "is it possible? Has all of London spent hours waiting in endless lines to view a fake emerald?"

Holmes rose from his chair. "That is the first thing that we must determine, gentlemen. If you are finished with your tea..."

⚜

Dalton was shocked at the scenario that was laid before him. "Gentlemen, it is not possible. The emerald was certified by an internationally recognized and renowned expert. The gem was then sealed, along with the certification, and shipped under twenty-four hour guard from Munich to this very office.

"In the presence of two German witnesses, as well as our Director of Security, I personally broke the seal and extricated the gem from the box. We then put it directly into the virtually unbreakable case in which it is exhibited.

"I will reveal one fact because of the exigency of the moment. That is that the emerald *never* leaves its display case. I put it into the case in the presence of witnesses and the whole display is moved in and out of the vault daily. It has never been opened. The only key to that case was sealed in the presence of the German overseers and is, at this moment, in a vault with the seal unbroken."

"Yes, Roger, we agree that your internal security is commendable, but the story..."

"I understand that the story says that it never arrived here, but I'm just giving you some insight into the handling of that emerald. The German security is every bit the equal of ours. I do not see any possibility..."

"Nevertheless, Roger, as I told you when we last met, everything our source has told us has turned out to be true."

If I had not seen the horror on Dalton's face a few years ago, immediately after he discovered the hanging corpse of Lord Balderston, I would have said that his countenance today was the most distraught I had ever seen it.

"I'm in a state of shock, Mister Holmes, at the very thought that this could possibly be true. I don't know if I'm still thinking clearly. What should we do?"

"Several things. First of all, is there a gem expert in residence in the museum?"

"No."

"But there is at least one in London..."

"There are several."

"Then I'd suggest that you send for the closest one immediately. Then I think that you should summon your Director of Security and the German overseers and tell them the whole story. When the expert arrives, we will have him examine the gem in front of all of these gentlemen as witnesses..."

Dalton had one objection. "Not the magazine representatives. This must be kept quiet while we sort it out."

Holmes just shook his head. "It's too late to even think about keeping it quiet. These gentlemen will not rush out and inform the world today, but bear this in mind. They already have the beginning of the story and it *will* be published. Even the Prime Minister could not prevent that."

"But..."

"Further, the Germans must be brought into the picture. If that stone in the display case is *not* the Green Fire of the Incas, it will be in headlines all over the world.

"Give no thought to trying to keep this quiet," Holmes continued firmly, "that could give the impression of some degree of guilt. You are going to have your hands full with the Germans if that gem is a fake, no matter what. Do not complicate your problem with any hint of secrecy."

Dalton nodded solemnly. "You are right, of course, Mister Holmes. As I said a moment ago, I'm in such a state that I am not thinking clearly. I'll get things started."

My eyes met Ian's as he looked up from the scrap of paper he was writing on. He smiled and winked, obviously excited to be in on such an adventure. Then he went back to writing his notes. It reminded me that

I had better be making notes of my own, and quickly, before I got too far behind. The Strand would be expecting a detailed account of this adventure, from Holmes' point of view as soon as it was concluded, if indeed it ever was.

Dalton was back in a few minutes with two large men in tow. It was easy to tell which was the German, by his glowering appearance and curt manner, and which was the Englishman, by his polite, but serious demeanor. Dalton's man was tall, sandy haired, and fair skinned.

"Gentlemen, may I present Hans Gertweiler, head of German Security, as regards the emerald, and Bruce Parling, the museum's Director of Security."

Dalton then introduced us. As would be expected, they both seemed a bit startled to be making the acquaintance of the eminent Sherlock Holmes, a little less so at the mention of my name, and not at all interested in Wainwright and McDonough.

The German immediately looked alarmed, and understandably so. The presence of Sherlock Holmes meant criminal activity and the presence of Gertweiler meant the emerald. That took very little thought.

Dalton addressed his remarks to the security men, seated side by side on a velvet sofa.

"Herr Gertweiler, Bruce, I have a remarkable story to tell you. It has been presented to me by Mister Holmes and Doctor Watson and could have earthshaking consequences." He went on to tell the story of the Magazine submissions, the first visit by our entourage to his office, and finally to today's events.

Gertweiler's eyes narrowed as Dalton came to his conclusion..."and so, gentlemen, Charles Winthrop is on his way at this very moment. I strongly suspect that within the hour we will all be laughing about this childish hoax being played upon us by this anonymous author"-Holmes had chosen not to mention Norma's name-"and we will recall it fondly in the years to come. I would add that the only reason I have even agreed to this investigation is that Mister Holmes himself brought the situation to my attention. Any less a personage would not have gotten into my office on such short notice."

Gertweiler spoke for the first time. "So that there is no misunderstanding, the gem that left Munich was, without question, the Green Fire of the Incas. If it is not now in that display case..."

Dalton interrupted quickly. "Hans, there is no need to speculate prematurely. That would only lead to acrimony."

"I do not speak acrimony, I speak truth. We gave you the most precious emerald in the world. There will be no excuse for not receiving the very same gem back."

"Herr Gertweiler," Holmes interjected, "I think we would all do well to heed Mister Dalton's advice. We will have proof shortly and can better assess our situation then. I would also remind you that the story states that the emerald was stolen in Germany, not England."

Before Gertweiler could answer, a sharp rap on the door heralded the arrival of Charles Winthrop, the gem expert. He was quickly introduced and Dalton asked Parling, "Has the case been moved?"

"We had to shut the line down, but allow those already there to view the emerald. I believe that it is on its way to the vault by now."

Holmes spoke to Dalton, "Roger, if I might suggest it, we should all go to the vault as witnesses for Herr Gertweiler that the seal on the box containing the key is unbroken. Perhaps Herr Gertweiler should inspect and break it himself, extricate the key, and open the display case. Then, in our presence, he should hand it to Mister Winthrop, who will make his determination in our presence."

"I quite agree," said Dalton.

By the time we arrived at the vault, the display case was being wheeled in. It turned out that in the random process of secreting the emerald, it was scheduled today for the same vault as the key. As we arrived before the safe within the vault that held the key, Bruce Parling turned the dial on the safe, heard it click open and stepped back.

"Herr Gertweiler, perhaps you should remove the key case and examine the seal."

Gertweiler stepped forward, pulled the door, reached in for the case and examined it thoroughly. He nodded, after a minute or two, and said, "This is the case and the seal is intact...untouched." He removed a pocket knife and cut into the wax seal, shattered it, and removed the key from the velvet cloth upon which it lay.

At Dalton's direction, Holmes and I lifted the top of the display case and held it while Gertweiler reached under and turned the key. Gertweiler and Parling slid the flat bottom free and set it on the table.

The eight of us formed a circle around the table and Dalton nodded to Winthrop. Winthrop stepped forward, picked up the gem and examined it briefly with the naked eye. He met Dalton's eyes with a grave look on his face, then picked up a jeweler's magnifying eye loupe for a thorough, professional examination.

Holmes and I, and probably all the others knew what the outcome would be. The grave look to Dalton was a clear message; the gem in his hand was a fake.

It did not take long. He raised his head and said, soberly, "Gentlemen, this is not only not the Green Fire of the Incas, it isn't even an emerald. It is a creatively designed, brilliantly crafted...piece of glass. An expert would not even need close examination. I knew it before I picked it up."

Although we expected it, we were stunned to silence. Truth to tell, I was almost convinced just by receipt of the story, since everything else had turned out as written. We were now faced with perhaps the crime of the century.

Gertweiler spoke first. "I must immediately report to my museum, which will immediately report to the government. That is my duty. It will be completely out of my hands. In fact, I expect that Schultz and I will be ordered to return home immediately. Higher ranking people than myself will be here soon."

Dalton just stared at him, apparently not knowing what to say next.

It was Holmes who took charge, giving Gertweiler a very hard look. "Tell me, Herr Gertweiler, how do you think this incident will reflect on you?"

Gertweiler looked surprised. "Why...not at all. We turned the Green Fire of the Incas over to the British and now they do not have it."

Holmes nodded. "A point of view. Allow me to present another that I think will be held in some quarters. Herr Gertweiler left Munich with the emerald. He is our Director of Security and he now returns without it. Even if the British government decided to steal it, a gross exaggeration, of course, to make my point. But no matter what, they will say, we expected Gertweiler to return with the Green Fire."

"I do not agree that that will be their point of view," Gertweiler said firmly.

Holmes nodded once again. "And what do you plan to tell your superiors happened?"

"Exactly what did happen. That the British had the emerald and now it is gone. That is all I know." He seemed less firm, shaky actually.

Holmes smiled sardonically, "And then you will seek employment at a different museum?"

"No! Why are you focusing this on me?"

"Because you are the one threatening rash, precipitous action without even the most cursory of investigations. The other seven of us are going to return to Mister Dalton's office to review every step in the process and try to understand where the security could have failed. I warrant you, sir, that your museum would rather have an intelligent response than a Director of Security throwing up his hands and saying he knows nothing."

Gertweiler looked down in cold fury. "I will wait until we...discuss it."

Holmes turned abruptly from harsh to amiable. "Excellent, we will be happy to have you with us." Turning to Dalton, he said, "I would suggest that we return this fake to the display case and allow people to view it as though it were genuine. Then we begin our inquiry."

Back in Dalton's office, Holmes led the discussion. "May we begin with a review of every step in the transfer process that took the emerald from the display case in Munich to the display case in London?"

Dalton turned to Bruce Parling. "Why don't you begin? Present it from our point of view, then Herr Gertweiler can point out any differences he sees. Is that acceptable to all?"

Gertweiler indicated agreement. The rest of the group did not matter in that decision.

Parling sat back and looked into space, as though trying to recall every step in perfect order.

"Yes, yes...well let's see, gentlemen. I first saw the gem in the office of the Managing Director of the Munich Museum, Professor Kleinschmidt. He and I, along with Herr Gertweiler were discussing, actually reviewing, the transfer plans. They had long since been negotiated, amended, and signed by all parties to the agreement, including the Boards of Directors of both museums. Believe me, gentlemen, it is an excruciating process.

"Professor Kleinschmidt had the emerald brought to his office by three armed guards and I was able to see it, hold it in my hands, actually."

No one said anything, so Parling continued.

"The gem was then taken to the cellar laboratory where they have all of the equipment for proper certification. There is a small room within the lab where the certifications actually take place.

"When Hans and I arrived down in the lab, Professor Kleinschmidt did not accompany us, the gem was there, still in the carrying case, still surrounded by the guards.

"Peter Sturtivant, a very renowned gem expert, from Amsterdam, was being shown a piece of new equipment by one of the lab technicians. He seemed quite excited about it. These people have such a passion for this work...Anyway, he came over, took the gem when the guards opened the case, and went into the small room. Hans and I gave the guards instructions regarding the transfer case and sealing equipment, which is kept in another room, and they left to fetch it.

"Hans and I then entered the room and watched Mister Sturtivant at his work."

"What exactly was he doing when you entered the room?"

"Hmm, as I recall, he had it under a large microscope, with a very intense light shining upon it, and was hunched over the scope. The emerald was in plain sight, though." He looked over to Gertweiler, who nodded agreement to this point.

"Sturtivant then measured the gem, from every imaginable angle, wrote his results down and compared them to a prewritten chart that had accompanied the gem. After at least a half hour of this, which both Hans and I thought was excessive, he announced that he was finished and would now prepare a positive certification. He told us to deal with the emerald because once he completes his evaluation, he does not touch the gem again."

Holmes asked, "Did he leave the area to prepare his certificate?"

"No, actually he had a preprinted form that he filled out and signed."

"Was Mister Sturtivant searched when he left the museum?"

Gertweiler answered that question. "Searched? No. Why would we search him? The gem was right before our eyes."

Holmes shrugged. "I have no reason to suggest that you should. As this meeting goes on, I will have numerous procedural questions such as that. It means nothing except thoroughness. I am picturing in my mind everything you say and looking for weaknesses in your system." That answer made sense to everyone, so Parling moved on.

"Next, we put the emerald directly into a small gem box and..."

Holmes interrupted again, "When you say 'we,' who exactly do you mean?"

"I mean Hans Gertweiler and myself He actually picked up the gem and set it in the box, but my eyes never left it."

Holmes nodded. "Then what?"

"We closed the box and put on a hot wax seal, set it in a larger box, and packaged the whole thing. We even put seals on several seams of the final crate, to be sure that it was never opened in transit.

Parling then went through the several elaborate steps to convey the crate by carriage, train, ship, train and a final carriage ride to the security entrance of the British Museum.

Roger Dalton stepped in at this point to conclude the gem's journey. "I was in the receiving room waiting for their arrival and I participated in the unpacking. Along with Bruce and Herr Gertweiler, I will certify that the package that was delivered had no broken seals, and I mean all the way down to the small gem box that held the emerald."

Next came another lengthy narration of the steps taken each day in displaying and securing the gem, all of which seemed to me to add up to an invulnerable system. I did not make that comment because I knew with metaphysical certitude that Holmes would assert that there is no such thing, and he would be right. I was left to wonder when and where the gem could possibly have been switched. But, of course, in that regard, I was in good company. We all wondered that.

Hans Gertweiler finished up, after Bruce Parling and Dalton had spoken, by saying simply, "I have nothing of significance to say. Mister Dalton and Mister Parling covered the subject quite thoroughly, and my observation is that everything occurred exactly as they said it did,"

Now everyone turned to Holmes, hoping for some miraculous solution to the problem, but none was forthcoming. "Gentlemen, assuming that Mister Parling and Herr Gertweiler did not conspire to steal the emerald," Holmes said, then smiled, "an assumption I join the rest of you in making, it would seem that we must go back to the very beginning.

"It would appear that the gem was not stolen prior to the agreement to transfer it, because Mister Peter Sturtivant certified that the gem he received to inspect was indeed the Green Fire of the Incas. Therefore, I think that I will have to interview him on several small matters."

Charles Winthrop spoke for the first time. "I may have some bad news on that, Mister Holmes. Peter may have died."

All heads snapped to face Winthrop. "That's a rather startling statement," I said.

"You said, 'may have died,' Holmes interjected.

"Right. Because I know nothing definitive. We had an annual gem certification conference several weeks ago in Luxemburg City, and Sturtivant's name came up, people wondering why he wasn't there. Someone said he had heard that Peter had died. That's all he knew. I don't know if it was just a rumor or not.

"I never looked into it because people come and go in this business and I never heard anything about him again."

Holmes waited until Winthrop was done before asking, "Were those his exact words? That he had died, or could he have said that he was killed?"

Winthrop took a moment to search his memory. "I'm sure all he said was that he had *heard* that he had died. Anything like he was *killed* would have gotten more conversation than that."

"How old a man was Sturtivant?" Holmes asked.

Winthrop shrugged. "I'm not certain, but I would say mid to late fifties. He seemed to be in good health, but one can never be sure of that."

"Did he say *when* he had died?"

"Not that I recall. Remember, the man said he had *heard* it, not that he was sure."

We all stood there in stunned amazement as Holmes pondered this development. "I'm sure you would all agree," he said, "that if Sturtivant really is dead, that casts quite a different light on this whole mystery.

"Gentlemen," Holmes said, "It will be necessary for me to spend a few hours pondering what we have seen today." To Gertweiler, he said, "Herr Gertweiler, I withdraw my objection to you informing your museum Director of this crime. Now that we have thoroughly discussed it, it is appropriate that you do so.

"We, of course, have no control over their reaction, but I would suggest a secret investigation. There will be plenty of time for recriminations after the gem is recovered or after we are forced to admit that it won't be.

"The architects of this scheme seem to be bent on gathering as much publicity as possible. Ergo, it would seem to follow in logic that if that is what they want, it would be best for us to deny it to them."

Gertweiler nodded, but said, "I agree, but once I inform my Director, it is out of my hands. All I can do is relay your message."

We stopped at the telegraph office on the way back to Baker Street and Holmes once again sent some number of messages. It is unlikely that anyone in the British Isles makes greater use of this method of communication than Holmes.

CHAPTER 15

LIGHTNING cannot strike or thunder roll on a clear, cloudless day. But if it could, it would be no more shocking than the announcement that Mrs. Hudson made in the early afternoon of a dull, uneventful Monday. Holmes and I were busily packing our small hand luggage for a short stay in Amsterdam.

"Mister Holmes, Doctor, there is a Norma Bainsteas downstairs asking to be shown in."

I know that my mouth fell open and I suspect that Holmes, who was rarely surprised by anything, was just as stunned as I.

"Great Scott!" I cried. Then looking to Holmes, "Is it possible?"

Holmes just shook his head. "We'll know in approximately sixty seconds." To Mrs. Hudson he said, "Please show our visitor in and prepare tea for five. Before preparing the tea, please fetch Wiggins and send him to the Strand office with a message for Mister

Wainwright and Mister McDonough to come quickly. Tell them "Urgent, Bainsteas here."

In short order, we heard footsteps on the stairs and into our rooms stepped a tall neatly dressed lady that I would estimate was in her mid thirties. She was moderately attractive and seemed surprisingly familiar to me. I quickly realized that it was because I had studied her picture at length on more than one occasion.

Holmes stepped forward and greeted her, not as a potential diabolical mastermind of crime, but as a guest in our rooms, and entitled to the courtesy that civilized people accord visitors. I, on the other hand, was prepared to tackle her if she should decide to bolt.

"Miss Bainsteas, I am Sherlock Holmes and this is my associate, Doctor John Watson. You are very welcome, but I must admit that we are very surprised to see you here."

She gave him a curious look and said, "First of all, my name is not Bainsteas any more. I am Norma LaMauret, and I can't imagine why you are surprised to see me. You have apparently been looking all over England for me, according to my brother, and some of my friends.

"Beyond that, I sent you a telegram telling you that I would try to call on you when in London. Didn't you receive it?" She had a somewhat aloof manner about her.

"We did, of course, but..."

"Then you should have expected me," She said firmly. We were into the conversation about a minute and the strength of her personality was already abundantly clear.

"Before I address that point, Norma, if you don't mind me calling you that..."

She nodded.

"Doctor Watson and I were surprised to get your first telegram, dripping with sarcasm, as it was, but even more surprised to get a second one. Why did...?"

"I sent you *one* telegram, Mister Holmes, not two, and there was no sarcasm whatever to it. I can't imagine what you are talking about. I simply wired you that I might stop to see you."

The three of us stared at each other for several seconds until Holmes snatched a telegram from his desk and handed it to her.

"Is this the telegram you sent?"

She glanced at it briefly. "Yes. Certainly."

He handed her another. "How do you explain this telegram?"

She read it quickly and handed it back. "I know nothing of this telegram. I did not send it and I have no explanation for it."

Before Holmes could respond, she demanded, "I would like *you* to explain, sir, the consternation you have caused my brother in Aberdeen by visiting him twice, once with a Police Magistrate, looking for me. When you complete that explanation, I would like to know why you sent the police to the home of my friend, Cordelia Lange, in Cornwall, and asked for a picture of me. You have made me look, to family and friends, like an escaped felon of some kind."

I don't think either one of us could have anticipated that when we finally came face to face with Norma Bainsteas, that she would be taking the offensive.

Again, before Holmes could respond, Mrs. Hudson arrived with tea. In the few minutes it took to get the tea poured, creamed and sugared, a breathless Nevin Wainwright burst into the room.

"Holmes!" he cried. He snapped his head toward Norma, then back to Holmes. "You said it was urgent."

Holmes smiled, "And urgent it is, but...where is Ian?"

"I sent him out on an assignment. I fear that he'll be devastated to know that he missed your summons." Wainwright once again snapped his head toward our visitor, "Are you Norma Bainsteas?"

"I was. I am now Norma LaMauret."

"These stories that you..."

"Mister Wainwright," Holmes interrupted sharply. "I will conduct the interview if you don't mind." His tone of voice said that he would conduct the interview whether Wainwright liked it or not.

"Interview?" She asked curiously. "I demand to know what is going on and I mean immediately."

Holmes sat before her and looked deeply into her eyes. "Let me tell you what I can at this time. Your name has arisen in connection with a very serious crime. Do you have any idea why that would be?"

She seemed genuinely shocked. I was getting a queasy feeling about this whole situation. When her name was announced by Mrs. Hudson, I had formed the opinion that she was here to gloat, to be as outrageous as imaginable, by confronting us and more or less daring us to prove anything against her. The kind of thing that Moriarty would have attempted.

But this woman before us did not seem to have any idea what we were after. On the other hand, she *could* be an accomplished actress.

Her shock seemed to change into fear, then quickly to combativeness. "What kind of crime are you referring to and how is my name connected to it?" she demanded. "And *who* connected my name to this...crime?"

Holmes answered her calmly. "A person calling herself Norma Bainsteas connected Norma Bainsteas to this crime. In other words, unless someone is using your name in an attempt to...embarrass you, you connected yourself to this crime."

"I know nothing of any of this business. I have not committed any crime and I most certainly have *not* connected myself to any kind of crime. In fact, if this does not start to make some sense very soon, I am going to leave and make certain that I never have the displeasure of seeing you again."

"Not a wise course to consider, Norma. With the evidence we have, I could easily send for Scotland Yard and have you arrested."

"Arrested? For what?" She demanded.

"For murder, for one thing. There are several other crimes of a very serious nature, but murder is the top of the crime list."

She seemed about to go into shock before our very eyes. In fact, she sat speechless.

"Mrs. LaMauret, Norma," Holmes said, "please understand that this is a very serious situation. We have been searching for you ever since we discovered a corpse that we were directed to by a Norma Bainsteas. It was a ghastly crime. However, the fact that you are here, and the guilelessness of your manner has given me very serious pause. We may have been searching all this time for the completely wrong person.

"I do believe, though, that we could clear this up in just a few minutes"

Holmes reached across to his desk and picked up the photograph we had received from the police in Cornwall and handed it to Norma.

"I assume that you will confirm that this photograph is of you. We received it through the Cornwall police from your friend Cordelia Lange in Cornwall."

"Of course it's me. As I have already told you, Cordelia and I went to college together."

Holmes took a sheaf of papers from his desk, which I immediately recognized as the original handwritten story from "Norma" that began this whole sordid adventure.

"Mrs. LaMauret, what I have in my hand is a copy of the document that caused our interest. It is in the handwriting of the person we seek.

"If it is not the same as your handwriting, we will have serious doubt that you are our suspect. If it is...

"So, are you willing to give us a copy of your script for comparison?"

Without hesitation she glanced to the quill and ink pot on Holmes' desk. Walking to his chair, she said, "What would you like me to write?"

Holmes dictated, "It was necessary for me to do this in order to avoid detection by the police."

She wrote quickly, then set the pen down and looked at Holmes, who made a final request. "Would you please give us a sample of your signature?"

She quickly signed it and handed it to Holmes, who held it beside the manuscript and smiled, "Not even close. The two hands could not be more different."

"Certainly not," she said, with what I would definitely call a sneer. "Can I now assume that I am no longer a suspect in your silly little game?"

Holmes smiled. "No, that would not be a correct assumption." We all blinked at that. As Holmes was about to elaborate, we heard heavy foot steps on the stairs.

"Ah, that would be inspector Lestrade," said Holmes, which also raised eyebrows all around the room.

Introductions were quickly made with warm handshakes and smiles, except for Norma, who did not shake Lestrade's outstretched hand, but looked at him with a combination of concern and disdain.

"Inspector Lestrade," Holmes said, "while you pour your tea, I'll finish the thought I was sharing with Mrs. LaMauret."

Lestrade nodded, seeming to understand the situation. Holmes must have spoken to him during one of his errands while I was busying myself with a Strand story.

Turning to Norma, he said, "Norma's handwriting is completely different from the script in the original story. Therefore, she asked if that meant that she is no longer a suspect. I had told her that that was not a correct assumption when you arrived, Inspector.

"To complete the thought, I will tell her that, in my opinion, she is one of two things; A diabolical killer with extraordinary hubris, as evidenced by her presence here, and a facility for deceptive handwriting, or," he now added with a touch of lightness, "completely innocent."

"I choose to be considered the latter," she said scornfully, and rose as if to leave.

Holmes raised a hand. "Norma, I'm afraid we can't allow you to leave just yet."

"Not leave? How dare you use a word like allow to me? Are you planning to arrest me?"

"Not at all, ma'am. We merely wish to prevent your assassination."

She turned white, gaped, and put her hand to her mouth. "Assassination? What in the name of all that is holy have I gotten myself into?" She was practically screaming by now. "I thought I had an opportunity to meet a famous man, so I came. Now I am accused of horrendous crimes and, even more incredibly, threatened with assassination." Her previously firm resolve shattered and she began to cry.

Holmes, for all of his ruthless pursuit of criminals, could be surprisingly tender to the feelings of innocent people. I had seen him at past murder scenes as tenacious as a Bull Mastiff in pushing away police and reporters who could "contaminate," as he called it, a crime scene. Yet in the next moment he could show the most touching compassion for family, especially children of victims.

I became convinced of his belief in Norma's innocence as he took her hand and gently tried to calm and reassure her. He most assuredly did not do this with genuine suspects. Quite the opposite, he always tried to bring them to maximum emotional stress to crack their facade of innocence.

Holding her hand in both of his, "Norma, if you are truly innocent in this matter, and I am leaning more and more toward that view, then something terrible has been visited upon you, either by coincidence or design. In either case, I believe that you deserve a better explanation than you have gotten to this point.

"Most of what I am about to tell you will be in print soon anyway, so I do not compromise our investigation by sharing it with you. Let me begin by asking if you have read the last two issues of the Strand magazine."

"I have not," she said simply.

Holmes nodded, "There is a serialized story, which will be concluded soon, about a case you may remember, having lived in Aberdeen at the time, about the murder of a young man named Carlton Mackenzie."

"Murder? Carlton was not murdered. I remember the case well. He stole money from our company and absconded. That is the last I have heard of him."

Two words in her answer stunned, I am sure, all of us. Lestrade leaned forward and Wainwright scribbled notes, while I waited for Holmes to pounce upon the words, which he did immediately.

"You said, 'our company?'" Holmes asked in undisguised amazement.

"Yes. I worked at the same company as Carlton. I was only there a few months, but it happened to be at the same time as the theft. I knew Carlton fairly well, and I have met his wife on a couple of occasions, the poor woman.

"But Mister Holmes, are you now saying that he was murdered? There was nothing like that in the case that I, or for that matter, anyone else in Aberdeen knows about. We were all amazed that he stole the money and ran away, but there was never a hint of him being murdered."

Holmes took a few minutes and explained the whole story, beginning with the original submission to the Strand, and including our discovery of the body.

Her face was one of astonishment as the story unfolded, but turned to puzzled as Holmes concluded.

"It's an amazing story to hear, Mister Holmes, but I still do not understand where I fit in. Are you saying that whoever did this actually signed my name to those papers?"

Holmes understood her consternation, as we all did. "That is exactly what I am saying. It has not been published in the Strand yet, but the letter that accompanied the story, supposedly from the perpetrator of the crime, was signed by a Norma Bainsteas

Another shock to her system. I should say another in a series of shocks visited upon her this afternoon. "That's incredible. I don't know what to say. How can this be?"

Holmes shrugged. "Very often when we get to the bottom of a puzzle, we find that of all the scenarios possible, the least likely is the one that actually occurred. In this instance, I can think of a few possibilities. First is that, if you are not involved, the mastermind of this plot picked your name out of thin air and has us pursuing an endless trail. I reject that out of hand. It would make no sense.

"Next, I would speculate that the extraordinary coming together of your name, your history, and the company that was victimized, and your personal acquaintanceship with Carlton Mackenzie, means that the crime was committed by someone who knew both of you and was familiar with the company, most probably even worked there. That is the avenue down which I choose to travel."

Holmes asked her several more questions over the next hour, having her tell us everything she could remember about every employee that she could recall interacting with Carlton Mackenzie. Amazingly, he wrote nothing down, but then again, I had seen that pattern for years.

To conclude the interview, Holmes asked, "Did you know a Garret Dickinson, who was also employed at your company?"

She answered without hesitation. "Garrett. Yes I knew him, not as well as I knew Carlton, but fairly well."

Holmes' ears perked up. "Please tell us everything you can recall of him."

"Is he involved in some way?"

Holmes shook his head. "We have no reason to believe that he is, but quite coincidentally, he resigned and left the day after Carlton disappeared. You notice that we have asked about as many of the employees as you can recall. Dickinson is one whose name we know, so please..."

"I don't know much about him, nobody did, but he was a very pleasant young man, very friendly. The more I think about it, though, I realize that he didn't say too much about himself."

Holmes asked, "Do you know why he left so abruptly?"

"I really don't know for sure why he left," she said, "but it wasn't what I would call abrupt. I knew for almost two weeks before he left that he was going to."

Holmes raised his eyebrows in surprise. "He told you?"

"Yes."

"Did he give any particulars?"

She pondered for a moment. "Well, I know that he did not like his supervisor, but then nobody did. He was a swine. I left because of that man also. He very brazenly suggested that I engage in some inappropriate behavior with him. I thought about slapping him, but decided against it."

Holmes nodded, "Probably a wiser course in the long run, but did you continue in contact with Dickinson?"

She shook her head decisively. "I've never seen him again and, to the best of my recollection, I've never heard or spoken his name again...until this afternoon."

After getting a physical description of Dickinson, as she remembered it, Holmes said," I believe that we are finished here, Norma, except for the possible assassin out on the street. I say 'possible' because we do not know for sure. The case that we are investigating is far more complicated and much larger than we are able to divulge at this point, but the person who signed your name to the letter is the linchpin in the whole story. She, if it is a she, could cause tremendous turmoil on the continent and we believe that the man who has been following us has actually been looking for *you*."

"Why haven't you arrested him?" she demanded.

Holmes smiled. "Two reasons. One, he hasn't done anything and two, he is inept and easy to keep track of. We have been content to let him follow us around, but we can no longer allow that. He undoubtedly saw you enter the building and will see you leave.

"If we are correct as to his intentions, you are in great danger. Therefore, we must deal with him. We had planned to allow you to leave, see if he followed you, and follow him, but there could be too great a risk in that."

"So, what will you do?" she asked nervously.

Holmes smiled again. "Inspector Lestrade will have him arrested immediately, and accuse him of multiple murders, in the privacy of a cell, of course, and see how he reacts. If we ask a suspect what his intentions are, he will always lie and claim he has done nothing wrong. If we accuse him of something serious, he will normally admit to whatever he was up to, assuming it was less serious, and be glad to be let go.

"No matter what, we will find out, confiscate his weapon, and put him on a ship back to the continent."

She seemed genuinely puzzled. "Is that how police procedures work?"

"Inspector Lestrade, Doctor Watson, and I have worked together for a long time. We have developed a variety of...unorthodox procedures. This one may be considered borderline illegal, but very effective, and implemented with the best of intentions."

Norma smiled for the first time. "The end justifies the means?"

"Actually, Doctor Watson wrote a story by that name a while back. The answer, we concluded then was... sometimes."

Lestrade left and in a few minutes Holmes and I, Norma and Wainwright, watched out the windows, with amusement, as four police officers conversed with the man on the bench, abided a few minutes of outraged bellowing until a police carriage arrived, and whisked him away. We would await Lestrade's report.

As we bade Norma LaMauret, nee Bainsteas, goodbye, Holmes promised to send her a final written report when the whole picture was clear and the miscreants incarcerated. The address she gave was in a small village in the French Dordogne region.

Holmes asked, at the door, "Norma, as we were trying to track you down, we received a report that a Denis LaMauret, about your age, had passed away, but the location was Honfleur. Is there any..."

"Yes." She nodded her head sadly, "We were living in Honfleur at the time. Denis loved the sea and did not fear it, even in the worst of weather. He went out alone one night and didn't come back. A fisherman found the empty boat, but it was three days before Denis washed ashore. I couldn't stay in Honfleur...too many memories.

"The home I live in was Denis' family farm. He was an only child and when his parents died, it was his. We sold most of the land to provide for our future, so I live in a comfortable old place on about twenty acres."

"Surprising that you don't return to Aberdeen, where you have family and friends," Holmes mused.

She shook her head firmly. "No. Perhaps someday, but not now. The memory of how most of my family treated Denis is too painful in light of his death. Whenever I visit Aberdeen, it's only to see my brother William, whom you gentlemen have met. He's the only warm heart in the family."

Her face seemed a study in sadness as she left. We all were silent for a while, perhaps pondering the sorrow of relationships shattered by intolerance, possibly never to be healed.

CHAPTER 16

IT was a rough crossing, as the channel often is this time of year, not at all ameliorated by the heavy wind and black, glowering clouds that enveloped Amsterdam. I estimated that I had not seen the sun or any hint of blue above me in eight days. I visited Amsterdam only by necessity, since it always brought out the pessimistic side of me. Being below sea level, with only manmade dikes holding back the raging tide, did not provide me with peace of mind or comfort of soul.

We took a carriage directly to the building that housed the Amsterdam Medical Examiner, Doctor Willem Schmidling, who turned out to be a short, rotund, rather garrulous, but quite amiable gentleman. He seemed very pleased, even excited, at the opportunity of involvement, however brief, in a case being investigated by the eminent Sherlock Holmes.

It appeared that he had prepared for our visit, but not necessarily professionally. He had a considerable pile of Strand magazines on his desk, and beside them a few of the monographs Holmes had written on various aspects of crime investigation. I had had them published through the Strand, as well.

On a sideboard was a Delft china tea set in the white and blue colors that I had always found so attractive. A tiny wisp of steam rose gently from the spout of the teapot, indicating that the steeping brew was made fresh for us. Beside it set a stout bottle of French cognac.

Doctor Schmidling set cream, sugar, and spoons on the table before us and poured tea, asking, "Gentlemen, this weather requires me to brace my tea with a drop of brandy. Can I do the same for yours?"

Holmes declined, but I gave him a vigorous nod. I noted with satisfaction that he poured much more than a drop in his cup and mine.

"Now gentlemen, you are here to inquire about the death of Mister Peter Sturtivant, you said. I have the file on my desk, but there is a complication that could delay its availability."

We both raised our eyebrows.

"You both would have to sign three or four of these Strand magazines, with personal inscriptions, and all three of your monographs, Mister Holmes."

"That is the complication?" I asked, "You want us to sign the magazines?"

He smiled warmly. "That is the complication and it would be a boon if you were to suggest that we worked together on something of significance."

Holmes was quite gracious. "We could do that in absolute sincerity," he said, taking the top two Strands from the pile. "Although it will not be evident, what we are here about is connected to the case being serialized in these top two issues."

Schmidling was delighted. Holmes and I complied with his request with alacrity and celerity as he opened the file. His manner changed abruptly from jolly and talkative to sober and businesslike as soon as the file was opened. Still friendly and cooperative, but very professional.

"Gentlemen, I fear that you will be disappointed with the file because it is rather sparse. Mister Sturtivant, who I knew personally, had been missing for four days when he was fished out of the Zuider Zee. In your professional endeavors, I'm sure that both of you have seen, or at least understand, what extended stays in the water do to a body. He was virtually unrecognizable. We did the best we could with a few minor birthmarks that his son could recall, but he had no scars or significant anomalies on his body. His son was certain, though, that the body was his. A ghastly affair, being present at such occasions."

We nodded silently, completely understanding.

"Gentlemen, rather than me trying to tell you the whole story, such as it is, why don't I let you peruse the file at your leisure. Feel free to take any notes you like. Being trained in such things, you may pick up something I have missed."

As we started into the report, he refilled our teacups and before I could stop him, generously fortified my cup with the cognac. I cannot, in good conscience, say that I regretted his generosity.

We finished the file and Holmes started into the blizzard of questions that often attended interviews such as these. He began by inquiring into Sturtivant's financial status.

"He wasn't a wealthy man, that anyone knew of," Schmidling began. "He lived quietly and modestly. Because of his stature in the field, he was able to charge high fees for his work, but gem certification is not an every day activity. I would say that he lived comfortably, but not lavishly, and did not show any sign of financial insecurity."

Holmes nodded. "And can I assume that he had no criminal record or background of illegal activities? No offense, Doctor, but we must rule out all impossibilities to arrive at the truth."

"I understand, Mister Holmes, but I am not aware of anything along those lines. He seemed a model of rectitude, but you could check with the local police."

Holmes said, "I've already informed them, by telegram, that I intend to stop and visit them."

The conversation continued for another hour and another pot of tea, sans cognac, going through family and friends, to the extent that Schmidling knew of such things.

Sturtivant's wife had passed away in the great influenza epidemic twelve years earlier and he was left with three grown children, all married, and living in Amsterdam. Schmidling knew that he had some grand children, but nothing of number or any names. Further, he had no idea where in the great city any of the children lived.

Our interest was piqued as Schmidling concluded his discussion of Sturtivant's family. "As I have mentioned, Peter lived alone, but he has been seen around Amsterdam in the company of a much younger woman of late. I have never seen her or heard a name, but others have mentioned her." He added with a smile, "We Dutch are a great lot of gossipers."

Holmes asked, "So nothing else of interest regarding the corpse has occurred to you?"

"I'm afraid not, sir. As I said, he had been in the water a long time. All we could determine was that he had not been shot or stabbed. There were no broken bones and no obvious signs of violence upon his person.

"Further, his clothes were not torn and his rather expensive pocket watch was still attached to the fob. So, with the corpse in the shape it was in, we had no choice but to declare it a drowning for undetermined reasons."

⁂

The visit to the police was uneventful. One did not sense a strong attitude of cooperation from them, perhaps fearing that Holmes would find something they had missed and thus embarrass them by proving that Sturtivant had been murdered. They did, however, state strongly that Sturtivant had no criminal record and no hint of scandal in his background.

The next day, we were able to find all three of Sturtivant's children easily, as well as several dealers in expensive gems who knew our man very well.

We were not able to learn anything of the young woman Sturtivant had been seen with, and nothing else of great interest.

The sailing back from Amsterdam was no better than the earlier trip over, but it was on the train from Dover to London that the case took a very dramatic turn.

CHAPTER 17

HOLMES was, by turns, relaxed as we sipped our tea, and pensive as he used the breaks in conversation to look inward and ponder where we were in this rather vexing case. The tea was excellent, as tea service on trains went, but the scones fell so far short of Mrs. Hudson's that she would be offended even by the comparison.

"Now Holmes, I know that you learned far more than I did in Amsterdam and you should be engulfed in profound shame if you do not share it with me."

Holmes pondered the opening move in my inquiry with amusement. "Engulfed in profound shame,' Watson? Are you now bringing your melodramatic literary proclivities into your every day banter?"

"It's called engaging your prey. If I simply asked what is new, you would regard it as idle chatter and give me an unsatisfactory answer as you slipped back into your ruminations. By startling you with syntax, I seek to knock you out of your train of thought and snatch you into a deeper conversation with me.

"It is not unlike your habit of beginning an interview with a known felon by making an outlandish accusation in order to jolt him from the offense to the defense."

He smiled broadly. "Brilliant, Watson, you have succeeded so spectacularly, that it will take me a moment to even remember what I was thinking about."

I felt triumphant, which was not a frequent occurrence in discourse with my erudite room mate

"Let's begin with the medical report, Holmes. Aside from its brevity, I found little else of note."

Holmes pondered and responded. "I agree that there was precious little there, but you can't have failed to notice in the statistical portion that followed the narrative report that there was no measurable water in the lungs."

"Great Scott! I was so numbed by the narrative that I skimmed over the numbers without studying them. That casts a completely new light on his death."

"Not really, old fellow, not for me anyway. What it means, of course, is that he was dead before he went into the water. Which means that he was murdered. But I was already certain of that. I viewed it as confirmation rather than revelation."

"But...you didn't challenge Schmidling about it," I observed.

"There was no reason to. We are now certain that he was murdered, which is what we went there to determine, and challenging Schmidling would do one of two things. It would either embarrass him professionally, which we have no reason to do, or...it would alert him if he has any nefarious reason for having given a misleading report..."

"Such as...?" I asked.

"Such as having accepted a bribe for laying the death to rest so quietly. If, at the end of the case, there is any reason to suspect him of skullduggery, we will make an issue of it. If there is not, we will point it out quietly and allow him to save face by discovering the error himself.

"If he has been bribed, I would like anyone who is monitoring our activities, and there is no doubt that we are being tracked by whoever the Norma Bainsteas writing these letters is, to think they have fooled us."

I digested that briefly. "That certainly is logical, but what about the bigger picture? Have we clarified anything there?"

Holmes mused a long while before answering. "I would not think so, Watson. I was convinced when we reviewed the security procedures that Sturtivant would turn out to be the scoundrel. Once the gem was turned over to Parling and Gertweiler, we had two men, whose job required them to be suspicious of each other, watching it. To suspect a cabal involving both of them seems beyond reason, given the timing and circumstance.

"Let's review the critical moment when the gem was taken from the display case and presented to Peter Sturtivant. What Parling and Gertweiler agreed on was that Sturtivant took the gem and went into the small room to begin his examination. I saw that as a potential problem immediately.

"Parling and Gertweiler stated that they gave the guards some instruction regarding the transfer case and the sealing equipment and then went into the room. They said that when they arrived, Sturtivant had the gem under a microscope already. I would venture to guess that the gem was out of their sight for almost a minute, perhaps more.

"A minute to palm and replace a small item like a gem is a virtual eternity. Anyone could do it. Moriarty could do it if he was blindfolded and being stared at.

"So now we have the real emerald tucked safely into Sturtivant's pocket, a fake being examined and ceremoniously turned over to our security experts"-he had a slightly derisive tone to his voice as he said it-"and they go blithely away, confident in what is in the sealed case.

"You will recall that I asked if Sturtivant was searched after his certification and they were shocked at such a notion. Why would we search the certifier? Why indeed?"

"He *would* seem to be the person in the mix that could be trusted," I said.

"The bank examiner syndrome," Holmes said, chuckling. "If the bank examiner says there is something amiss in the accounts, no one questions him. They question the bank officers. He is the last to be suspected of any mischief.

"I recall to your mind a monograph I wrote several years ago entitled *Delusion by Expectation.* We expect auditors and examiners and certifiers to be legitimate, and we always look to them last if a problem arises. Whoever our Norma Bainsteas is, he or she certainly understands that. Always get a trusted authority figure to do your dirty work."

I was taken aback by the audacity of the act. "The reason they are trusted, though, Holmes, is their past record. It takes years to build a reputation in such fields."

"Agreed, old fellow, but that makes them only slightly less susceptible to bribery, and absolutely no less susceptible to blackmail, extortion, or intimidation."

I wasn't completely convinced of that, but who am I to debate Sherlock Holmes?

"I suppose you're right, Holmes, but where are we then?"

"We take small steps at a time in this case, Watson. It's not like some that we've solved on the very day the crime was committed.

"We see a possible pattern arising in two of these cases, which I'll get to in a moment. First, about Sturtivant. It's clear that our mastermind had a way of knowing that the gem would be loaned to the British Museum. We don't know yet, but speculate that either he was in a position to influence the decision of which gem expert to engage for the certification, or he reacted quickly once the decision was made.

"Possibly the appointment with him was made several days or weeks in advance. It's also possible that he does all of the certifications for the Munich museum. We'll have to inquire about that.

"A point to look into later, but for now, we'll begin with the fact that our mastermind knows who will do the job. Next, he either intimidates, blackmails or bribes him into switching the gem and turning it over to him. I suspect that we will not find that out until we have made an arrest.

"So, either way, Sturtivant switches the gem as the security men are occupied, gives it to our perpetrator, and for his effort, he is murdered. Bear in mind what I have said numerous times. Very simple, ten second actions are far less detectable than long drawn out charades. Sturtivant switches the fake for the real gem almost the second he touches it, in the wink of a eye.

"For the security men, it's also the wink of an eye. Sturtivant takes the gem, turns his back, they give quick instructions, and within seconds they turn and see the gem under the microscope. From their point of view, everything is perfectly normal, no time has passed. Besides, their expectations would be that any threat to the gem would come from the outside.

"Now, the pattern that we see emerging is that in two cases, Carlton Mackenzie in Aberdeen, and Sturtivant in Munich, our mastermind finds a weakish person, forces or induces him to commit a major theft, appropriates the loot, and kills the only person who could identify him and possibly testify against him.

"It's diabolical, Watson, in that he never exposes himself. He plans the crime, executes it through surrogates who are implicated in the crime and therefore neutralized, scoops up the proceeds, killing the only threat to him or her, and disappears. As people are running around helter-skelter to recover their losses, our man is in another town, possibly another country, planning his next caper.

"The pattern doesn't quite hold in the bank fraud in Zurich, but in its difference, we can find logic and perhaps a bit of similarity. In this case, rather than killing his puppet, Mundt, he neutralizes him by putting him in a position where revelation of the crime ruins him. He chooses not to kill him at this time because he sees future usefulness for him.

"But that might only be a matter of time. If I were Mundt, I would not feel too sanguine about my long term survival if my usefulness ever recedes."

We drifted into a period of silence, for which I'm sure Holmes was grateful. I sensed a desire to return to his cogitations. Truth to tell, my eyelids were growing a bit heavy and I welcomed a respite from the rather frenetic pace we had been maintaining.

The steady clicking of iron wheel on iron track, the frequent bouncing and the occasional jolt as we rounded a bend without sufficiently reducing speed, kept me from slipping into a restful sleep, so I contented myself with closed eyes and meandering thoughts. Unlike my partner of so many years, I tried not to think about the case, or any other case for that matter.

I found contentment in the tiny villages or fields of wildflowers zipping past the window whenever my eyes fluttered open.

Suddenly, I was jarred back to the moment during one brief flutter as I glanced at Holmes and found a look of deep shock on his face. His mouth was literally hanging open.

"Holmes...?"

I noticed that he had the manuscripts before him and the first letter from the bogus Norma Bainsteas.

"Holmes? I repeated.

He raised a hand to ward me off for a moment and wrote something on the back of one of the sheets of paper. He stared at the paper raising it to his eyes as though in disbelief.

He put the paper back down, snatched up his pen, and wrote a few more lines. Then he stared again and buried his face in his hands for a long moment. Finally looking over to me, he said, "Watson, I do not know whether to laugh at what I am about to show you, or to cry."

He shook his head again and said, "We have been made sport of by the rascal claiming he or she was Norma and I should hang my head in shame and cry for my criminal obtuseness...but, I choose to laugh instead. If I could send him a brief message right now it would congratulate him and say 'well done."

"Whatever are you getting on about Holmes?" I demanded.

"Anagrams," he said simply. "I have found something vaguely troubling about Rene LaDier's name right from the outset. It didn't have the ring of a genuine name to me, almost like a made up name or a stage name for one of those distasteful types that dance in shows."

I shrugged. "There are countless combinations of syllables that make up names all over the world. I pay very little thought to them."

Holmes nodded agreement. "Normally, I do the same, but..."

"You mentioned anagrams?" I asked.

He smiled ruefully. "Look at this."

I snatched the paper and found two vertical columns of names, a quickly scratched line connecting each

name in the left column to one in the right. The first set
of names startled me;

Rene LaDier—Irene Adler

"Holmes...Irene Adler? What in heaven's name
does that mean?"

"Read the second set and all will be clear," he said,

Norma Bainsteas—Sebastian Moran

I was stunned. "So the names are made up from
past associations we have had? He is simply playing with
us and Norma Bainsteas just happens to be an anagram
for Sebastian Moran? Nothing more than that?"

"I believe that that is the case with Rene LaDier and
Irene Adler. Norma will take bit of thought. There may
be more to her name appearing than that."

CHAPTER 18

B Y prearrangement, Lestrade, Wainwright, and McDonough were in our rooms in Baker Street when we arrived at three p.m. Holmes had sent telegrams informing of them of our arrival, promising a report on our activities in Amsterdam.

We had stopped at the British Museum to inform Roger Dalton that his worst fears were undoubtedly a reality; That the emerald was not only taken by the gem certifier, but that it had passed out of his hands into the hands of a master criminal.

Even if he was eventually apprehended, the likelihood was that he had sold the gem in exchange for an enormous amount of money and covered his tracks. Since Sturtivant was the only one who knew who the gem was given to, and Sturtivant was now an unpleasant memory, it would seem virtually impossible that the gem would ever be seen again.

Moreover, since Sturtivant was dead, his duplicity could probably never be proven. Therefore, the Germans would assert that they had passed the genuine emerald to the British Museum, and would have an internationally accepted certification to support their claim.

Dalton was almost in tears. He paced back and forth, burying his face in his hands numerous times, lamenting the damage to, if not the complete destruction of, his reputation.

"Even though we will tell the press what we believe, that we never received the genuine emerald, history will record me as the man who lost the Green Fire of the Incas. The Munich Museum will be merciless in pressing that story because my counterpart there does not want to be remembered as the one who lost it."

"There must be insurance for this kind of situation," I said.

Dalton dismissed the point. "Of course, there is insurance, Doctor Watson, but for the emerald, not for my reputation. No one insures that."

Though we made an effort to comfort and reassure our crestfallen friend, it was to no avail. He was inconsolable.

≈§≈

We found a happier group of faces at Baker Street, all of them eager to hear what had transpired in Amsterdam. Holmes and I greeted them warmly and shook hands before pouring tea.

"Good afternoon, gentlemen, and thank you for coming. Ian, we missed you at the interview of Norma Bainsteas."

"It broke my heart not to be here, Mister Holmes, but Mister Wainwright had given me an assignment all the way over in Canterbury. To compound my distress, I had an atrocious steak and kidney pie for lunch on the return train and it must have been bad. I couldn't return to work for two days."

Holmes smiled warmly, "Well, we're all happy to see you feeling better. We'd hate to have a lapse in your journal."

"Mister Wainwright's notes were as complete as mine would have been. I have an update for you and Doctor Watson."

At their collective insistence, however, Holmes agreed to give our report before any of them presented any new material.

It didn't take long, because Holmes reported the sparsest of facts. He did not mention the absence of water in Sturtivant's lungs, basing his insistence that he had been murdered on the circumstances. As we would soon learn, there was no benefit from omitting the water in the lungs.

When Wainwright began his report, the first sentence out of his mouth was, "Sturtivant stole the emerald. Norma...it seems silly to keep using that name, since we know it isn't her, but we don't have any other. Anyway, the story says that once the jewel was in his or her hands, Sturtivant was of no further value to them. Therefore he was 'dropped out of the picture.' That's an exact quote."

"Further, he says that Sturtivant accepted a healthy bribe to do it, so any sympathy for him is wasted."

Holmes pondered the story, then asked Wainwright what he planned to print next.

Wainwright practically gushed, "Everything. The final chapter of the story of Carlton Mackenzie and the unhappy business in Aberdeen will be published in Wednesday's edition. We will also have a story that introduces the theft of the emerald, without giving any specifics.

"We will simply say that the crime of the century will be revealed in the coming weeks, beginning next Wednesday. We will say that the crime is so secret that the police don't even know about it yet, and so spectacular that it will be included in future history books."

Holmes frowned. "You gentlemen certainly dip deeply into hyperbole in marketing your product."

"But this is not really hyperbole, Mister Holmes. The things we say are exactly true. We don't embellish by a degree..."

Holmes smiled sardonically. "The crime of the century, Mister Wainwright? In the same century as the Whitechapel Murders?"

"Well, I'll have to give you that, Mister Holmes. Nevertheless, this *is* the biggest story since Jack the Ripper and we have to go with it. If I didn't, I would certainly be sacked and my successor would publish it.

"We will be, once again, printing three times the normal number of copies. In fact, we received an order from America, of all places, that we had to place with a private printer. Our regular company is working around the clock to finish Wednesday's issue."

Holmes just shook his head. "It's almost a form of voyeurism. People wanting to see the distress of crime victims and read all the gory details. How will you say that Sturtivant was killed?"

"We won't. We'll wait to see if Norma gives us any description."

Holmes was clearly unhappy with the international attention that was building on this case.

"And how," He asked, "will you report the missing emerald when the time comes. Where will you place the emphasis as regards the gem's substitution?"

"I'm not sure i understand, Mister Holmes."

"There will be a torrent of acrimony passing between the British Museum and the Munich Museum. The Germans will not react well and will be trying to place blame. Doctor Watson and I are certain that the Green Fire of the Incas never came into the possession of the British Museum. Therefore..."

"I see the point you are making and I agree. The gem was lost by the Germans and that is how we will state it. After all, sir, we are all Englishmen here."

Holmes asked, "Your plan, then, is that you will not let the news of the emerald's disappearance be made public for at least ten more days?"

"That is correct sir."

As Wainwright and McDonough left, Holmes watched out the window, then excused himself, went into his room, and closed the door.

❧❧

The London Times, the following morning, ran a headline that could be read from across the street;

Green Fire of the Incas Stolen!

The story had a remarkable number of details, including the trip to Amsterdam taken by Holmes and myself. I was stunned. How in the world did they get that information?

CHAPTER 19

I THOUGHT that we were now completely out to sea on the investigation that had consumed so much of our time over the last few weeks, and feeling a curious mix of frustration and embarrassment.

The newspapers were now hanging on everything that Nevin Wainwright had to say, assuming that as the addressee of the communications with the author who had previously identified himself as Norma Bainsteas, he would be the first to learn any new information from the dark side. He was becoming a celebrity in his own right, by virtue of his position.

My embarrassment arose from the fact that it was looking increasingly as though the point was to embarrass Sherlock Holmes and we had been unable to do anything about it.

Although the stories were sent to Wainwright, the anagrams for the names of Irene Adler and Sebastian Moran were clearly directed at Holmes and the taunting telegram and the Gaulois cigarette package that had been sent over the name of Norma Bainsteas was delivered to Baker Street.

Moreover, it would be impossible to forget that the very first letter that began this whole adventure specifically cited Holmes' work and asserted that there were some, if not many, operating on the dark side of the law and never receiving "credit," as bizarre as that sounds, for their accomplishments. It was, certainly, a malevolent gauntlet thrown before England's greatest detective.

To those unfamiliar with the difficulty of solving intelligently conceived crimes, and for those spoiled by the adventures, previously published, of Holmes solving complex crimes within days, it seemed as though the cretin had a point,

In fact, questions were beginning to emerge as to whether my illustrious room mate had indeed met his match. A respected columnist in the London Times opined that the sanguinity of the denizens of our capitol city about their safety, because of Holmes' vigilance on their behalf, may turn out to be in some degree unwarranted.

Fortunately, such sentiment was in a miniscule minority to this point, but if this dragged on for too long, one could never be confident of the staying power of a fickle citizenry. None of which seemed to be of any concern to the master detective.

Over our Port, a few days after our return from Amsterdam, I brought the subject up.

"Holmes, I am not at peace about where we stand in our search for a solution. I was content earlier on to be seeking Norma Bainsteas because we learned within a few days that there was such a person. I know that a squirrel could not hide from you in the Sahara once you knew who he was. Your ability to track down felons is unquestioned.

"But now that identity that we thought we had has turned out to be a mirage, which vexes me to no end. Are we now completely back to the beginning? Do we now know nothing whatever about the person or persons we are looking for?"

Holmes seemed no less relaxed today than normal. He smiled patiently at my consternation. "Peace of mind when seeking a murderer is not necessarily a good thing, old fellow. A sense of urgency is what we need and we both are gripped by it. You wear your emotions on the surface more readily than I, but I am no more peaceful than you.

"I have learned over the years that some things take longer than others and my confidence that we will catch this insidious chap remains absolute. So I will counsel patience and hope that you will soon have some peace of mind. As to where we are, I would say that we are *not* back at the beginning.

"What you have to bear in mind, Watson, is that sending these stories to the Strand is not a capricious whim on the part of our perpetrator. If it were, we'd have him already. Each of the three crimes that he has boasted of, the theft of the ninety thousand pounds and murder of Carlton Mackenzie in Aberdeen, the bilking of Karl Mundt's bank in Zurich, and the theft of the Green Fire of the Incas, all were meticulously planned and meticulously executed.

"Two of them were offenses that could lead to the gallows, yet he has now brought them to public attention, at least theoretically, at great risk to himself. So does it make sense that he would approach these revelations without sufficient purpose and with any less care in planning?

"I think not, sir. If anything, it would be all the more carefully planned, since his risk here would seem to be far greater than potential rewards...*it would seem.* But until we know what he is truly up to, we can't really make such judgments."

I interrupted by saying, "Holmes, you continue to refer to our criminal as 'he,' even though he or she uses a female name, Norma, and the only one who has been seen, that we know of, Rene LaDier, is clearly a woman."

"All part of the game, Watson. When all is said and done, there is no doubt in my mind that a man will have been the planning and driving force in the whole plot."

I was not convinced, but having no evidence to put forth, I could not pursue the point. "But as I said, Holmes, it does appear that we are back at the beginning, without a clue to the perpetrator's identity."

"Not really, Watson. We know that we are dealing with a superb intellect and meticulous planner. We can be relatively certain that he knows Norma Bainsteas, whether or not she knows him.

"If we did not know for certain that Professor James Moriarty is dead, I would have a strong feeling that he was involved. This crime spree has all the earmarks of Moriarty planning, if you think about it, old fellow.

"Crimes against hugely profitable targets, crimes that go virtually undetected, crimes perpetrated by others, but he the main beneficiary, and an arrogance beyond limits. Who else but Moriarty?"

Holmes sighed deeply. "The only possibilities would seem to be my previously unknown brother, Linville, who we saw die with our own eyes, and Moriarty's protégé, the almost equally brilliant, yet curiously more cruel, Colonel Sebastian Moran."

Memories of Moran flooded back. He was, indeed, the one to be more feared personally. No one, not even Moriarty, caused chills up and down the spine as did this cold hardened killer.

I had chronicled his story and published it in the Strand as *The Empty House.* Although the account that I published was factual and accurate, there was a significant omission. No one, not even Holmes knows, because I never told him, how close I came to killing Sebastian Moran.

If one recalls the story, he knows that Holmes and I were hiding in "the empty house," across the street, waiting for a sniper to arrive. Holmes had placed a wax bust of himself in the window of our Baker Street rooms, so that it could be clearly seen in silhouette.

Moran crept into the room in which we awaited him, snapped together the malevolent air gun he had used in other murders, and fired a shot into the head of the wax bust.

Holmes leaped upon his back and wrestled the arch-villain to the floor, only to be thrown off by a display of animal strength. He grasped Holmes by the throat, with an intention of choking the life out of him, when I intervened by striking him on the head with the butt of my revolver.

That is what happened and that is what I reported. What I did not report was the moment that I stood with the barrel of the revolver at Moran's temple, my finger tightening on the trigger, determined to remove this threat to Holmes' life forever.

To this day, I do not know exactly why I did not do it. There would have been no injustice, so it wasn't that. There was no inability on my part to discharge a weapon at another human being, since I had done it in the past. Perhaps in my subconscious, I realized that Holmes would not have done it that way, so I quickly smashed his head with the gun. He was easily subdued after that.

Whatever held me back, I am grateful for it because, justifiable circumstances notwithstanding, I know that for the rest of my life I would have regretted it as a murder.

Noticing Holmes' steady gaze at me, I snapped back to the present. "Sorry, old man, I let my mind wander back to our last encounter with that villain, Moran. Where were we?"

"We were reviewing those whose dark skills would have made possible crimes of this magnitude. I was about to say that, all things considered, this has more the feel of Moran's handiwork than Moriarty, "the Napoleon of crime."

"I would agree with that, Holmes. Moran would do his own killing when necessary. Moriarty would send Moran to do his. I still am taken aback that a man who had lived a life that could almost be described as heroic would have turned to crime."

Holmes seemed not as surprised by it as I. "We have solved too many cases of dire crime committed for profit for me to be surprised anymore. That said, I do agree that there have been far more likely candidates than a man who had served her majesty so well in military service and had written at least two rather engaging books. I took the time to read both of them."

I shook my head in agreement. "Having served in Afghanistan, as he did, I was drawn to read the one he entitled, *Heavy Game of the Western Himalayas.* I found it fascinating, as well."

Holmes' face took on a more serious appearance. "I would speculate aloud, Watson, that when we run this fox to ground, he will turn out to be, in some way, a disciple of the infamous Sebastian Moran.

"Now, Watson, if you'll excuse me, there are a few trains of thought I have decided to pursue, but need more information about. Therefore, I will be dispatching some telegrams this afternoon."

CHAPTER 20

$\blacksquare$ ◆ $\blacksquare$

ROGER Dalton arrived unannounced as Mrs. Hudson was serving breakfast for Holmes and I. We insisted that he join us, but he only picked occasionally at the little he allowed her to serve him.

He had taken a carriage through a steady, depressing drizzle that had lasted for the better part of forty-eight hours. Dark and gloomy as the day was, his mood made it look like sunshine. The intense pressure of the daily lambasting he was taking from the newspapers was clearly wearing him down.

"Mister Holmes, is there anything you can do to help me? I have served the museum well for over twenty years and now I have to abide snotty reporters half my age questioning whether I have outlived my usefulness. It's appalling."

Holmes was not without sympathy for our old friend. "How could I best serve you?" he asked.

"Two things come immediately to mind, sir, if you would be so gracious. Now that the theft of the emerald has been made public, against your expressed wishes, perhaps you could speak to the writers who assemble daily at the museum and tell them that in your opinion, the gem was stolen in Germany. They would accept that from a man of your acknowledged integrity and put this unbearable pressure back where in belongs, in Munich.

"That should not compromise Mister Wainwright's ability to sell Magazines in the least. Besides, it is the truth and the right thing to do. Come to think of it, it might even enhance the sales."

Holmes shrugged, "I have no interest in the Strand's sales except to the extent that they benefit my friend and associate across the room."

He smiled and nodded to me.

"Then you'll do it?" he asked urgently.

"To be sure," Holmes answered, "now what is your second request?"

"Come to the Museum tomorrow afternoon. The Germans are sending a delegation to investigate this fix we find ourselves in and they will arrive with a predisposition of guilt on our part.

"Perhaps you could join Bruce Parling and myself as we try to explain what happened. If you could bring the magazine story..."

"That will not be possible. Wainwright has the story and it's unlikely he will let it out of his sight, even for so noble a cause as rescuing you. Besides, whether I have the story or not is immaterial. I will be happy to come and present the situation forcefully, and yet, truthfully."

❦

The Germans were a bit taken aback by the presence of Sherlock Holmes at a meeting of what they thought would be museum representatives, mainly counterparts to their own positions. They were further taken aback by his strong presentation of the facts as he knew them.

One had to be sympathetic to their situation. They, in good faith, had agreed to loan the most valuable emerald, and one of the most fabled gems in the world, to the British museum.

Having done so, they were now aware that it had been stolen and, to their unbearable chagrin, that it may have been stolen from them, not the British.

They demanded proof, if such be possible, to which Holmes calmly replied. "We have a document that describes the manner in which the gem was stolen. It is from the same person who has admitted to other crimes of a very serious nature, including at least two murders, and whose accuracy has been firmly established."

Before they could react, he continued, "We also have a written narrative of the exact movements of every person involved in the security of the stone, including Herr Gertweiler. There is no question that the theft *could* have happened in the exact manner described in the story. I would say that, given the fact that everything our master criminal has said has turned out to be true, there is little doubt that the story is accurate."

The head of the German delegation asked numerous questions, in an apparent attempt to discredit Holmes' account of the events, including, "Herr Holmes, you insist that Peter Sturtivant was murdered. Yet you seem to be basing it entirely on the possible coincidence of his death and the theft of the stone occurring at almost the same time. What if his death was an accident, or even a suicide?"

Holmes nodded respectfully. It was a reasonable question. "That fact, by itself, could almost convince me, but it is not the only basis for my judgment of murder. Unfortunately, I am not at liberty to divulge the physical evidence at this time.

"My suggestion is that you have the Munich police contact Scotland Yard and commence a cooperative investigation. Inspector Lestrade has been informed of everything that I know. It is his judgment, as well, that the theft occurred in Munich; therefore he has no authority to begin an investigation here. If the German police ask for assistance, there is no doubt that Scotland Yard will cooperate. If asked, I will also keep them apprised of my progress."

The question that brought the most discouraging answer to the Germans was, "Herr Holmes, what chance is there that you will apprehend these criminals and effect the return of the gem?"

"I am certain that I will apprehend the criminals, but in truth, I don't foresee a great likelihood that the emerald will be recovered. It was very likely sold before it was stolen and is now in a remote hiding place. It could literally be in any continent in the world."

The news was disheartening, but not nearly as shocking as what we found upon our return to Baker Street.

CHAPTER 21

IT was not the next package of Gaulois cigarettes delivered to Baker Street that shocked us, although they produced diametrically different reactions from Holmes and myself. Holmes was amused, while I hoped that when we caught this arrogant guttersnipe, I would have an opportunity to thrash him with my cane before Scotland Yard arrived.

It was the now bi-weekly visit from the ashen faces of Ian McDonough and Neville Wainwright.

"Mister Holmes," Wainwright began, without the amiabilities normally attendant to our meetings, "as we prepare to publish the last installment of the theft of The Green Fire of the Incas, we have received the first portion of the next story and I must tell you that it has shaken me to my very core.

"The malevolence of his intent is horrifying, but the vastness of scope is breathtaking."

I quickly hopped mentally from one crime of the last decade to another in anticipation of what Wainwright was about to reveal, but could only think of the Whitechapel murders as an example of the scope he seemed to be describing. Maniacal crime of that kind did not fit the pattern of the shrewd crimes of profit we had seen from this man. My perplexity was short-lived.

"Mister Holmes, our man has now gone from revelation of crimes of the past to threats of crimes in the future...crimes that would make headlines world wide. I can't bear to even describe what he is threatening, so I'll let you read it yourself."

He stood before Holmes, the sheaf of papers in his shaking left hand, as he pointed halfway down page one. "Up to this point, Mister Holmes, he engages in insincere greetings, but gets down to business here."

As I expected, Holmes started at the top and read silently through the insincere greetings, as Wainwright had described them, and began to read aloud when he arrived at the meat of the story.

> *"There are political forces in England unalterably opposed to the continued reign of Queen Victoria. These forces are willing to pay a king's, make that a queen's ransom, to see her either abdicate or be assassinated. The former being an unlikely hope, I will therefore accept the bounty of elements even darker than myself and assassinate Queen Victoria."*

OR...

"There are criminal forces abroad in the land that would see England, in the absence of the meddling of Mister Sherlock Holmes, as a veritable land of milk and honey. Without the unpleasantness of one of his investigations of our enterprise activities, they would merely have to brush aside the not very formidable threat that Scotland Yard presents in order to drink deeply of the milk and sup luxuriously of the honey.

"Mister Holmes would be flattered by the sum that has been offered to insure his retirement. Since those on the dark side more closely resemble kin to me than those on the side of the angels, I will accept their munificence and effect the elimination of this odious obstacle to our dark entrepreneurship."

OR...

"There are international forces who would find Great Britain's rigidity in military, economic, and political arenas more malleable if the current Prime Minister were to be replaced by a gentleman more to their liking. Since some petty princes may be involved, along with industrial interests whose value exceeds whole countries in Africa, for instance, the treasuries available boggle the mind. Being a citizen of the world, with no more loyalty to Great Britain than, let's say Nepal, I have no hesitation in accepting the largesse of these nefarious financiers."

OR...

"Being an individual of monumental, make that boundless, greed, I may choose to do all three. To a man of my proven accomplishments, none of these tasks seems particularly daunting. The greatest problem that I would face would not be tactical, but financial. How could I hide or account for such vast sums of money, given that I have never had gainful employment for more than very short periods of time.

"On the other hand, how many people would love to have such a vexing problem?"

Holmes raised his head from the paper and smiled enigmatically. "We'll gentlemen, it would appear that the parrying is over and the thrust is imminent. To that, I would say, it's about time."

I was startled, and in some small measure, nettled by the sangfroid Holmes was displaying. I had long known him to be, or at least seem to be, fearless in the face of any threat, but this was too perilous to ignore.

"Holmes!" I said more loudly than I had intended, "this is a threat to the stability of our nation, not to mention a dire threat against yourself. How can you take it so lightly?"

The smile remained, but the tone of voice belied it. "Do not be deceived, old fellow. I do not take it lightly. Our antagonist in this struggle has accomplished all of the goals he has set, as far as we know, and would not make this threat if he did not intend to carry it out.

"The lives of the Queen, the Prime Minister, and myself are now in mortal danger. I would add, Watson, that because of your frequent close proximity to me, that your life could well be included in the threat."

Turning to Wainwright and McDonough, he said, "It is also a possible threat to your lives, as well. If our man's weapon of choice happens to be a bomb, propinquity to his target is a serious risk."

Wainwright seemed to turn to concrete, while McDonough appeared to be edging toward the door.

Holmes continued, "When I say 'it's about time,' I'm merely saying that we have suffered through several weeks of his toying with us from a great distance. We do not know where he is or where he has been, because his activities did not require him to be very close.

"But now, he is threatening some lives that are not very accessible. He will have to come out of his lair and get quite close to any of us that he intends to kill. That adds a large degree of vulnerability to his position."

I was more taken by a different point of view. "It also adds a large degree of vulnerability to *our* position, Holmes. That concerns me more than *his* vulnerability. In fact, what I find most disconcerting is that of the three targets of his evil designs, you are by far the most vulnerable, which makes *me* very vulnerable, as well."

Holmes shrugged. "Perhaps, perhaps not, but the observation could be made that once we discovered the body in the hills of Scotland, this moment was inevitable. There was a plan in place before the first revelation or the revelation would not have occurred. Had we walked away from this puzzle, it would never have been solved, which made our participation mandatory."

"I suppose," I mumbled.

"Our antagonist began with crimes from a few to several years past, but in the emerald theft, he appeared to predict a crime not yet committed. In point of fact, it turned out to be another crime already accomplished, but very current. Now, he truly is looking to the future."

I grimaced, I'm sure, before saying, "And many innocent lives in the balance."

"Be calm and of good cheer, old fellow. As we have said in the past, and equally true today, the game is truly afoot. Things will now begin in more rapid order and in greater levels of violence. Frightening, to be sure, but in a curious way, exhilarating.

❧

The "things to come in more rapid order and in greater levels of violence," were not long in coming.

❧

The snow began in the middle of the night and was at least three inches deep by the time I awoke. Holmes was already dressed, but wearing slippers and reading the papers, a cup of tea at his side. I noticed traces of moisture near the door and on his shoes next to the umbrella stand.

"I say, Holmes, have you been out this morning?"

"Briefly, old fellow. I sent Mycroft a brief sealed note via courier. I could not trust the telegrapher with something as sensational as threats to the Queen and Prime Minister. It would be all over London by noon if I had. I also sent Lestrade a telegram asking him to join us for tea late this afternoon so that he could be apprised of the threats. Obviously, I used guarded language."

"Yes, obviously, but I'm amazed that you gave him until late in the day. Normally you ask people to arrive more quickly than is humanly possible. You're not getting soft are you?"

Holmes smiled. "Not at all. It's just that I expect us to be summoned to the Diogenes Club for lunch as soon as Mycroft reads my note. I'd counsel you to go easy on breakfast, considering your fondness for the club's menu."

I limited myself to one buttered scone and three cups of tea, the last of which I was pouring as the courier arrived, summoning us to lunch at the club at eleven.

"Rather early for lunch," I observed crustily.

"Lunch is not the point, Watson."

I walked over to the window to check the progress of the snow, which had not abated in the past hour.

"A bit of a problem out in the street, here," I said.

Holmes came to the window next to me and we both observed two carriages, apparently headed in opposite directions, which had gotten too close and had locked wheels. Traffic was building in both directions, and although we could not hear them, we saw a lot of angry words being exchanged.

It seemed that we both lost interest at the same time. I returned to the sideboard to replace my tea cup, and Holmes headed toward his chair. With my back still to the window, I was suddenly startled by breaking glass.

As I whirled and saw the window that Holmes had been looking through shattered, *my* window was suddenly obliterated.

"Stay back, Watson," Holmes cried, "Do not go near the window." He took a revolver from the desk drawer and crept toward the window, but in the protection of the section of wall between the two windows.

He poked his head slightly into the open, looking straight across the street, then down into it. Turning left, he did the same at the other window. After a few minutes, he walked briskly away from the windows, and toward the door.

"Let's go down and look around, but I fear that our assailant will have fled." I grabbed my own revolver and followed him down the stairs. Mrs. Hudson, who was dusting pictures on the walls of the hall was stunned at the sight of Holmes and I coming briskly down the stairs with pistols drawn.

"Don't be afraid, Mrs. Hudson, I don't think that there is any immediate danger, but I'd like you to go to the kitchen and stay there until we say otherwise." She didn't have to be told twice.

We took up positions on opposite sides of the door and moved the curtains back as unobtrusively as possible to look into the street. The wheels of the two carriages had not yet been disengaged, but the focus seemed to be more on getting them free than on blaming each other.

I could not see anything threatening to 221B, or even a person looking in our direction. Holmes had apparently come to the same conclusion because he let the hand holding his gun drop to his side and started back up the stairs, speaking loudly to Mrs. Hudson that the danger had passed.

⁂

Back in the room, Holmes conducted a thorough investigation and came to some firm conclusions about what had just happened. He sketched it for me briefly, holding a complete analysis because I would be present when he apprised Mycroft of the events.

"For now old fellow, let's get our coats and see what we can find in or on the building across the street."

⁂

We arrived at the Diogenes Club, our appetites none the worse for the adventure the morning had brought, but with a keen sense of urgency. Mycroft had been a member of the club for virtually his whole adult life, having at a relatively young age gathered together a band of men sharing his seemingly misanthropic tendencies and molded a set of rules that fit their personalities perfectly'

First and foremost, no member was allowed to acknowledge the presence of any other as they passed in the halls or rooms and, with the exception of the Strangers' room, no human utterances were to be heard.

Moreover, to the best of anyone's recollection, no woman had ever crossed the threshold of the club since its incorporation.

Violation of this august club's rules had, over the years, resulted in more than one expulsion. Not that many women in this Victorian age would have any interest in entering a club so intensely male.

The woods were dark and somewhat bulky, and great maroon velvet drapes stood poised at the windows to shut out any sunlight that might issue from London's perpetually sodden skies.

When everyone had his newspaper or magazine, and there were no members afoot, the club had the ambiance of an undiscovered tomb. Exactly as the members wanted it.

Mycroft was his curmudgeonly self as we arrived but was, as always, gracious in his manner toward me.

"I've taken the liberty of ordering the crab bisque and jugged hare since both of you showed such great zest for it in the past. I've also sent for a bottle of that Madeira you introduced me to a few years back. Now Sherlock, where shall we begin?"

Holmes began with the threat to the Queen and the Prime Minister, allowing Mycroft to read the letter and ponder it. We then discussed enhanced security for both potential targets for the better part of an hour. A grim-faced Mycroft was not anxious to tell both the Queen and the Prime Minister that they were possibly targets of a murderous mercenary, a highly efficient one at that.

As we concluded this portion of the conversation, Holmes was quite concerned about the number of people, security and otherwise, that would have to be made aware of the situation.

"Pressing crowds of reporters and sensation seekers make it much easier for a potential assailant to blend in, work his way closer. Then if shots are fired or a bomb thrown there will be such chaos that a well planned escape will be that much easier."

Mycroft agreed, but faced reality. "We have a queen and a Prime Minister that will never submit to bullying from a terrorist like this. They will expect to go about their duties unfettered and demand that we do our job in protecting them."

As we sat in silence for several minutes pondering our dilemma, Mycroft picked up the letter and read it again.

"He does seem to take the whole business with at least a dollop of lightness, almost humor," Mycroft observed.

"Yes," Holmes replied, "and I do not see that as a good sign. As I've said in the past, a sense of humor in the presence of great intelligence often indicates a stable, balanced mind, the innate malevolence notwithstanding. However, we cannot allow that to lull us into any stage of complacency.

"He has shown himself to be a ruthless killer and implementer of whatever vile plot he has put his hand to. If he says that he is determined to kill me, the Queen, or the Prime Minister, perhaps all three, we can be sure that an intelligent plan to accomplish it has been put together. There is a more than reasonable chance that one of us will indeed die."

"He almost did it today," I interjected.

"*What?*" Mycroft's head snapped around to face me.

"He shot out two of our windows just seconds after we moved away from them. If he'd fired five seconds earlier, we might both be dead."

"Great heaven, that is appalling. Why didn't you mention that earlier?"

Holmes took the floor in answering the question. "It is true that if we had been standing there five seconds longer we might have been shot, which leads me to believe that he did not intend to kill us just yet. He certainly did not arrive there just as we were stepping away from the window and commence firing.

"He saw us, waited until we were clear of the windows, then shot them out."

"Why would he do that?" I demanded.

"I can't be sure of that yet, but I am sure that I am right."

Mycroft asked, "Do you know where he fired from?"

Holmes nodded, "The roof on that red brick rooming house directly across the street. He fired a single shot through each window. The bullets went into the carpet and embedded themselves in the floor beneath it. I was able to dig them out.

"I assumed that the bullets entered the window approximately two inches below the section of glass that remained intact. Placing a fishing pole where the bullets entered the floor and aiming it directly through the hole in the window gave us an angle that led directly to the roof."

Mycroft interjected, "And on the roof you found...?"

"Not very much of value, only confirmation that it was indeed where he had fired from. There was an area with a direct line of fire to the window where the snow was trampled, indicating that that was the spot. But the whole area and the path back to the fire escape appeared to have been dragged with the rascal's coat to obliterate any usable footprints."

Mycroft nodded, "And in the alley?"

"About the same," Holmes replied, "footprints roughed up, carriage tracks not distinctive and blending right into normal traffic when they turned into Regency Street."

"Thorough bugger," Mycroft said, beginning to pace the floor. "Now Sherlock, about the weapon, you haven't mentioned any panic or chaos in the streets below and..."

"Precisely," Holmes replied.

"But it isn't even remotely possible," Mycroft said with a quizzical look on his face.

"Absolutely not possible."

"Dead," said Mycroft.

"As a doornail," Holmes replied, and I knew it was happening to me again, as it had several times in the past.

"Gentlemen," I said in a chiding tone, "if I may interrupt you for a moment. You are once again slipping into that form of dialog that is completely inscrutable to any third party in the conversation.

"You are exchanging thoughts without expressing them, knowing exactly what each other is talking about. You have agreed on three things and I have no idea what they are, so I must ask three questions.

"What about the weapon you alluded to, what is absolutely not possible, and who, for heaven's sake, is dead?"

They both smiled patiently, as Holmes took up the explanation. "Sorry old fellow, as I've said in the past, Mycroft and I have been brothers for a long time. Now, Mycroft noted that there was no disturbance in the street below, when the sound of bullets being fired should be heard all over the neighborhood.

"What that brought to his mind was something that you and I discussed recently...Sebastian Moran and that insidious air rifle that he had invented and used to kill several people, including the honorable Ronald Adair. It fired real bullets, yet it was virtually soundless. That was the weapon.

"Now as to what was *impossible*, that would be that it was fired by Sebastian Moran, the *reason* for which leads to question number three. The answer to that is that Sebastian Moran is dead, quite dead, deader than a doornail, actually. And now, your three questions being disposed of, we'll move on.

"Our next quandary is where the air rifle came from because the one used by Moran is in the archives at Scotland Yard. To the best of our knowledge no other air rifle has appeared on the criminal scene."

In further conversation, we were all forced to concede that if Moran could put together such a device, there were certainly others who could do so as well. But the idea, the method of operation, was still eerily reminiscent of the unquestionably dead malefactor, Sebastian Moran.

The excellent luncheon dispatched, the increased need for security around the Queen and the Prime Minister agreed to, and the sense of urgency reaffirmed, we agreed to part company for the day. Holmes would have to apprehend this monster if he were to be apprehended, since we all agreed that Scotland Yard would not be quite up to the task

Slipping into our coats, Holmes and I promised once again to be in contact soon.

"I do have one suggestion," Mycroft said.

"Don't bother to offer it, Mycroft. I am already spending full time on this case and any urging by you to do so will be redundant," Holmes replied

"Actually, I was going to suggest that you spend more time looking out the window, Sherlock. Perhaps if our rascal shoots *you*, he won't find it necessary to try to assassinate Her Majesty or the Prime Minister."

I assume that it was said in humor.

CHAPTER 22

———◆———

IN our long years of association, one thing that I could count on from Holmes was inconsistency in dispensing unverified information, unsupported speculations, or even hunches whose logical, underpinnings had not yet crystallized. I say inconsistency because at times he told me virtually nothing unless I stumbled over it, but at other times he would pour us a Port and begin by saying something like, "Watson, I do not think that you are in a current status on this investigation, so allow me to elucidate."

At other times, he would make a veiled allusion to some arcane facts or historical episode, like the amazingly coincidental discovery of the planet Neptune by two different men in two different countries or the lack of straight lines on the Parthenon, and leave me as befuddled as a man lost in the Sahara at night.

Other times, he said nothing at all and I learned of the occurrence of a crime and its solution at the same sitting. These, of course, were rare, and the one vital consistency was that at the successful conclusion of a case-there were almost never any other kind-he would invest the time to give me a complete, unabridged, and unhurried explanation. He answered every question thoroughly and chided me in an amused fashion if I failed to ask an important question.

"Watson, you seem to clearly grasp the role that the watchman played in the theft and subsequent violence, but you haven't asked why he did it. That opens the door to the depth of the malevolence at play." This is a typical prodding question by the master detective.

At times I would dismiss him with a flourish, point to an imaginary line on my papers, out of his line of vision, of course, and assert that that was my next question. What I'm uncertain about is not how many times I fooled him, but whether I *ever* did. Probably not.

This aspect of our relationship is topical because this morning I peered at him over a cup of tea and a plate of rashers and eggs, and became convinced that something had startled him. I quickly glanced at the document in his hand and realized that it was the most recent pages of the journal that Ian McDonough was maintaining about our current investigation.

"I say, Holmes, is there something in those pages that is of interest?"

He turned quickly to me as though my voice had broken some sort of reverie that he had drifted into. He looked at me for a moment, then to the papers in his hand, as though just coming to the realization that they were there, and shook his head brusquely.

"No, no Watson, nothing here that we haven't known about, but something popped into my head that I have been pondering for a while. It bears investigation, and there is never a better time to investigate something than right now." With that, he was gone.

But as Holmes headed north on Baker Street, he pondered the journal, despite what he had said to me. As he would later reveal, Holmes was pondering a brief, seemingly innocuous entry in the journal, something no one else would have picked up.

Actually, it was surprising that even Holmes had. Had something been accidentally revealed, or misinterpreted, and unknowingly recorded by the young witless, Ian McDonough, and inadvertently been included in the journal?

⁂

Mycroft Holmes' emotions were clearly on the surface as we arrived at his Whitehall offices in response to an urgent summons.

"Sherlock, this is becoming very tedious. Why in heaven's name have you not solved this problem?"

Holmes sipped his tea, seemingly blithely indifferent to his brother's anxiety.

"Actually, Mycroft, I've been much too busy doing those little puzzles they call crosswords in the daily newspapers. Then there is my ongoing analysis into the lives and practices of England's honey bees, which is how I will spend my retirement. Then there is..."

"This is not amusing, Sherlock," Mycroft snapped. "What if one of them had gone off?"

Holmes turned quickly away from the window, suddenly very focused on his brother. "Suppose what had gone off?"

"Aha, there you are! You didn't even know about it! And you call yourself a consulting detective. Perhaps I should be consulting you on crossword puzzles and bees."

Holmes shook his head impatiently. "Now, who is being tedious, Mycroft? Pleases tell us exactly what you are talking about."

"I am talking," Mycroft said emphatically, "about the two bombs that were found on the route the Prime Minister takes to visit the Queen at Buckingham Palace. Two carpet bags were leaned against lamp poles, packed with enough black powder to sink Her Majesty's whole navy.

"That is what I am talking about. What if one of them had exploded?"

Holmes slipped into a momentary concentration that excluded Mycroft and I. He stared out the window once again. It was a short-lived reverie. Without changing expression, he asked, "Why didn't they?"

"We don't know why. First of all, they were found by security personnel traveling the route in advance of the Prime Minister, but the curious thing is that…"

"There were no detonating caps in the bags," Holmes said pensively.

Mycroft's mouth fell open. "How would you know that?"

Holmes didn't answer, continuing to stare out the window.

Mycroft went on, "That makes no sense whatever, no detonators...and makes the whole thing even murkier."

Again, Holmes waited a long while to answer. Mycroft was about to address him again, when he finally spoke. "Au contraire, Mycroft, it makes perfect sense and it does not make things murkier, but actually begins to make them clearer, to bring them into focus."

"What the devil does that mean?" Mycroft demanded.

Holmes allowed a small smile to emerge. "Mycroft, this is unseemly of you. You are allowing your angst concerning the security of the Queen and the Prime Minister to break your normal pattern of logical, dispassionate analysis. Take a moment and review in your head the contents of the most recent threat we received and relate it to your upcoming schedule."

Mycroft did as Holmes instructed, seeming puzzled at first, then squinted as though trying to bring a distant object into focus. Finally, his eyes widened and his mouth practically fell open. He stared at Holmes, still computing in his mind, "Oh, my Lord in heaven."

⚜

As we sat in London at Mycroft's urgently called meeting, another was taking place in a sparsely attended park in Zurich. The quiet beauty and peace of the place, even in a flowerless season of leaf-bare trees, was in marked contrast to the conversation taking place on the only occupied bench in the park. Winter had not yet quite set in, but one needed an overcoat to stay out of doors for very long.

Karl Mundt was practically sputtering as he vented his wrath at a very hard looking man.

"If you think you are getting even one franc for that imbecile you sent to London, then you are as obtuse as he is. You guaranteed me results and that dolt comes back with his tail between his legs, his weapon confiscated, his travel privileges to the United Kingdom revoked, and feeling fortunate that he is not in prison. If you think that I am paying for performance like that..."

"I don't expect my fee, but there were expenses..."

"Not a franc! Nothing! You're lucky I'm even here speaking to you. The only reason I am is that I have another assignment that has to be carried out. I will give you another opportunity, but with one important condition, which is that you carry it out yourself." Mundt glared hard at him..."as you led me to believe you were doing the last time."

"I never said that," he protested.

"I am not getting into any childish verbal squabbles. It was clear to me that you were going to handle it, no matter what you say."

"But I..."

"Enough of this! Listen to me carefully. If you accomplish this task successfully, I will pay you for the last job, as well as doubling your fee for this one. Do you understand?"

He could scarcely believe his ears. Just as he was becoming resigned to no fee and no reimbursement of expenses, a treasure was laid before him. "I understand completely, sir. I apologize for the ineffective agent I sent and I promise you that I will handle this assignment myself.

"If I fail for any reason, I will not present myself for payment. Is that fair enough?"

Mundt just nodded, thinking that if he failed he had better not present himself for payment, anyway. That should go without saying. He'd be lucky if Mundt didn't send someone to assassinate *him*.

"What is my assignment, sir?"

Mundt took an envelope out of his pocket and set it on the bench between them. "Here is a down payment on your expenses...a generous one at that. I want you to use the best...equipment, whatever you need.

"Also included is a complete narrative description of your assignment and the date certain by which this transaction is to be consummated."

The man extracted the note and read it quickly, raising his eyebrows, then tucked it away without counting the money. It was clear that there was quite a bit of it.

Mundt then picked up a package that he had brought to the meeting and handed it to his now well compensated employee. "Take this and see if it is of value to you. I have examined it and formed the impression that it could be very useful. If not, use your own equipment and return this to me at our next meeting."

⊰ઙ⊱

Holmes, Mycroft, and I sat in silence for a long while. I was anxious for the conversation to resume because I still did not understand what was happening. Holmes had reasoned out that the explosives planted on the Prime Minister's route were not equipped with exploding elements and said it made sense, refuting his brother who had said it did not.

Holmes had told Mycroft to ponder the written threat that we had received and compare it to, of all things, Mycroft's upcoming schedule. Mycroft had apparently experienced a frightening epiphany. My task was to garner some understanding without appearing obtuse. No small task, given the gargantuan intellects arrayed. before me.

"Mycroft, I am not privy to your schedule as your brother apparently is, so I am a little lost in this."

Mycroft nodded understandingly. I had, on more than one occasion, chided the pair of them for speaking in what seemed to be either a code or a window into each other's thoughts.

Mycroft addressed me with great patience, perhaps sympathetic to my struggles in trying to keep up with a pair of brothers who sometimes had full conversations, and complete understandings, with a tantalizingly few words.

"Sherlock is not privy to my schedule either, Doctor, but he could probably recite most of it from pure speculation about whatever is going on in Great Britain at any given time.

"He has made reference to the threatening letter we have reviewed and, as you will recall, it promises to assassinate the Queen, the Prime Minister, Sherlock himself, or all three."

I nodded, "I recall that much."

"There were shots fired into your rooms and bombs set along the prime Minister's route, which, of course, could be interpreted as assassination attempts, however ineptly done."

I nodded understanding again.

"Sherlock does not believe that they were serious attempts and I agree. But then why make them?"

I noticed Holmes watching Mycroft's explanation with an amused smile.

"It would appear that our killer is either trying to make us think that these were serious assassination attempts or he is continuing to toy with us as he has with the Gaulois cigarette packages he posts to you once in a while. Clearly the latter option is true.

"As regards my schedule, you undoubtedly are aware that the Queen's son is to be wed in a state ceremony next month."

"Of course, "I replied, beginning to see what he was getting at.

"The Queen, The Prime Minister, and Sherlock will be in attendance, as will I. This may be the first time that Sherlock has ever attended an event in the company of both such illustrious personages." He glanced to Holmes, who nodded verification.

"So," I said, "your conclusion is that these seeming attempts are mere pranks and that his true intent is to perform all three assassinations on the same day, namely the upcoming wedding."

Mycroft smiled for the first time. "Doesn't that make sense to you?"

"It does, of course. But what if he made these haphazard attempts to give that impression, while he organizes a more serious try, thinking our guard may be down in the weeks prior to the wedding?"

They both seemed to shrug in unison, Holmes saying, "We certainly can not rule anything out, but I am inclined to lean heavily toward the wedding day. It has a certain élan, a panache, to it that I think appeals to our man. Nevertheless, as you suggest, Watson, we must be extra vigilant in everything we do."

CHAPTER 23

S T. Paul's Cathedral is the largest church in London and one of the most magnificent in the world. I say this with unabashed pride as a citizen of the British Commonwealth, and more specifically, of Great Britain.

Few things elicit the warmth I experience in strolling up Ludgate Hill, in view of this awe-inspiring edifice at its crest, with the second largest church dome in the world, only St. Peter's in Rome exceeding it. It has been my great pleasure to conduct a walking tour of the city with numerous friends over the years, making St. Paul's the highlight of the trip.

Holmes has a small pamphlet describing the history and wonders of this holy place and I am completely without contrition as I use this Strand article to laud what is arguably Christopher Wren's masterpiece. Holmes, of course, has some book, tract, or pamphlet on almost any subject imaginable and I use them with greater frequency than does the master detective, who probably stores as much information in tidy divisions of his brain as the British museum does in its great galleries.

I borrowed the pamphlet several times years ago and saw no good reason to continue returning and re-borrowing it, so it now resides in my own book case.

I was delighted almost a year ago to be visited by General Sir Malcolm McQuillen, a Scotsman who was my commanding officer in Afghanistan decades ago, prior to becoming a general officer. He was enthralled with the cascade of information I showered upon him, and undoubtedly impressed with my scholarship.

Of particular interest to Malcolm were the tombs for, or monuments to, such great Englishmen of history as the Duke of Wellington, Sir Joshua Reynolds, John Donne, Generals Gordon and Abercromby, Admirals Howe and Collingwood, and Doctor Samuel Johnson, to name just a few.

I would risk boring the reader, no doubt curious about this description of the Cathedral, if I were to include the story of his amazement at St. Paul's area exceeding 87,000 square feet, or some of the historical events recorded within its walls.

John Wyclif was tried for heresy here in 1377, and in 1527, William Tyndale's translation of the New Testament was publicly burned in a rash display of intolerance. Some of the splendor of the lovely church was stripped away when the rascalous Henry VIII made off with many of its treasures.

St. Paul's is relevant to our story at this time because it is thought by Holmes to be the scene of not only *his* assassination, but that of the Queen and the Prime Minister as well. The date was less than a month away

∗ॐ॰

It was only two days after the meeting in Mycroft's office that he once again convened a meeting to plan security for the royal and political leaders of our great nation.

Mycroft himself presided over the meeting with the directness of a monarch, his imperium, flowing from the office of the Prime Minister, was absolute. He deferred to Geoffrey Barnhill, a very tough-minded, rather taciturn, career security officer on matters of personal security for the Queen and Prime Minister, but made clear that even Barnhill would be required to submit detailed security plans for his personal written approval.

At Holmes' suggestion, Mycroft designated Inspector Lestrade as the leader of the ad hoc force handling the criminal aspect of the event. While Barnhill's job would be the protection of his eminent charges, Lestrade's job would be to capture whoever had designs on their destruction.

If you have read my past body of work in the Strand magazine, then it should go without saying that Lestrade's appointment did not arise from his brilliance or his crime prevention prowess. It arose strictly from Sherlock Holmes' refusal to embarrass Scotland Yard by accepting an overt leadership role, a role that by any reading of state protocol clearly belonged to them.

No one intimately familiar with the proceedings, and precious few were, had any doubt regarding who would be the final word on investigative matters. Despite only a tepid admiration for Lestrade's abilities, Holmes had found him an indefatigable worker when properly directed, apparently fearless, and more than willing to accept Holmes' quiet leadership. Lestrade's acquiescence to said leadership had been very beneficial to his career, probably the salient factor in the prominence he now enjoyed.

Fascinated as I always am with criminal matters, especially owing to my association with Holmes, I nevertheless grew quite weary of the endless details discussed over an eight hour period, interrupted only once for refreshment.

Mycroft's first decision was that all of the numerous entrances, with the obvious exception of the west-facing main entry, would be locked and guarded from dawn of the wedding day until the last guest had left the Cathedral.

The chapels of St. Dunstan on the left and of Sts. Michael and George on the right would also be closed with a covertly armed guard inside and outside of each. Those were the easy decisions and were taken within the first half hour. By noon, instructions for every washroom, office, and niche were discussed to the point of tedium, but it got even worse as the day wore on.

In the general meeting, Mycroft stressed that Security's mission was not simply to protect the Queen and Prime Minister, but to do so without an overt presence and to allow the wedding to flow in an orderly, regal was one of the words he used, manner.

This was, after all, a historic ceremony, royal nuptials always are, and it was not to be marred by an oppressive police presence. That said, and with no intent to visit undue pressure on those assembled, Mycroft pointed out that their careers would end in disgrace if any harm befell the wedding party or invited guests.

But in a private meeting with Holmes and myself, he displayed a frequently seen petulance in chiding Holmes for not having caught our perpetrator. Holmes responded with a patient nod and an insouciant smile.

"You *must* cease smirking at me, Sherlock, and take this more seriously. This ceremony will have visitors from literally all over the civilized world. We will be the laughingstock of the international community if we have to parade a regiment of soldiers up and down the aisle to protect our nation's leadership, and even worse if something happens to them when we knew in advance that an attempt would be made."

Holmes accepted it as would one who has had the very same conversation numerous times in the past.

"Very well, Mycroft," he said with feigned patience, "I will begin to take this more seriously."

CHAPTER 24

O UR preparations began in earnest the day after Mycroft's security conference. Holmes walked the length and breadth of the great Cathedral more times than I could estimate, much less count. He had at his disposal a three man crew with a ladder and extensive tool box, both of which were used frequently.

He had simultaneous lists in progress through out the day, such as one for danger points, one for places to locate armed guards, one for sites to be utilized by agents with binoculars to unobtrusively scan the crowd for anomalies of any kind, and others too scribbled for me to decipher. I later found one directing the placement of armed snipers.

The highlight of the day for me was the opportunity to climb the North tower with Holmes and others and touch the legendary "Great Paul." Cast in 1882, and weighing sixteen and a half tons, it is the largest bell in England. I will not bore the reader with a compendium

241

of other famous locations and objects in this vast place of worship, but I found the day to be equal parts exhilarating and exhausting.

⁂

Even Holmes seemed content to savor Mrs. Hudson's cuisine and settle into chairs by the fireplace with generously poured brandies beside us and note pads on our laps. Unfortunately, I would soon learn that he was not.

"Holmes," I said, to begin our post-meal discussion, "what did you conclude from your day's activities?"

He smiled congenially. "That the Queen and the Prime Minister are in mortal danger."

I waited for a moment to see if that shocking statement would be followed by a smile, but it was not. He was serious.

"But Holmes, you spent the day examining the Cathedral at great length and, I assumed, plugged any potential gaps in our security. I concluded that you had completed your work there."

He shook his head slightly. "Not completed, old fellow, barely begun. Today was too acquaint myself with the Cathedral as a detective, rather than as a tourist. Those are vastly different approaches."

"Well then," I said, "I'm sure you listed the most dangerous points...I tried to do that and I came up with four, but it seemed to me that you corrected them. How many did you come up with?"

"Twenty-three."

"Twenty-three? May I see your list?"

He handed it to me without comment. Thankfully, he had brief written notations describing the danger that each location presented so that I did not have to ponder it or, worse yet, be forced to ask.

"So are you now going to prepare solutions for these weaknesses?"

"Not tonight, Watson. There will be ample time for that."

I was quite surprised to hear that. Holmes normally attacked a problem the moment he realized that it existed and didn't stop for food or rest until he was through.

"What are you doing tonight, then?" I asked.

"I will spend the evening, old fellow, making plans to assassinate the Queen and Prime minister myself."

I chuckled, thinking that I knew what he meant by that. Confirmation was quickly forthcoming.

"Our killer, Watson, will have a plan. Of that, there can be no doubt. Therefore, I must not only examine the Cathedral virtually inch by inch, to prevent it, but to try to put myself in his head. If my assignment was to assassinate three people, not sitting together, in a dense crowd of, let's say, three to four thousand people, how would I go about it?

"That would be a Herculean task by itself, but made incalculably more difficult by the desire to escape after the deed.

"As we have discussed in the past, Watson, killing a person of great prominence is not a terribly difficult thing to do if one is willing to give up his own life in doing so, or if one's zeal is such that he does not care whether or not he is caught.

"There is no doubt in my mind that our fiend is not interested in either dying in the Cathedral or being apprehended afterwards. There is a clear narcissism at work here, old fellow. Our man wants the wealth and comfort that a successful life of crime will afford him, but he also wants the recognition of his genius.

"If he were to accomplish his bizarre goal, he would immediately write it up in flowery terms, glorifying his foul deeds, and submit it to the Strand. Even a grieving nation would flock to the magazine stalls to secure a copy... in record numbers, I'm sure."

"But Holmes," I practically cried out in frustration, "how much money does this monster need? He must be very wealthy from the crimes he has already committed. Why would he undertake such a risky project to accumulate more money, when he probably will never spend the money he already has?"

Holmes nodded apparent agreement with my point, but then dismissed it. "I don't believe that money has any part in this, Watson. If it were just the money, he would certainly never announce the crime he intended to commit and allow us to prepare to thwart him and capture him.

"For that matter, he would never have admitted to the crimes he has published in the Strand because they have been set aside by the authorities as unsolvable at this point. They would need new evidence to even know where to start.

"No, Watson, there is far more than money at play here. I mentioned the obvious narcissism as a trait in our man's makeup. He boasts of crimes that were never even discovered. It bothers him that they weren't discovered, even though at the time of commission, he took great pains to conceal them.

"I think he sees himself as a modern day DaVinci, but not using media like oils or marble. Instead, he sees himself crafting crimes as works of art...models of planning and execution beyond the capabilities of most men. And having done so, he wants them recorded... visual evidence of his genius. Whereas DaVinci left us the Pieta and the Mona Lisa, tangible objects, he wants at least printed evidence to remain.

"When he expires someday, a full book-length manuscript chronicling his whole career may be found among his personal effects."

I shook my head in dismay. "You are worrying me, Holmes."

"Not to worry, old fellow, he isn't after you...that we know of," he added with a clever smile.

"Holmes, I wasn't thinking of myself..."

"Of course not, my dear friend, I tease you, but let me add one more element to the gloomy mix, a ray of hope at that."

I raised my eyebrows in anticipation. "Thank God there *is* a ray of hope. What is it?"

"We talked about money and I've speculated that narcissism is a more important factor than money. I now speculate that there is something even deeper than sick pride driving him. He is gripped with hatred or an insatiable thirst for revenge...perhaps the first leading to the second.

"What he is doing, has done, displays the fanaticism of a Jack the Ripper. Our man is not quite as savage as that, that we know of, but he is every bit as driven.

He could not stop himself, even if he wanted to. I am amazed that he has been able to exercise the patience that he has, but our man in Vienna, Freud, says that these things grow in power to grip and impel.

"As the mind grows sicker, the mania takes firmer hold, and the urge becomes less controllable and possibly more diabolical. And in that, Watson, are the seeds of his destruction. And although we are being especially careful with the safety of his putative targets every day, we are focusing our efforts on the final day, the Armageddon, as I suspect he views it.

"To have shot me as I stood before the window several days ago would have accomplished very little for his ego. Assassination with a sniper's rifle, vile as it is, is a rather pedestrian crime. It happens too frequently all over the world for anyone to view it as anything but a horrendous crime. He has something in mind that will put him in history books."

It all made sense to me so far, albeit a warped, perverted kind of sense, but that was Holmes' point. That is the only kind of sense that would explain this dark plot.

"But Holmes, what vengeance does he seek? And against whom, exactly? Perhaps he has a hatred and desire to kill one of you, but what could all three of you have done to him to make him seek such revenge? Especially since you don't even know what it could be."

"Very insightful, Watson. That is indeed the question, the answer to which will be the undoing of our prey. I can think of numerous criminals and ex-criminals who would be delighted to kill me, but so far none who would obsess about proving himself more brilliant. Moriarty would have fit the bill, so would Sebastian Moran, but they are verifiably dead. So who else is there?"

The question hung in the air for a long while, then dissipated as an aroma that eventually drifts away. We lapsed into a long silence, Holmes in deep meditation and I in note-taking. As I set my pen down at the end of the evening, I realized that taking the notes was an act of faith.

If we did not solve the crime, indeed if we were killed trying to, they were worthless. In retrospect, I realized that I had invested a whole evening of my life in the at least subconscious confidence that the master detective across the room would eventually produce the same result he had in countless other cases; An innocent victim saved, a malevolent predator imprisoned or dead.

⁂

Across the Thames, in a dingy home in a poor neighborhood, a man studied as intently as Holmes. He looked up from a thick stack of blueprints, to the unassembled equipment on the broad bare table before him, then back to the prints.

He had purchased this house for a single purpose, to plan and execute a horrific crime. Because of the nature of his undertaking, he could not keep the necessary papers and hardware in his home. They could be seen.

Because of his great, albeit unearned, wealth, he could buy a small headquarters, use it in complete isolation from those he knew and who knew him and abandon it upon completion. The equipment would be left at the scene of the crime and all papers burned to ash in the tiny fireplace.

Assuming he survived the test of wills and intellects with the famous Sherlock Holmes, an assumption with which he was supremely confident, he would simply take a carriage ride home and resume his life in complete normalcy.

Eventually he would move again, in maybe a year, perhaps two, but he would be missed by very few and quickly forgotten. Just as in Aberdeen and Zurich, just as in Paris and Prague, just as in Barcelona and Florence.

St. Paul's is world famous for many good reasons, including the grace and symmetry of Christopher Wren's design and the skill and meticulous care to detail of those who implemented his plan.

The Cathedral in Canterbury is arguably as beautiful as St. Paul's, the killer thought, but if it is thought about or mentioned, it is not normally because of its beauty.

Something that happened there has become the defining characteristic, the memory jogger. In 1170, the Archbishop of Canterbury, Thomas a' Becket, as a result of a lengthy dispute with his king, Henry II, over the "Constitutions of Clarendon," was brutally murdered. He was slain by four knights as he prayed in the Cathedral, a crime that the passage of centuries has not forgiven.

As a crime had changed the world's perception of Canterbury Cathedral, so will I, he pondered, change forever the world's perception of St. Paul's. Future generations will think first of what happened there and thirst to know who I am, or was, just as they thirst to know the now unknowable, the identity of the author of the Whitechapel horrors, the truly infamous Jack the Ripper.

They will think they know me, but they will only know me as Garret Dickinson. Unless I arrange for a posthumous memoir, or reveal everything through a Strand story, my true identity will never appear in any history books. But *I* will know what I have done and why. Accounts will be settled then, wrongs made right, vengeance savored.

He studied his placements and smiled at the preparations he had made before giving up any clues, any indications of the venue for his date with destiny. There was still a little to do, but it could not be done yet. But when it was...

❦

As Sherlock Holmes and I sat on Baker Street planning for the near future, and an obsessed criminal turned off the lights in the seedy hovel he would be embarrassed to admit owning, and headed for his permanent home, another very determined man boarded a train in Zurich.

He would go directly to his compartment and lock the door. It was nearly eleven o'clock in Zurich on a cold, dark night and he would not be seen again unless someone noticed him debarking in Paris in the morning. From there, he would immediately board a morning train and proceed to the sea coast, at Calais, leaving him a short sailing to the Port of London.

For tonight, he would uncork a bottle of the Belgian brandy that he so enjoyed, limit himself to two stiff drinks, and pore over his assignment once again. The package of unassembled equipment that Mundt had given him in Zurich had turned out to be easily snapped in place and quite unique. He would do his best to avoid returning it to Mundt upon his return.

For now, he found the instructions easy enough to follow, but the point of it difficult to understand. On the other hand he was being paid handsomely and, he conceded, his was not to reason why.

⊰§⊱

Holmes had determined that the method of assassination, assuming the Cathedral truly was the venue, would almost have to be a bomb. That, of course, also assumed that the attacking party would be a single person, no more than two. He had completely ruled out a reckless, guns blazing charge into the assemblage.

It could not succeed in striking all three targets because of their dispersion and the army of armed police officers, Scotland Yard agents, and military personnel within and around the church.

It would also be a suicide charge because the defenders would have been instructed to fire before taking any chances on an apprehension. The possibility of failure and the concomitant risk to the targets was too great.

⊰§⊱

Mycroft Holmes kept his brother informed of any security steps he took, but felt no need to seek anyone's permission or concurrence. Therefore, two weeks prior to the wedding ceremony, an army of unobtrusive, plainly dressed, well-armed, specially recruited soldiers began to patrol the streets of London daily.

They were armed not only with their firearms, but with vital, but secret, information in the form of the day by day schedules of the Queen and the Prime Minister. Any place they were scheduled to appear, and the routes to and from, were examined with a meticulousness that would have impressed even the master of detail, Sherlock Holmes.

They looked up and down alleys, in any empty boxes or bags strewn about. Many strange or suspicious looking men had been followed all the way to their homes or places of businesses for no better reason than that they didn't look quite right to an inspector.

They were a dedicated crew, reporting their daily activities to group leaders, who reported to department heads, who reported directly to Mycroft Holmes.

What they couldn't realize, of course, was that their efforts were useless. The killer, as Sherlock Holmes had speculated, had indeed picked that date, that event, that place, St. Paul's Cathedral, on the day of the Prince's wedding, for Armageddon, the final battle between good and evil, driven by his perverted view of what good and evil really were.

Many trash bins may be looked into, and several people followed or even questioned, but they really didn't know where to look. Garret Dickinson could not be found, or understood, until much later.

CHAPTER 25

NEVIN Wainwright and Ian McDonough seemed to be fuming as they stomped up the stairs, and fell into chairs without even removing their coats. They shook their heads brusquely at our suggestion of tea and got right to the point. Wainwright was practically sputtering as he tore a small sheaf of papers from his breast pocket. Ian was no less irate.

"Mr. Holmes, there is no limit to the arrogance, hubris, pomposity..." he looked to Ian, who said, "gall."

"Yes, *gall*,...of this monster. He has sent us another story and I need read you only the first sentence to give you the flavor of the rest of it."

Holmes nodded, an enigmatic smile on the corners of his mouth. "I am anxious to hear it." It was hard to determine whether he was amused at the consternation of our guests, or did not expect very much from this communication.

"Here is what this...this..."

"Monster," interjected Ian.

"Exactly. Monster. He writes, 'Following the daring assassination of the haughty Queen of England, the stuffy and treacherous Prime Minister, and the pompous, overblown Sherlock Holmes, I reveled in the vengeance that was mine and set about planning a historic crime that would be remembered almost as long as the last one."

Wainwright slammed the papers to the floor and looked wildly at us. "Is this not the most appalling claptrap you have ever heard? He begins his story by casually claiming credit for one of the most bizarre murders in history, with no remorse or contrition...he's proud of it.

"And he speaks so confidently, knowing it has not happened, and yet showing no doubt as to his ability to accomplish it...past tense! He should be horse whipped and then drawn and quartered...without mercy."

Holmes seemed not too greatly concerned. Ian had gathered the papers from the floor and put them back in order. Seeing Holmes' outstretched hand, he quickly passed them on. Holmes read them quickly, then set them on the table at his elbow.

"Watson, old fellow, you will be amused at the third and fourth sentences, which reveal the "historic crime," to which he alludes. "I next turned my attention to further exposure of the nation's arrogance and incompetence by a theft even more significant than the "Green Fire of the Incas." Laughing to myself at the ignominious state to which Scotland Yard would sink without the great Sherlock Holmes, already defeated by me, I planned the theft of the Crown Jewels from the Tower of London.

"Then he adds, 'I neither need nor want the jewels. In fact, my disdain for them is such that archaeologists a thousand years from now may find them at the bottom of the Thames, but I will have accomplished my objectives; an arrogant monarch removed, an inept government exposed, Scotland Yard laughed at, the great Sherlock Holmes brushed aside, and a shameful atrocity avenged."

Holmes looked up from the papers. "So Watson, how would you assess our man's mental state after reading this?"

I had to take a moment to ponder such a question, knowing that Holmes would allow me the time. "Well, my first reaction is that there is a terrible anger inside of him. Also he seems to have become a little less objective and quite a bit more...oh...obsessed."

"Less objective, Watson? How so?"

"I would say he seems more focused on the *results* he hopes to achieve from his newest intended crimes than he is on the crimes themselves."

Holmes seemed to nod agreement, but pushed a bit further, "Results?"

"Yes, results, Holmes. He seems to want to embarrass you and Scotland Yard more than he wants gain from the crimes. Why else would he put the authorities and yourself on guard by telling you what he plans to do?"

"Excellent, old fellow. I agree, but with some small reservations. I've looked through the remaining sheets while you were talking and see nothing about how he actually accomplishes our supposed assassinations, or about how he plans to steal the jewels, so he is not becoming reckless in his zeal. That said, he continues to reveal a little more about himself."

"Such as...?" I asked.

"Most telling is that he is seeking vengeance for what he perceives to be an injustice from the past. This from a murderer, a thief, a swindler, and heaven knows what else. I'm sure that he didn't turn to a life of crime because an honest man, perhaps an acquaintance of his, was mistreated by our government.

"And including me in his vendetta almost certainly points to the culture of crime. I have precious little contact with the world outside of 221 B Baker Street that is not related to crime investigation.

"Therefore, it seems that it must arise from someone I apprehended, Scotland Yard dealt with, and the government was involved in"

"Marvelous," I said sourly, "that reduces our list of possible suspects from everybody in Europe to maybe a thousand."

"And with only a week to go until the wedding," Wainwright added, equally sourly.

Holmes laughed aloud, something he rarely did. "Gentlemen, you should see your faces. Brighten up, it isn't that dire a situation. The Queen and the Prime Minister will be well guarded and I am not overly concerned with my own personal safety. Some very brilliant people have had designs on my life and did not succeed.

"Besides, the list that I have in mind is considerably shorter than Doctor Watson's."

"Oh? What can you tell us about that?" asked a suddenly perked up Nevin Wainwright.

"I'm afraid nothing at this point, gentlemen, but soon enough."

"But my journal," Ian said, practically in a whine.

"Be of good cheer, Ian, you will have some startling conclusions for your journal. I've already promised that I will reveal as much as possible to you and Mister Wainwright because of your cheerful cooperation in this whole investigation.

"But, having said that, gentlemen, I trust that it goes without saying that this information must be kept secret. We do want not reporters or excessive security to cramp us in our investigation and we do not want our villain to see any of our preparations." Both men nodded agreement.

As they rose to leave, Wainwright asked, "What do you make of the name he uses on the manuscript, Mister Holmes?"

Holmes turned to the last sheet, looked bemused for a moment, then smiled. He read the name aloud, addressing me, "He signs it, 'Chidiock Tickbourne,' Watson."

It meant nothing to me. "Are you sure you are reading it correctly, Holmes. I've never heard of a name like Chidiock. Have you?"

"Just once. I read a poem several years back entitled 'On the Eve of His Execution.' It was written by a young man who would be executed the following day for a very serious crime. It was a message to his mother as I recall and had a rather unusual meter to it.

"Nevertheless, it was a very creative and very moving piece of work. I'm sure I have the book around here somewhere. Anyway, Chidiock seems, *by this one poem,* to have found his way into England's corporate literary memory. It's been published in more than one obscure anthology. I've never run across anything else that he wrote."

We were all puzzled until Ian asked, "But Mister Holmes, what does a nice poem have to do with a monster stealing the Queen's jewels after murdering her?"

"A bit of irony on his part, Ian," Holmes replied. "The crime for which young Chidiock was being executed was...attempting to assassinate Queen Victoria."

CHAPTER 26

ON Monday morning of the week that the Queen's son would be married, Holmes and I were back at St Paul's. To my great surprise, Holmes started by revisiting every place he had previously examined in exhaustive detail. It was not until Tuesday that we began in areas previously ignored.

It turns out that these areas were the ones most likely, in Holmes' estimation, to be the true problem areas. When I inquired as to why they were the last ones examined, Holmes simply frowned and told me to think about it. I have surmised in retrospect that the killer would be most likely to set his traps, or whatever apparatus he would be using, as close as possible to the events to avoid discovery.

While that certainly made sense, it was also true that the closer to the date, the tighter the security. Holmes did not feel that the security precautions were a concern of our prey, who seemed surpassingly confident.

It was a pleasure for me, in the first two days, to visit places within the massive walls that I had never seen in all the years I have been in London. If one takes the staircase from the South transept up to the triforium space over the aisles, one finds a delightful array of historical treasures. In the library are centuries-old manuscripts, books, and autographs in a room enveloped in the most graceful, yet powerful, wood carving.

In the trophy room are relics of very early origin, and some of the models of St Paul's that Christopher Wren made, or had made, during the design phase of this magnificent edifice. There is no end to the history of this place as reflected in the artifacts that abound in virtually every corner of the upper reaches. There is a dizzying array of passages, niches, alcoves, unopened doors, and lurking expanses of darkness.

Testiness is not a normal aspect of my demeanor, but I must admit to a slight elevation of my temperature as I watched Holmes pore over dusty old folios of church plans. I would have to admit to taking pleasure in reviewing prints that bore the actual signature of Christopher Wren, but there is a time and place for everything.

This time of fear and dread seemed not the most appropriate for pleasure reading. There were lives at stake, as I reminded Holmes. He gave me a patient smile and seemed to admit that I was right.

What I could not have known, and I doubt that Holmes could have either, was that the killer we sought had studied these same plans with the same assiduousness as Holmes, but at a much earlier date.

We may never know what he found, for sure, but what he did with his discovery had a profound impact. Since I considered Holmes' incredible focus to be a waste of very valuable time, I never really knew for sure whether he had found the same thing. It all began in the crypt.

※

As I took to my bed on Tuesday night, things began to change in my psyche. For reasons at first inexplicable, then painfully clear, I was overwhelmed with dread, foreboding.

By Wednesday morning, it was worse. A strange feeling, an ominous eeriness, gripped me as we awoke, and I suddenly understood why. I realized that we were only two days removed from the events to come and Holmes had not found anything that could lead to our killer's apprehension.

It had been easy to retain some peace of mind earlier, when we had a few weeks and were convinced that we knew the time and place of our tormentor's attack, but those two weeks had now evaporated and we seemed no closer to a solution.

There had been times in the past when such feelings had besieged me, such as the cold dark walks across the moors of Dartmoor when that fiendish hound was bedeviling Baskerville Hall. With Holmes back in London I was responsible for the safety of young Baskerville and he would not take what I considered normal precautions. It almost cost him his life.

This situation was even more cause for worry. In Dartmoor, we at least seemed to know what we were up against. A hound, no matter how large and vicious, could not withstand bullets and by its very nature, it would herald its approach. If we failed, a single man would lose his life. As disappointing as that would be, national catastrophe would not ensue

In our current dilemma the head of the royal family, the leader of the English government, and my closest friend of many years were now under a threat of imminent violent death. If they were to die in the Cathedral, with literally thousands of innocent citizens within and without, we could only guess at how many other casualties there might be.

Holmes' demeanor did not lend much in the way of reassurance. While laboring tirelessly, often out of my sight because of the fatigue that eventually overtook me, he did not evince the normal confidence that I had come to expect.

❧

Back at Baker Street in the evening, Holmes' mood seemed to lighten after reading several telegrams and two letters, both seeming to contain legal documents of some sort. They seemed not to be connected to the search of the church, or any other aspect of the current case, at least as far as I could discern, so I proceeded with another project.

Had Holmes given me any indication of progress in the day's activities, I would have pursued him with the diligence of a bloodhound.

As it was, I was happy for the opportunity to finish my first draft of *The Adventure of the Three Garridebs,* which would prove to be one of my favorites.

I particularly liked it because it came at a time when Holmes had inadvertently shown the depth of his character. As I have revealed numerous times in these Strand pages, Holmes' primary, indeed only, interest was the case at hand. He shunned applause and praise for his accomplishments, almost disappearing before one's eyes after the capture of the perpetrator and the revelation of all of the relevant details.

As I neared completion of the Garrideb work, I could not resist the urge to include the fact that Holmes had recently declined one of the highest honors an English citizen can receive, a knighthood. What I did not reveal was that he tried to have it offered to his brother, Mycroft, who, it turned out, wanted no more to do with it than his illustrious brother did.

With my eyes growing heavy and my thoughts riveted to the innate modesty and depth of purpose of the Holmes brothers, I looked over to him and started to take my leave for the evening. "Well Holmes, I am going to begin my rest for what I assume will be a very busy day tomorrow. I regret that today was not more successful."

Holmes smiled warmly. "To the contrary, old man, today was a remarkably successful day."

Several things happened simultaneously; my mouth fell open, my eyes widened, my body stiffened in my chair, and my fatigue was washed away.

Staring at him, speechless, for several seconds, I finally collected myself enough to ask, "How were we successful and why haven't you told me?"

"I would have told you the whole story if we had been able to return to Baker Street in the same carriage. Unfortunately, your fatigue seemed such that I thought it advisable not to ask you to accompany me on a few critical errands.

"After you left, I spent two hours with Lestrade on security arrangements..."

"I thought they were in place, Holmes."

"Revisions, Watson, revisions. Then he and I spent an hour dictating a story to the editor of the London Times. It will be the subject of tomorrow's headlines."

"Great Scott, Holmes, why didn't you tell me after supper?"

"The night would not have passed without a full summary, you may be sure. It's just that I had so much important mail and you were engrossed in your work..."

"I would have wanted you to interrupt...but enough of this! Tell me what you have uncovered."

"The string of bombs came first..."

CHAPTER 27

THE morning edition of the London Times ran a headline in perhaps the largest print it had ever displayed. PLOT UNCOVERED TO KILL THE QUEEN, it screamed. The banner beneath it said, in only slightly smaller type, P.M. ALSO TARGETTED.

The story began in normal size print and gave me an immediate chuckle. "Inspector John Lestrade of Scotland Yard revealed today that an ongoing investigation by the Yard had uncovered a sinister plot to assassinate the Queen and the Prime Minister by a series of bombs found in the centuries-old crypt in St. Paul's Cathedral.

"Lestrade was vague as to whether he had actually found the bombs and exactly where they were. A veteran reporter for the Times was able to elicit the fact that the eminent detective, Sherlock Holmes, was somehow involved in the investigation. Mister Holmes was not available for comment.

"What has been determined is that the bombs were constructed of dynamite in substantial quantities. The caches were secreted in the crypt and cleverly disguised, according to Lestrade, but not beyond the scope of Scotland Yard's investigatory powers. The explosives were secretly concealed in the ceiling of the crypt and arranged around stone pillars supporting the floor.

"Lestrade estimates that the explosive power would be sufficient to destroy the pillars, collapsing the floor, burying perhaps a thousand of the guests, certainly the most eminent, at the front of the Cathedral, under tons of debris."

The story went on to say that no indication of motive had been revealed or that Scotland Yard had any idea who was behind the loathsome plot. "Early speculation has centered on the vile international anarchist movement, which seeks to bring down governments around the world.

"Anarchist murderers have taken the lives of five sitting heads of state, most recently the American President, William McKinley."

Neither Holmes nor I had spoken over breakfast, both of us engrossed in the newspapers. I broke the silence by saying, "Holmes, they are suspecting that the anarchists are behind this."

"Yes," he said, "that is convenient for us."

"Ah," I said, "it sounds as though you may have pointed them in that direction." He merely smiled.

Reading further, I found mention of a rifle of sorts being discovered somewhere in the church. It said that they could not determine if it was a toy, a model, or a real weapon.

"I say, Holmes, they now say that they have found a possible rifle, but can't figure out exactly what it is."

Holmes nodded, "I found it and I know exactly what it is, although I didn't give them any information about it. I want our man to know that it has been found, but I'm not yet ready to reveal what it is."

That surprised me a bit. "What is it?"

"It's a copy of that air rifle that Sebastian Moran used in a couple of assassinations, years back, undoubtedly the same weapon that was used to shoot out our windows two weeks ago.

"Where was it?"

"Very cleverly hidden through out the library. It was disassembled, with each part out in the open, but seemingly a part of other innocent objects. Looking for a weapon, one would be checking under things, or inside of things, not investigating items in plain view. Also having it out in the open provides easy and fast access. It can be assembled in less then thirty seconds by someone familiar with it."

"How did you find it?" I asked.

"Two points. One, I am very familiar with it and every part of it, and two, I was looking for it."

"Even though you knew of the bomb?" I persisted.

"Especially knowing of the bomb. This chap has made It clear that he is determined to succeed, and on this particular day. Lethal as they are, dynamite systems can be unreliable. Too much moisture...a gap in the fuse or wiring...improper execution. Any number of things can go wrong, although given our man's skill and efficiency he probably wired it right, and it would go off if he had a chance to detonate it.

"The air rifle is his backup weapon in case the explosive ever failed to work. He could fire from several different vantage points up there without being seen. Also, it provides for a partial explosion...part of the system failing. In the chaos that would ensue, he could fire all day from the highest reaches without being detected.

"There are such places up there?" I asked.

"The upper levels of that building are like a rabbit's warren, a maze of passages, rooms, staircases. A person could get lost up there. I would say that it is the perfect setting for someone of such malevolent intent."

I shook my head in equal parts astonishment and disgust. "The hatred that men can feel toward their brothers is almost unimaginable. Some of the cases that we have worked have had some very unsavory characters, but there is nothing in my memory to equal this. This monster is prepared to kill a thousand or more people to be sure that he kills the three that he is after."

Holmes could only nod his agreement.

"So Holmes, what will we do today? If everything is as you speculated, isn't our work in the Cathedral pretty much completed?"

"I'm afraid not, old fellow. In fact, today could be a more important day than yesterday."

"How so?" I asked.

"Really, Watson, that should be a bit elementary. The morning papers have told our culprit that we have found his deadly weapons and disarmed them. If he is to be successful, then he must come up with another plan. And since the wedding is tomorrow, he must do it today.

"You will, of course, recall that the Times article you read said that Sherlock Holmes was unavailable for comment."

"Yes..."

"At noon today, the Times will issue a special edition promising to reveal an exclusive interview with "the great Holmes." He said it with a sardonic chuckle. "In the article, I will excoriate the editor of the Times for printing the story, saying that they have now alerted the killer that the plot has failed and robbed us of our opportunity to apprehend him.

"He will now remain free and in a position to attempt an assassination at some later date. In an egregious excess of hyperbole, they will say that I charged them with responsibility for any future mishaps that may befall the Queen or Prime Minister at the hands of this monster.

"They will also quote an enraged Inspector Lestrade as threatening to arrest the whole Times staff if anything befalls our illustrious leaders. He also says that he will track down the source of the leak to the Times and put him in chains, as well."

I had to chuckle picturing Lestrade making such threats. His temper and impatience with malefactors was very well known, but of course this was a charade.

"So Holmes, the point is to reveal to our chap who used to be Norma Bainsteas, but is now Chidiock Tickbourne, that we have discovered his plot and disarmed it...in order to lure him into trying again? You hope to nab him in the Cathedral some time today?"

"Yes..."

"And you feign this outrage and these threats in order to make him think that you expect him to cancel his current effort, to wait before trying again...that the Queen and Prime Minister are now safe, at least during the ceremony? And thus embolden him to come to the Cathedral and into our waiting arms?"

"Yes again." Holmes said, but I have known him too long not to notice something in his eyes. Before I could press on, Holmes bolted to his feet, pulled the door open and yelled down for Mrs. Hudson to try to track down young Wiggins, the leader of his pack of young delinquent commandos.

By way of explanation, he said, "I promised Wainwright and Ian that they would be a part of this for the whole way. I will need them now to play an important role in the closing scene in this drama, which will hopefully be played out in the next thirty hours."

He wrote a quick note, addressed the envelope to Wainwright and handed it to the breathless Wiggins, along with a handful of coins.

"This must be put into the hands of Mister Nevin Wainwright, Wiggins. If for any reason he is not there, then you will ask for Ian McDonough, and you will tell him that no one is to see the note other than he and Wainwright. I trust it goes without saying that you will not leave it with anyone but those two."

"I understand, sir."

"Good man, now be off with you." He was down the stairs and up the street in a flash.

"Now, Watson, we must also be away. There is much at the Cathedral which will need our attention and..."

"Holmes, a moment please. I have a very strong feeling that there is more to this than you have told me so far." He smiled that enigmatic smile that even our long years of close association has not helped me to decipher.

"My dear Watson, surely you, of all people, should understand that things are never exactly as they seem."

CHAPTER 28

LESTRADE'S crew had to cajole, then threaten and even push newspaper reporters out of our way in order to allow us into the cavernous old Cathedral. Once inside we experienced a relative peace, even though the place seemed to be a gigantic beehive.

St. Paul's was closed to the public, most particularly the newspaper people, our current nemesis, but the cleaners, repair men, and decorators hurried in every direction like a swarm outside an anthill. Fortunately, none of them had any interest in the investigatory activity in their midst.

Every staircase was manned by two armed guards, and no one, with the exception of Sherlock Holmes and myself, whose appearance was known to the officers, was permitted up the stairs. Anyone else wishing to go up would have to be presented to the guards by Lestrade personally.

※

The day went rather quickly, despite the growing tension in my mind. I had to frequently stop and breathe deeply and attempt to relax. Such was my anxiety, I found myself checking my own pulse on more than one occasion.

Holmes remained, well, methodical through out the day. He displayed his normal calm demeanor and, to my great surprise, he agreed to spend a few minutes, along with Lestrade, in answering questions from reporters.

The reporters were gathered in the broad vestibule of the Cathedral with repeated instructions that they were not allowed into even the rear of the vast nave. Lestrade said that anyone who attempted to enter would be promptly arrested.

Holmes allowed the Inspector to make an opening statement, while he stood in the background, a pleasant smile gracing his normally taciturn public countenance. Lestrade reveled in the attention that Holmes had thrust upon him, but was discomfited by the questioning period. Everyone who made an inquiry addressed it to Holmes.

Holmes answered as briefly as possible, lauding Lestrade's diligence and attempting to deflect credit for foiling this most reprehensible of plots.

As Holmes stipulated that the next question would be the last, I noticed Wainwright and McDonough slip in the door and seat themselves on a bench barely within earshot. They both made eye contact and displayed broad smiles.

They saw no point in crowding up close because they were secure in the promise Holmes had made to them that no one would learn any significant details before they did.

Holmes concluded the last answer with his most expansive answer to date, adding a not too gentle castigation at the end.. "Even though we have not yet captured the fiend behind this horrific plot, we have successfully uncovered and thwarted his plan. Whether he will try again at some future time, I can not speculate, but with the help of Inspector Lestrade and my associate Doctor John Watson, I can guarantee that we have found all of his pernicious apparatus and deactivated it.

"The Inspector and I would still like to know who it was that revealed the threat to the Times. This is not information that should have been made public and the result is that the Times has probably cost us an opportunity to apprehend our killer tomorrow. Rest assured that we will be *almost* as diligent in tracking you down as we are in finding the author of this plot. Good day, gentlemen."

As Holmes stepped away, there was a flurry of shouted questions, but one voice was a tad louder than the others. "Motive, Mister Holmes! What motive could he have?"

Holmes turned back and answered, loudly enough to be heard by all, "We have not uncovered anything on that, but when we get our man, I'm sure his motivation will be clear."

Another shouted question as we moved toward the door to the nave, "Are you absolutely certain that the Queen will be safe tomorrow?"

The question hung in the air as we passed into the cool semi-darkness of the vast Cathedral. Not wanting Lestrade or He or I to be engulfed with questions once again, Holmes dispatched a uniformed Bobby to fetch Wainwright and Ian and bring them to us.

Lestrade was called away by an officer on some matter as our guests arrived. We exchanged warm greetings and took seats near the east wall, out of anyone's way, but also out of their range of hearing.

Wainwright began with profuse thanks for being allowed in, as well as congratulations for the accomplishments that had been ungraciously revealed in the morning Times.

"Even though the Times may have set back the date of this villain's capture, it is no less a certainty, sir. Her Majesty's empire owes you a profound debt of gratitude."

"Thank you, Mister Wainwright, but I hope that you and Ian were not deceived by that little charade."

They both seemed taken aback as Holmes continued, "It is true that we found the bomb and the rifle, and that the rest of the Cathedral is secure, but we are by no means certain that the monster will not try something else tomorrow.

"Doctor Watson and I have reason to believe that there is more going on here than meets the eye, and that we may have an inkling of who is behind all of this. For that reason, and because of the reliability you have both shown through out this ordeal, we must take you into our confidence.

"Even more than that, you will have roles to play, if you are willing to accept them."

The delight in their eyes would be difficult to describe. Ian particularly gushed with enthusiasm, "Anything, Mister Holmes. Anything you want, I will do, regardless of the risk."

"We appreciate that, Ian, but I hope you know that I would never put you in a dangerous position. Your task will be important, make that vital, but out in the open and perfectly safe."

He reached into the breast pocket of his coat and withdrew a thick envelope, handing it to a curious Nevin Wainwright. "What I would like you gentlemen to do is take the eight o'clock sailing to Calais this evening, and the night train to Zurich as soon as you arrive."

Their mouths practically fell open, but Holmes ignored it. "You will arrive in Zurich early in the morning and proceed immediately to Herr Karl Mundt's bank. Now, the timing in this is critical. You will determine that Herr Mundt is in his office and you will spend whatever time you have in and around the lobby of the bank.

"Tomorrow's ceremony will begin promptly at one p.m., with the actual vows being taken at approximately two. At least that is the schedule as it currently exists. It is one hour later in Zurich.

I would like you to present yourselves to Herr Mundt's secretary at exactly two-forty-five Zurich time, fifteen minutes prior to the vows being taken here, and not let him out of your sight for as long as possible. He will undoubtedly offer you tea or coffee. Accept it and drink it slowly. It will be uncomfortable, perhaps, but he will eventually insist on knowing exactly why you are there.

"At that time, you will give him this envelope." Holmes produced a smaller, thinner envelope. "Is everything clear?"

"I'm sure it is, sir, but I am bewildered," said a clearly puzzled Nevin Wainwright. "Of course, I am thrilled to be involved in this, and I hope that I can speak for Ian as well, that we will be willing to carry out this assignment, but...isn't there anything more that you can tell us?"

"Much as I would like to, I am afraid that I can not. Even Watson does not know what is in that envelope, and you have no doubt about the level of trust that I have in him."

"But, Mister Holmes," they seemed to whine in unison.

"I'm sorry gentlemen. Much depends on this mission being carried out, but if your hearts are not in it, I know that Inspector Lestrade has a couple of volunteers available."

That was all it took. With no more than hurried goodbyes, Wainwright and McDonough were on their way to Zurich.

CHAPTER 29

THE day dawned heavily overcast, but the forecast was for a pleasant, even sunny, afternoon. Perfect for the royal nuptials. The prospect of a lovely breakfast, a stroll in Regent Park, then an invitation to a regal event, the likes of which I had never attended, obviously did nothing to quell the ominous foreboding I felt.

It was like waking from a deep sleep rested, refreshed and hopeful, only to recall that you were suffering from a cancer that would claim your life shortly. One was never very far from the harsh realities he faced.

Although the sun was still a good hour below the horizon, Holmes, as I expected was already gone. I ate a few buttered scones and drank a few cups of tea as I dressed and was soon standing in the rectory of St. Paul's Cathedral.

Holmes and Lestrade were issuing last minute instructions and checking the precise deployment of the roughly one hundred agents assigned to the day's security detail. Some were uniformed, some formally dressed, as though they were guests, some wore the overalls of the huge maintenance staff, while still others were dressed as uninvited citizens standing outside the Cathedral hoping for a look at the dignitaries.

❧

At Buckingham Palace, the royal family had not yet risen, but their staffs had. Clothes were being laid out and examined meticulously for any hint of a stain or blemish. Caterers were carrying in supplies for the lavish reception scheduled for the several hours after the ceremony and decorators, all known personally by their supervisors, were preparing the great room for the festivities.

Security at the palace, under the direction of the crisply efficient Geoffrey Barnhill, was as tight as it was at the Cathedral. As an added precaution, and to cut down the exposure somewhat, the Prime Minister and his family had spent the night at the palace and would travel in a heavily guarded caravan, along with the royal family, to the Cathedral at the appointed hour.

❧

In Zurich, Karl Mundt drank his morning coffee, Turkish, black, thick and strong, snickering as he read the daily newspaper. Today's royal wedding in England covered virtually the whole of the front page. He had long felt nothing but scorn for the whole apparatus of royalty. A Queen who really doesn't rule. A population that practically worships her, but turns the governance of their daily life over to venal politicians.

If the people really wanted to do something for their poor, as the politicians pretended, how many thousands of mouths could be fed every day with what they spent on their monarchy every day. Or how many small homes could be built for them on the vast lands that the British royalty had confiscated over the centuries. Not that Mundt cared any more about the poor than the politicians did.

At least I am honest in my indifference, he thought. At least I am willing to look in the mirror and admit that Karl Mundt is primarily concerned with his own welfare and that the others who shared the planet with him were responsible for *their* own.

But setting aside his disdain, Mundt was focused on something else that he hoped would happen today. If not today, then very soon, he was sure. He refilled his cup with the steaming brew, pondering what really was almost within his grasp.

❦

The killer, a man of several names, currently Garret Dickinson, stretched lazily, surprised that he had actually managed a few hours of sleep. He smiled at the thought of all the preparations the authorities, not to mention the great Sherlock Holmes, had taken to try to thwart him. Heaven only knows how many Bobbies, even soldiers, dressed in civilian clothes, guarded, or surreptitiously patrolled, every possible entrance to the Cathedral. A host of armed and determined men assigned to keep him out.

The poor fools, he chuckled. How he wished that he could whisper into each one's ear and tell them how laughable their efforts had been because he was already inside the Cathedral.

On the other hand, Dickinson did not know of a small precaution Holmes had taken. Childishly simple, but potentially effective, and known to literally two people on earth, Sherlock Holmes and the Queen of England.

Dickinson slipped his watch from his hip pocket and checked the time. Still only eight-twenty. He would have to bide his time for several more hours. He would move into position approximately thirty minutes before the ceremony was about to begin, execute his plan, and be on his way. They would never know what hit them.

The riches, down payments of which he had already received, would make no real difference in his life. From previous crimes, he had already amassed more money than a thousand men could spend in a lifetime, but the satisfaction, the shaming of the entire government, and the abject humiliation of Sherlock Holmes. Those treasures would enrich him as no fortune could and the memory would last forever.

❧❧

Mycroft Holmes finished dressing and prepared to go to the Cathedral, several hours early, to be sure, but on duty, if needed. He would have had a bed brought in and spent the night in the great nave if he had not had such complete trust in his better known brother. Sherlock would accomplish his task today, if it were accomplishable.

The only nagging doubt in his mind was that. Not whether Sherlock could do it, but whether the task was doable at all. Outstanding as it was, Holmes' record was not perfect. Many years ago, young Openshaw had placed himself in Holmes' care and had not survived.

Mycroft had not carried a firearm out of his Pall Mall flat in over twelve years, and that only to show it to Holmes and Watson over lunch at the Diogenes Club.

It was an American Colt revolver, finely hand made, as accurate as the art of weapon making could render it, and resplendent in it's African elephant tusk handle. "Pearl handled," his benefactor had called it, but Mycroft knew it to be fine ivory. It was a gift from an acquaintance from the Southwest of America, given in appreciation for Mycroft's discreet handling of a problem the man's wayward daughter had caused while visiting in England.

Mycroft carefully loaded the weapon, feeling somewhat foolish, given the number of professional gun bearers that would be in attendance, but also gaining a measure of reassurance from its feel in his pocket.

He looked down to the street and saw his carriage and chauffeur waiting. With a final look in the mirror, Mycroft picked up his top hat and headed for St. Paul's.

❦

It was still only nine forty-five, and we were all assembled, Holmes, Lestrade, Mycroft, Geoffrey Barnhill and myself. We had discussed some of the security arrangements so often and in such detail, that I was weary from it.

I wished the organ was playing and the bride was making her stately walk down the aisle. Better yet, I wished it was late evening and it was all over, that Holmes and I were sitting in front of the fireplace, brandy snifters in hand, discussing a successful conclusion to the whole sinister business that had occupied our time for too long. A pleasant reverie that I could easily have lost myself in.

As we broke up, Mycroft took a temporary seat right in the middle of the nave, where he could view the entire visible portion of the cathedral and receive constant updates from the security officials without the exertion of walking from place to place. Mycroft had a greater aversion to walking, his corpulence a great burden, than he had to the French. Few who knew him would have believed that there was anything he liked less than the French.

Lestrade left for a final stroll around the perimeter of the church and a final chat with those in charge of each area. He did not mind his visibility in the least, or that the killer may be watching with binoculars, or was even closer, for that matter. Truth to tell, Lestrade would rather scare the killer away and pursue him after the day was successfully over, than take a chance on something marring this royal event.

It was eleven o'clock by the time everyone was satisfied that everything that could be done, had been done. Holmes led us up the great stone staircase at a pace that was not to my liking, but actually a bit slow for Holmes. Lestrade and I, along with two uniformed Bobbies, and nine plain clothes Bobbies, followed.

We passed into one of the least frequented, least attended, portions of the maze of halls and passageways in the upper rear of the cavernous cathedral. Remote as it was, it did afford, through a small window, a view of the altar, the long choir area, the North transept, and at least a third of the nave. The portion of the nave that could not be seen was of no consequence. The targets of our madman would be up front and visible from here.

Before entering the room for the final time, Holmes personally positioned each of the nine plain clothes Bobbies and reiterated his instructions. Once Holmes, Lestrade, the two uniformed Bobbies, and I went into the room the door would be shut and observed from the hidden positions. The first person who attempted to enter was to be allowed in, then all of the police were to converge upon the door, blocking any possible escape.

The force inside would be sufficient to deal with the killer. Hopefully, the trap was set, but doubts were impossible to quell. Time crept and we were now less than an hour from the beginning of the ceremony and there was no hint of the presence of our quarry. I pondered the unthinkable; What if Holmes was wrong? What if he had truly been outsmarted? All in the law enforcement community considered that Sherlock Holmes was the transcendent intellect fighting crime in England.

But what if the original premise that began this whole frightening ordeal was correct? I have read the original letter from Norma Bainsteas so many times, seeking clues that even Holmes may have missed-not likely, I concede-that I involuntarily committed to memory the few sentences that defined her purpose;

> *"...to let your readership know that,*
> *brilliant as Sherlock Holmes may*
> *be, if all the stories are true, there is,*
> *nevertheless, a greater intellect abroad*
> *in the land."*

To prove that *single point,* this person calling himself or herself, appalling that we do not yet know which, Norma Bainsteas and now Chidiock Tickbourne, had gone to all this effort, and undertaken all this risk. We stand today in a semi-dark room after months of investigation, ninety minutes from its culmination, not even knowing if it is a man or a woman that we seek and, at least to my own mind, whether he is right. Could there truly be a "greater intellect abroad in the land?"

⚜

The minutes passed slowly, but my angst was not relieved by the apparent inactivity of our man. Indeed the tension grew.

"Holmes, we are only twenty minutes from the arrival of the wedding party..."

"Not really, old fellow. We are an hour and twenty minutes from their arrival."

"But it's..."

Holmes held a hand up to stop me. "In a private conversation with the Queen, when we had our last strategy meeting at the palace, I suggested that she plan to arrive one hour later, but that she not tell a soul, literally. As we sit here amidst the growing anxiety of everyone else in the palace, she is dillydallying and offering no excuses. No one will have the temerity to prod her."

"Well, you might have mentioned that to us," I said, with no small measure of asperity.

"My apologies, gentlemen. I intended to tell you as soon as the door was closed, but I got off on a different line of thought and it slipped my mind. Nevertheless, we must now come to point in the fashion of hunting dogs. Our prey does not know about the Queen's stalling."

"Holmes," I said nervously, "we are in a very remote area of this cathedral."

"Indeed we are."

I waited to see if he would elaborate on that, but nothing further was forthcoming so I persisted. "If he has other plans, then we are in the wrong place."

"Indeed we are."

"Holmes, your answers are very exasperating. Are we in the right place or not?" My level of tension was matched only by his aplomb.

"Indeed we are." But this time he said more. "We will now go to absolute silence. The time has arrived when he must make his move. We will draw our guns and be still as statues. The next person through that door is our killer, and it won't be long."

Holmes had explained earlier why this was the room from which the villain would strike. The explosives hidden in the crypt and the air rifle, also cleverly deployed, were mere feints to mask his purpose. The instruments of death were not in the church, but ringed around the outside of the dome in small rain drainage channels. They were almost impossible to detect, but Holmes had either come across them, or reasoned out their existence.

The fuses for the explosives were routed to this remote room where the perpetrator could light the wicks after he had ascertained that his victims were below the dome. He would then leave by the same devious route that he arrived by and be completely out of the cathedral as the largest church dome in the empire came crashing down on heaven knows how many innocent lives.

It made perfect sense to Holmes that he would use more than one method of attack, expecting them to be found, lending a sense of security, allowing a lowering of our guard, providing an expectation that the problem had. been solved.

This room from which the fuses were to be lit felt dusty, smelling of mustiness mixed with rodent droppings and was now completely still, all eyes on the door and fingers tensed on handles of hand guns.

But he didn't come through the door.

CHAPTER 30

AT exactly ten minutes to one, we heard a scraping of stone from a rounded portion of the wall. From a great distance we heard the great organ begin to play and a hearty applause issued from outside the cathedral. Perhaps some member of the royal party, unaware of the Queen's tardiness, had arrived.

The only light entering the room came from the small window that looked down on the nave, but it did dimly illuminate the section of wall from which the scraping issued.

As we stared at it, one of the large building blocks slid from view, being pulled to the other side of the wall. Another was quickly removed and the top half of a body squirmed through the aperture. Pushing against the wall, he forced his body through and rolled over, rising to his feet.

He held a small hand torch, playing it around the room and finding nothing out of place until the beam rested upon the face of Sherlock Holmes.

The man gasped, "What the..."

Immediately, the torches in the hands of Holmes, Lestrade, two uniformed Bobbies, and myself flashed on. I had waited for several days now to see the wretch that had bedeviled so many lives over the years, to see the face and look into the eyes. For some unexplainable reason, even though Holmes and I were sure that Professor Moriarty and Sebastian Moran were dead, I half expected to see one of them standing before us. Perhaps even the ghost of one of those despicable criminals.

My eyes focused on the face before us and my heart almost stopped. It was not a hardened criminal at all. It was Ian McDonough. How in the world could this be?

"Ian," I said, "What in heaven's name are you doing here?"

Holmes stepped forward, reaching into Ian's inside pocket to extract a revolver. "His name is not Ian, Watson. You are looking into the face of Ferdinand Moran, the son of one of the most heartless killers that it has ever been our pleasure to incarcerate, the malevolent Sebastian Moran. He is also known as Garret Dickinson, among other identities."

"Moran...?" said Lestrade.

"Dickinson...?" I said.

Ian, now to be known as Ferdinand, stood before us, everyone silent, staring at each other. He glanced over his shoulder quickly, as though he might bolt back through the hole, but he knew it was not possible.

Setting aside the revolvers Lestrade and the police were pointing at him, he knew instinctively that if he had been lured into a trap, that complete precautions had been taken. The room would now be sealed off by officers in the hall and the cathedral surrounded. Everyone's top priority would be the brilliant, but now hopelessly surrounded, young man we had known as Ian McDonough, but would now remember as Ferdinand Moran.

Holmes lit the room lights and illumination flooded in, perhaps metaphorical to the light now being cast upon the case we had been striving to solve.

I was briefly disconcerted by flashes of memory of our recent past. The onset of the adventure, the seemingly witless, naïve Ian, elated to be involved in the trip to Aberdeen, euphoric at inclusion in the hunt, alongside Sherlock Holmes, the most renowned master detective in all of Europe, perhaps the world.

Now the almost cherubic looking young man stood before us, exposed as a master criminal with pretensions of greater brilliance than the inestimable Sherlock Holmes.

He appeared to me to have lost none of the audacity that had allowed him to commit such brilliantly conceived crimes or the confidence he had evinced in dropping a gauntlet before Holmes. In fact, he smiled the smile of a sportsman.

"It appears that you have the best of me *this* time, Mister Holmes."

"This time?" Holmes asked. "Do you think there is a possibility that there will be a *next* time?"

Ian smiled confidently. "Oh there will be a next time, sir. Do you really think that there is a British prison extant that can hold me?"

"I do," Holmes replied, "but the point is moot. I was thinking of something more permanent, like the gallows."

"Ah, there is that, sir, but even more unlikely than a long stay of her Majesty's hospitality."

Holmes managed a sardonic smile. "We shall see, Ian. I would be considerably less sanguine about my long term prospects if I were you."

"You mentioned the gallows, Mister Holmes. Would you like to mention any charges that you think you can prove that will get me there?"

Lestrade grabbed Ian by the wrists and snapped manacles around them as the conversation continued. He motioned to the officer holding the other set of manacles. He quickly went to one knee and bound Ian's ankles.

"The first charges will be the murders of Carlton Mackenzie and Peter Sturtivant, two that we know of. Sadly, I'm sure that we will ferret out others, perhaps several.

Ian shrugged insouciantly. "It will be interesting to see how you plan to connect me to those crimes. The stories that were sent to the Strand are the only link to the perpetrator of those misdeeds and you really don't have any way of linking me to them."

Holmes was unfazed by the denials. "You will be surprised at what evidence we will be able to produce at trial."

Holmes made a motion to Lestrade and we started out the door of the foul-smelling room, none too soon for me. Because of the chains on Ian's ankles, we proceeded down the dank stone hallway to a rugged stone staircase with black iron railings. Thin slits of light slipped through long narrow windows as we passed in and out of shadows, finally reaching the outside door.

We burst into sunlight and a beehive of activity. Bobbies carrying the traditional clubs had formed a moving periphery and beyond them, three police carriages formed another barrier. The horses stood patiently, unaware of the drama being played out around them.

As Ian stepped into the sunlight, he smiled at the extent of the preparations Scotland Yard had gone to, to insure his apprehension. "Are there any Bobbies in London today not assigned to me?" he asked. No one bothered to answer.

The manacles binding Ian's legs allowed for very short steps and almost no maneuverability. Perhaps it was the fact that his eyes were not adjusted to the bright sun or that he had an expectation of an obstacle free route to the middle carriage that caused the problem. Neither he nor anyone else noticed the three-inch long metal hook that had been embedded in the stone to hold the door open when necessary.

On only his second step, the hook caught a chain loop, instantly stopping Ian's leg while his upper body surged forward, then straight down. Ian reacted as best he could, turning his head sideways trying to avoid collision with the stone pavement, but his right elbow and both knees landed with a scraping thud. Ian winced in pain, rolling to his side and moaning slightly.

At Lestrade's direction, the police lifted him gingerly and set him upright on a visitor's bench along the grey wall. I knelt to assess the damage. The first things that met the eye were nasty bleeding scrapes on both knee caps and a slowly bleeding wound on the side of his head. The knees of his trousers were torn away and blood was soaking the pant legs.

"Some clean water and clean rags," I said, "and quickly."

"My knees aren't the problem," Ian whined, "I think something is broken in my elbow." He screamed in pain, "Please, I have to straighten it out! Unchain me, I can't possibly escape!"

Lestrade looked to Holmes, who glanced around the area and nodded. In seconds, his right wrist was unchained and allowed to hang free. It seemed to help considerably. Before long, two Bobbies emerged from the door carrying a basin of water and long strips of white cloth. The patch up didn't take too long.

We all agreed that a few minutes of recuperation on the bench were in order.

Ian breathed deeply and looked to Holmes. "Please tell me that you have not known all along that it was me."

Holmes smiled. "Of course not, I would have arrested you. I *have* suspected you for a short while, but in point of fact, I was not certain until we shined the light on you in the upper room."

"Why did you suspect me? Did I make a mistake?"

"Only one, but it was not serious. It was more a matter of circumstances adding up. My suspicions began when I received telegrams from three people that I had contacted who knew Garret Dickinson. The physical descriptions they gave me were remarkably detailed and remarkably alike. They seemed to fit you perfectly.

"Now, on a stand alone basis, that means nothing. I'm sure there are countless young men in England that closely resemble you, but it was a starting point. Next, when you did not show up at Baker Street with Wainwright when Norma Bainsteas arrived, my suspicions were further piqued. Wainwright said that he had sent you on an assignment, but your absence seemed telling. I could not be sure whether you had uncovered something about Norma, perhaps had had a tail on her for months or whatever. And obviously, I could not rule out that you had hurriedly arranged the assignment that Wainwright dispatched you to.

"Obviously, you could not face Norma because she knew you as Garret Dickinson, so it was not a mistake on your part, but was another indicator if one had a hint of suspicion.

"The mistake that I alluded to was small, but significant. Most people would have missed it. In your journal pages you clearly described a telegram that I received from Harrison Samuels in Aberdeen regarding a sighting of Norma up there. Neither Watson nor I had ever told you about that telegram, and no one else knew about it. So that information had to come from your sister or someone else you had monitoring the progress in Aberdeen."

"A sister?" I asked.

"Yes, Watson, a sister. A very significant person in this morass, but I will get to her in a moment."

Turning back to Ian, Holmes said, "Then there is the matter of your lineage, Ian...pardon me, I should be calling you Ferdinand now. Actually, your lack of lineage. You are like the biblical Melchizedek in that he had no lineage and neither does Ian McDonough. That has been researched and verified by Scotland Yard, at my direction. You, as Ian McDonough, came into existence shortly before securing a position at the Strand."

Ian smiled in a cruel, sardonic manner. "Perhaps you are a little smarter than I thought you were, Mister Holmes, but you will not win in the end."

"We shall see, Ferdinand, but since we have you now, would you like to reveal your motive for all this carnage?"

"Surely you do not expect me to confess to any crime that you can not prove I committed, Mister Holmes."

"What can you tell me about your sister?" Holmes asked.

"I'll tell you everything about her. Shortly after my father died, she was adopted by a couple that moved to Canada and I have never seen or heard from her again."

He and Holmes shared unpleasant smiles.

"...or was it Russia she moved to?" Ferdinand asked sarcastically.

"Are you ready to walk, or do the police have to carry you? I'm sure the discomfort that that would cause an injured man would not be very distressing for them."

Ferdinand tried to rise but winced in pain. "Two more minutes. Please."

"Holmes," I interjected, "you have mentioned his sister twice. What about her?"

"They are twins, Watson. Ferdinand and Isabella. I don't know if there is some irony in the choice of names that have some historical significance, or not." He looked to Ferdinand for confirmation, but got only a disinterested shrug in return.

"Anyway, Watson, I'm confident that Isabella Moran will turn out to be the Rene LaDier we seek and probably many other aliases. She is spewed from the same gene pool as our monster here and is probably of the same moral turpitude. I will be very surprised if she does not turn out to be every bit as ruthless as her malevolent sibling."

Ferdinand smiled evilly "And maybe even a better shot than me. I wouldn't sleep too comfortably if I were you, gentlemen."

Holmes returned the harsh smile. "You gave the same advice to the Queen, the Prime Minister, and myself and here you are on your way to the gallows. Allow me to return a threat to you. It's only a matter of time before she joins you there."

Turning to the others, Holmes said, "It's time, gentlemen."

Suddenly there was a commotion near the three black police carriages. We'll never know for sure what caused it, a bee sting on one of the horses, a sharp noise that startled it, but for some reason one of the horses kicked the one next to it. The result was a series of angry neighs and snorts and a halfhearted rearing by one of the beasts. It was quickly calmed and the horses were gentled back to their normal docile state.

I looked back to Ian, now Ferdinand, and was jolted to find a wide-eyed stare on his blank face, a look, seemingly, of amazement. He was holding his chest as he stared vacantly forward and suddenly a spreading red stain covered his shirt. As I started toward him, he toppled to his left and rolled to the ground, an empty stare in eyes looking to the sky. Ferdinand Moran was clearly dead.

Those nearby quickly drew their weapons and began looking around. The officers on the perimeter hardly noticed and I immediately understood why. The air rifle! There had been no sound of a shot being fired. We knew nothing of it until we looked back from the horses and found young Moran desperately clutching his chest.

Holmes reacted instantly. He ran to the perimeter officers and barked orders. "Go to the back of that whole row of buildings"-he pointed across the street-"and detain anyone you see, man, woman, or child. Accept no excuses from anyone. Get moving."

To the group of officers closest by he said, "Quickly, one of you to the roof of each of those buildings. If there is anyone up there, bring him down. If not, look toward the front for shell casings."

Turning back to me, he said, "Watson, I know how it looks, but please be certain that there is not a small spark of life remaining in him.

It took me twenty seconds to check and shake my head. There was no heartbeat and no pulse.

Holmes and Lestrade conferred briefly and agreed that we must gather up the body, send it to the morgue, and instruct everyone present to say nothing of what had happened. There was no point in marring the state ceremonies when nothing could be accomplished by it.

Within a half hour, all of the officers were back in the remote courtyard, having brought with them seven people found in the alley, on back porches, or in one of the gangways between the buildings. Four of the people, two men and two women, looked docile and frightened. The other three were elderly ladies and all irate. Lestrade had to raise his voice to calm them down.

With just a glance at them, I could see no reason for optimism that any of them were our shooter. That being the case, whoever shot young Moran had made a clean escape.

Holmes dispatched Lestrade to gather up all the officers and use the direst of threats to assure that nothing of what had transpired, not even Ian's capture, much less his assassination, was whispered to a soul. Holmes used his time taking each of the captive neighbors aside and grilling them extensively.

The streets were filling up around us, even here in the rear and we could tell that the time was growing short. The royal family would be arriving, probably in minutes.

I was surprised to see Mycroft Holmes step out of one of the side doors and head directly for his brother. It turned out that Holmes had sent for him discreetly, and would need to inform him of the stunning events of the last hour. I joined the conversation in time to hear Mycroft summoning Lestrade and instructing him to deploy his men in a two or three deep cordon around the royal family and the Prime Minister's family.

Rather than taking his place as an honored guest in the cathedral, Sherlock Holmes spent the entire time of the ceremony prowling first the crypt, repositioning armed men with shoot to kill orders in the event of any form of attack, then the upper reaches of the vast church. I, unfortunately, felt compelled to join him in these endeavors, not because of my instincts as a journalist, but my responsibility as a friend and aide.

⚜⚜

No one was happier than the Holmes brothers, John Lestrade, and Geoffrey Barnhill to see the last guests leave St. Paul's Cathedral, except for, possibly, myself. I have described earlier the dread that enveloped me as the fateful date approached. I was in a semi-controlled dither through out the day and desired nothing more than a peaceful night at Baker Street discussing the events of the day.

Though my confidence in Holmes had remained steady, I was, alas, forced to ponder the possibility that he would be outdone in this fearful adventure. What I was most confident of, though, was that if we managed to apprehend this unknown murderer, the case would be closed, once and for all. He was our target and capturing him would end the threat, or so I thought.

As Holmes and I rode silently in the carriage on our way to the Diogenes club, where we would be joined by Mycroft Holmes and Inspector Lestrade, I realized that our fears were far from resolved. We now had, not one, but two killers abroad in the land, and this after capturing one and seeing him murdered before our very eyes.

The subject of the emergency session over a meal at the Diogenes club would be the identification and apprehension of the sister of Ferdinand Moran, *and* his murderer. The possibility that they could be the same person crossed my mind, but no motive for Moran's sister to kill him presented itself. I would let Holmes steer any conversation along those lines.

With the customary reminders from Holmes about absolute silence when passing through the club, we made our way to the rear where we were shown into a well-appointed meeting room, one that Holmes and I had visited several times in the past.

We found two large pots of tea with cups, cream and sugar in the middle of the table. On the sideboard was a platter with assorted sandwiches, but no one had an appetite.

We took our seats and, as was the custom in meetings such as these, everyone looked to Holmes to lead the conversation.

"This is truly an astonishing event, gentlemen," Holmes began, "completely inconsistent with the whole case to this point, an abrupt departure from the whole flow of things, and could conceivably call some of our previous assumptions into question.

"The German General Von Clausewitz once said, 'When preparing war plans, expect the unexpected.' I normally abide by that principle and I had other plans to lure Ian into a trap if we didn't capture him at the cathedral. But him being assassinated, in truth, never crossed my mind.

"I felt certain that when we knew for sure who the killer was, and caught him in the act, so to speak, that the case would be concluded. Wishful thinking, I'm afraid.

"The question before us then, obviously, is how to proceed from here. I spent the ride over from the cathedral pondering that exact point. We must ask ourselves, first of all, who are the possible assassins?"

Holmes looked around the table to see if anyone wanted to step in, but no one did, so he resumed.

"I begin with the direst of possibilities, that the young man we knew as Ian McDonough, and subsequently found to be Garret Dickinson, but in truth is Ferdinand Moran, that that man is not the true mastermind of all this. That he is intimately involved but another person or persons is actually pulling the strings.

"Assuming that to be true, we would speculate that the motive for his assassination is that he knows so much that the true mastermind could not allow him to be captured and interrogated. Having failed to carry out the assassinations in the cathedral, and then being caught there, makes him expendable. More than expendable actually, it becomes essential that he is eliminated before he can lead us to the top of the pyramid.

"If that is true, then we must take our mallets back to the first wicket and begin again. We are virtually back at the starting point.

Holmes paused as we pondered this frightening scenario, which would mean that the threat of danger to the Queen and Prime Minister, not to mention Holmes himself, had not abated in the least.

"However, gentlemen...I do not make that assumption. I continue to believe that the brains of all of this, and the perpetrators, are Ferdinand and maybe Isabella Moran, which leads us to the next possibility; that the assassin was indeed the sister, Isabella. Her motive would be the same as I speculated a moment ago for a different mastermind, but like the first scenario, I set this aside also. Neither of these scenarios can be dismissed, but I find them less likely than the one I will now put before you."

Sherlock Holmes, as I have mentioned in more than one of my Strand articles, can demonstrate some very nettling proclivities, such as the unearthly odors and clouds of smoke he introduces to our rooms with the various weeds he calls tobacco.

I will not go into others except for the one just displayed. He brought us to the height of tension by saying that he will now put before his true and current theory of what has transpired, but then proceeded to leave us hanging.

In an absent minded fashion, he rose from the table, went to his overcoat and fetched a pouch of tobacco. After the interminable packing, tamping, and lighting of his pipe, he turned his attention to the tea pot. It was too much for the normally impatient and irascible Mycroft.

"For heaven's sake, Sherlock, will you forget about the tea and tell us what you think happened?"

It jolted Holmes slightly, as though he were still pondering it. "Of course, Mycroft," he said, as he continued to pour the tea, then add cream and sugar. "Now let me see...we were about to..."

A sharp rap on the door and Mrs. Hudson entered. "Pardon me, sirs. There is an Officer Craig here to see Inspector Lestrade. He says that he is expected."

"Thank you, Mrs. Hudson, please show the officer in."

He went directly to Lestrade, handing him a small canvas bag. "This contains everything in his pockets, sir, and this was around his neck." He produced a fine chain, with a small key attached,

As Lestrade emptied the bag onto Holmes' desk, Holmes reached out and snatched the key, examining it carefully, and nodding understandingly. He set it on the table beside him and looked over to Lestrade.

"Anything of interest, Inspector?"

"Nothing meets the eye," he mumbled, continuing to move things around on the table.

"I would like to examine everything when we are finished, but for now, I think I have found what I need. Now, where were we?"

"You were about to tell us who you think did it," Mycroft snapped, "and we would appreciate it if you would get to the point."

Holmes took no offense at Mycroft's testiness, an admirable quality that I had seen in both brothers, but proceeded calmly.

"I believe that we have a smaller remaining plot than either of those possibilities. It is my as yet insufficiently considered opinion that the major case has indeed been concluded. That young Ian, now Ferdinand, truly was the mastermind and that all of it lead up to his desire to kill the Queen, the Prime Minister and myself. We will flesh out the motive in greater detail later, but it will ultimately turn out to be the arrest and lengthy incarceration of his father that drove him. There are, however, more specifics to be learned there.

"We now turn to a completely new crime, the murder of Ferdinand Moran right before our eyes. I believe that the roots of this murder are deeply embedded in the previous plot and if we determine the motive, we will have our killer very shortly.

"The question that we must address is; who benefits from Ferdinand being dead? If we rule out informing on a different mastermind, including his sister, we come back to the basic element of criminal activity, financial gain. No matter how convoluted the plot, most major crimes, that are not crimes of passion, turn out to have money as the driving motivation.

"In the case at hand, we know that young Moran had accumulated vast amounts of money. Whoever has access to that fortune, aside from his sister, is very likely our assassin, or the puppet master of our assassin."

"And do you have such a person in mind?" Mycroft asked.

"I do." The name he put before us did not knock us back on our heels, but for the life of us, we could not develop any possible means of access to Ferdinand's money available to him. Holmes simply said that because we could not see it, did not mean that it was not there. But then, with an enigmatic smile on his face, he dangled the small key on the fine silver chain before us.

"Mycroft, we will need the quickest and most detailed analysis by your immigration service."

CHAPTER 31

MYCROFT did indeed react quickly and by three o'clock the following afternoon we had the information Holmes requested. By four o'clock, he had analyzed it and narrowed the search we would make to two men. By six o'clock we were on the late sailing to Calais, and by three the following afternoon, we were strolling out of the Zurich train station.

I assumed that we would head directly up to the Lindenhof esplanade on the way to Schneller's hotel to engage a room. I envisioned a lovely repast at Braun's Café, an evening of relaxation, and morning visits to the two addresses on Holmes' short list.

My years of association with the master detective, unfortunately, should have taught me not to expect the creature comforts that normal people enjoy. At least *when* they enjoy them, which is usually as soon as possible. Holmes regarded bodily needs as trifles and unproductive pleasure as even worse.

Therefore, we were headed through the banking district, north, to the first address on our list.

What Holmes had had Mycroft prepare for him was a list of everyone who had entered England from the continent within the last week and had returned at any time after the murder of Ian/Ferdinand Moran. He felt confident that he knew who would benefit most from the crime and would pursue that line of inquiry before any other.

Only two men had arrived from Calais in the week prior, *and* had presented Swiss passports, with addresses in Zurich. They had come on separate days, and did not seem connected to each other in any way, but both had returned on the late sailing after the tumult at the cathedral. That is all we knew of either of them, but they fit Holmes' criteria for consideration as suspects in the murder of young Moran. They would be our first contacts before confronting Karl Mundt.

We arrived at a neat two story brick home on Rolfs Strasse and, as I would expect, Holmes strode directly to the door and delivered several brisk strokes of the knocker.

The lady that answered was sprightly looking, pleasant and attractive. Guessing, I would place her in her early fifties.

"Good afternoon, are you Frau Moeller?" Holmes asked.

"I am, and you are...?"

"I am Sherlock Holmes and this is my associate, Doctor John Watson."

She seemed to ponder that response and gave us an amused smile, then said, "Actually, I'm not Claire Moeller, I'm Marie Antoinette."

We both chuckled, and Holmes returned her humor. "History does not record Mademoiselle Antoinette as being nearly as attractive a lady as yourself, but I assure you we are who we say we are."

The smile changed to welcoming, though I was not certain that she was convinced.

"And what could I do for you gentlemen?"

"We would like to speak to Herr Moeller, if we may."

A wave of concern crossed her face. "May I ask why?"

"It is in connection with an inquiry that we have been asked to conduct, and I'm afraid that I can't say more than that until I see your husband."

She assumed a more serious mien, but invited us into her parlor and had rich black coffee before us in just a few minutes.

"Franz should be home in half an hour at the most, and I am now prepared to believe that you are Mister Holmes and Doctor Watson. She produced a not inconsiderable pile of old Strand magazines, all printed in German.

"There are no pictures of you, Mister Holmes, but several of the issues have a picture of the Doctor. Franz reads and keeps every issue, except for the ones that he passes on to our children. We have a daughter and three sons who also read the magazine. If they happen to miss an issue, Franz lends them one of his." She smiled broadly. "To the best of my recollection, none of them has ever returned a copy."

She said, more seriously, "Mister Holmes, I know that when you are involved, it is a very serious matter, so I must confess that I am quite concerned at your being here...not that you are not welcome."

Holmes tried to put her at ease. "Contrary to the impression one would gain from the Strand articles, I am involved in many mundane matters." He produced a business card and handed it to her.

"As you can see, I am not a policeman, I am a consulting detective. I often get requests to find missing relatives, find lost or stolen articles, or verify backgrounds of people for myriad reasons. Obviously, Doctor Watson only publishes the most sensational of our engagements in the Strand. Lost puppies don't sell magazines."

We all smiled and she did seem more at ease, but I noticed that Holmes had not told the *complete* truth. While what he said was accurate, he failed to mention that it had been the better part of twenty years since he had accepted one of those 'mundane matters' as an engagement.

Before Claire Moeller could ask whether we were there on a mundane matter, her husband arrived home. It seemed to me, at first glance, that he could not possibly be our man. He was shorter than I would have expected, speculating on what type of man this lady would have chosen, and quite a bit heavier.

His handshake and manner were very firm and he looked directly into the eyes of whomever he was addressing. One had the impression that he had been trimmer, possibly an athlete in his youth, but had not been as fastidious with his dieting and exercise habits over the years.

"Herr Moeller, I will get directly to the point, since I'm sure you are tired after a day's work and in need of your supper."

Moeller just nodded.

"May I ask what your relationship is with Karl Mundt?"

"The banker?"

"Yes."

"I *have* no relationship with Mundt and I have never seen him in my life. The only reason I know his name is because it is in the newspaper frequently. Why would you ask me that?"

"I'll get to that in a moment," Holmes said. An evasion, I was sure, because I had heard him say that in the past and never get back to it.

"May I ask what your work is and why you were in London on Friday?"

"You may. I am a vendor of pharmaceuticals and was in London in that regard. Now, I must insist that you tell me why you are here. While my life is enjoyable and productive, it would also make a very dull story for the Strand. Do you suspect me of something?"

Holmes brushed past the question and continued with others before Moeller had a chance to object. For his part, Moeller seemed to realize that he was not going to get any answers until Holmes had asked all of his questions, and he accepted that. There is something disconcerting about the presence of a law enforcement officer in your home, even if one is without guilt.

After half an hour of gentle interrogation, Holmes seemed to come to the end. "Herr Moeller, I have just one more question and we'll take our leave. Please do not read anything into the question. It is routine and must be asked. Will the gentlemen you said you were with all day Friday, Smathers and Craddock, verify your story...there will be no gaps in time?"

"There were no gaps and they will absolutely verify it."

The interview wound down to a sincere thank you from Holmes and I for the gracious patience both of the Moellers had shown.

As we rose to leave, Claire Moeller first invited us to stay and share their evening meal, but as Holmes pleaded the need to get to another interview, she snatched the Strand magazines and had us sign copies for all their children and several friends.

This seemed to happen every time we interviewed anyone who read the Strand, but I suppose it is understandable and, given their cooperation, the least we could do.

Back in the cab, I was appalled to hear Holmes give the driver the other address rather than direct him to Schneller's hotel.

"Holmes, this is absurd. It's late, we don't have a room for the night and..."

"We do have a room for the night, old fellow. I booked us into Schneller's by telegram and asked them to reserve us a table for a late seating at Braun's Café. I doubt that we will see Herr Friedrich tonight, but I would like to take a quick look at his home. We will then see him in the morning."

The class of neighborhood and the quality of the homes on Friedrich's street were quite similar to the Moellers, upper middle class and comfortable.

To my great satisfaction, if not elation, the house was completely dark. We traveled around to the back and saw nothing there either. To my chagrin, Holmes actually mounted the porch and unabashedly stared through the chap's windows.

Eventually he gave up and returned to the carriage with a dour expression on his face. "Too dark to see a thing." I suppressed a grateful smile. We would soon discover that there was nothing to smile about in that home.

⚜

The morning brought rain and a stale croissant with my tea. As usual, I had to eat hurriedly, trying to ignore Holmes' impatient grunts and snorts.

To my surprise, we did not head directly to the home of Meyer Friedrich, but to the office of Gerhard Schmidt, the Director of the Zurich branch of the Swiss National Police. Holmes had been of great assistance in the solution of a crime wave in Zurich several years earlier, deflecting the credit to Schmidt, as he did so often with Inspector Lestrade.

Needless to say, we were greeted enthusiastically upon our arrival. As tea was served, Holmes laid out for Schmidt several of the details of the assassination attempt upon the Queen and Prime Minister, concluding with the murder of the young man Holmes identified as Ian

McDonough. He did not mention that he was the son of the infamous Sebastian Moran.

As Holmes concluded his narration, Schmidt shook his head, and recapped his understanding of what Holmes had just laid out.

"So Holmes, you are saying that this deranged young man, McDonough, planned to kill the Queen and Prime Minister, but was apprehended by yourself... and Scotland Yard," he added with a knowing smile.

"Correct," Holmes replied.

"And you think that McDonough was then murdered by Meyer Friedrich?"

"That is the line of inquiry that we are following, although everything that we have in the way of evidence for McDonough's murder is highly circumstantial."

"Can you connect Friedrich with McDonough?"

Holmes shook his head. "We do not, at this point, know of any connection. We believe that Friedrich is merely a hired assassin."

Schmidt breathed deeply, digesting the story. "That is a complete story, Mister Holmes, except for the one detail that you can not have overlooked, but have chosen not to tell me. Who hired Friedrich?"

Holmes smiled. "As you can understand, Director Schmidt, I am loath to sully a man's good name without something at least approximating proof. We have only a theory at this point, although it is not baseless. We have a strong feeling."

"How can I be of service if I do not know everything?"

"Let me suggest that we proceed in this fashion. You accompany Doctor Watson and I as we interview

Friedrich. If I learn anything that points to the accuracy of my theory, I will tell you the complete details and we will go immediately to confront the man responsible for McDonough's murder."

"I suppose that will have to be good enough," Schmidt said unenthusiastically.

⚜

We arrived at the corner of Meyer Friedrich's street in a police carriage, with another close behind, and disembarked. Schmidt dispatched three uniformed officers to approach the house from the rear, but not enter. Their assignment was to be certain that no one exited as we approached from the front.

The rear covered, Holmes, Schmidt and I, accompanied by two other uniformed police knocked loudly on the front door. With no answer forthcoming, Schmidt knocked again, this time jiggling the door handle as he did. As expected, it was locked.

I watched as Holmes looked through a large window to the left of the door and Schmidt to the right. Schmidt quickly said, "Mister Holmes."

Holmes walked over, peered in, and looked back to Schmidt. As I went to take a peek, Schmidt looked to one of the uniforms and nodded his head toward the door. The officer quickly forced the door open and we entered. An immediate right turn into the living room brought us to a ghastly scene.

A large, fully dressed man lay flat on his back, obviously dead, with a massive pattern of blood covering his chest. As a physician, I approached the body and tested for a pulse, finding none. It was not necessary to ponder the cause of death since there were clearly three bullet wounds to the chest, at least one of which had to have penetrated the heart.

I stepped back, knowing that Holmes did not like even the smallest of disturbances of a crime scene until he had examined it in detail.

There was a small white envelope standing on end and leaning against the left side of his body. It appeared as though the killer had dropped it on the dead man's stomach and it had rolled to the side.

Holmes picked the envelope up and glanced at the front. At first his eyes seemed to widen in amazement, but a small wry smile quickly crossed his face. He held the envelope up for Schmidt and I to see. Two words had been written on the front; "Sherlock Holmes."

Holmes opened the unsealed envelope and read the note aloud, "Mister Holmes, I will be very surprised if you are not the one to open this note. I should be disappointed in you if the police figured anything out before you.

"If you are here, you know that this man killed the man you have known as Ian McDonough. Since you arrested Ian at the cathedral, you undoubtedly also know who he really was.

"I understand that Friedrich here was not the puppet master, but a paid assassin. Nevertheless, he has received an assassin's just reward. Hopefully, by the time you receive this note the puppet master will also have been rewarded."

"Great Scott! Schmidt, we haven't a moment to lose. We must get to Karl Mundt's bank immediately!"

As we raced through the streets of Zurich, Holmes revealed to Schmidt everything that he had not yet told him, the salient point being that Mundt was the only one that stood to benefit from Ian's death, unless there were much broader dynamics at play than those presently known.

"The mastermind of this plot was indeed the young Ian McDonough, although he is not quite as young as he looked. His *precise* motive will not be known until we catch his sister, and possibly not even then. But all of that is a discussion for another time. Ian's sister, alias Rene LaDier, in truth, Isabella Moran, was probably very close to the scene when Ian was captured. No one, save Karl Mundt, knows what she looks like, so she could have been anywhere.

"She was undoubtedly as surprised as we were at her brother's murder, and perhaps even quicker to conclude who was responsible. For all we know she could have seen him flee, possibly even recognized him, given her likely underworld connections.

"Whatever the case, she tracked down Meyer Friedrich, possibly the same way we did, and assassinated him. She also announced that her next victim will be Karl Mundt, unless we are able to save him."

"I'm afraid I'm lost in all of this, Mister Holmes. How is Karl Mundt connected to any of this? He is a very respectable..."

"I believe less respectable than you think, but here is the connection." Holmes then went through the bilking of Mundt and his bank by the young Morans, particularly Isabella in the role of Rene Ladier.

"We'll have to suspend the explanation for now," Holmes said, as the carriage arrived in front of the bank. We hopped out and raced up the stairs to Mundt's office.

We all seemed to breathe a sigh of relief at the normalcy we observed as we passed through the large glass doors directly in front of his secretary's desk. On closer inspection, she seemed worried and upset and was looking back at his closed door, as we burst into the foyer.

"We are here to see Herr Mundt," Holmes said curtly, "please announce us."

"I'm sorry, sir. That is impossible. He is in an important conf..."

Holmes started for the door, as she jumped to her feet, "Stop! The police are in there! You can't go in."

That did stop Holmes. He turned to face her. "Why are the police in there?"

"I can't tell you anything, but he can't be disturbed."

Director of Police Schmidt held his badge up as he hurried toward the door. "We are also the police."

We pushed through the door, startling a distraught looking Karl Mundt and two officers seated facing him. They turned at the sound and were amazed at the sight of their superior entering the room.

"Director..."

"What has happened, Hans," he said to the officer closest to him, "why are you here?"

"We were sent for, sir. An associate of Herr Mundt's was murdered less than an hour ago and we are investigating. Your deputy sent us out in your absence, sir."

"Who was murdered?" Schmidt asked, "and how?"

"His name was Herman Boelking and he was shot. Since he was sitting beside Herr Mundt..."

"Where?" Holmes interjected.

"Across the street, sir. It was a business luncheon and both Boelking and Mundt were scheduled to speak. As Boelking was being introduced, he was shot."

Holmes went to the window, looking in every possible direction. He seemed to be satisfied with what he found and returned to Schmidt's side. I assumed he was making sure there was no available vantage point from which to take another shot at Mundt.

"And did you apprehend the shooter?" Schmidt asked.

"No sir. Nobody saw a thing. Amazingly, no one even claimed to hear the shot fired, but as Boelking rose he grabbed his stomach and fell to the floor and everything was suddenly chaotic."

"What? In a crowded room, no one hears a shot? That's absurd, " said Schmidt.

"I can explain that, Director." Holmes said. We had not mentioned the air gun for which Sebastian Moran was so notorious.

Schmidt turned to Holmes, who shook his head quickly. "Not now."

Turning to Hans, Holmes said, "Let's recap. Are you saying...?"

"May I ask who you are, sir?"

"Pardon me, I should have introduced myself. I am Sherlock Holmes and this is my associate, Doctor John Watson."

The officer stared for a moment, then turned to Schmidt, who gave him a brusque nod.

He turned quickly back to Holmes. "A recap, sir?"

"Yes, Hans. As I understand what you have said, Mundt and Boelking sat side by side, Boelking rose to address the audience and fell to the floor, clutching his chest. A quick examination revealed that he had been shot, but a crowd of...?"

"About a hundred, twenty-five, sir."

"A crowd of over a hundred and no one knew that a shot had been fired."

He said it as a statement rather than a question.

"That is correct, sir. Several thought he had had a heart attack."

Holmes nodded. "And no weapon and nothing suspicious was seen by this large crowd."

"That is correct, sir, as amazing as it seems. But with no gun shot sound, it could have come from anywhere in the room. For that matter, there are several doors and a balcony. It is quite a large room. We are still trying to determine where the shot was fired from, sir."

"Why are you here with Herr Mundt? Out of all the others?"

"He asked to be escorted back to his office, and being next to the murder victim and the fact that we would want a statement from him anyway..."

Holmes looked hard over to Mundt. "And has he given you a statement, officer?"

"Nothing of any value, sir. He says he has no idea why someone would want to shoot Herr Boelking."

"I don't find that in the least surprising," Holmes said with an edge in his voice that seemed to surprise the officer. Mundt did not look up, staring at his desk, seemingly frightened and confused.

"Is there anything else you can tell us?" Holmes asked.

"Just that there are four officers in the room where the murder occurred. About fifty of the guests were still there and they are being questioned. We have a list that supposedly has the names of everyone who registered for the affair, but as I said, there is very easy access to the room from several directions"

Holmes walked over and whispered something in Director Schmidt's ear. Schmidt nodded and dismissed the officer we knew only as Hans, and his partner. They left with instructions to report back about anything that may turn up in the investigation of the murder scene.

As the officers left, all eyes turned to Mundt, who still had not lifted his head. We took seats facing him, with Holmes in front and the closest to the forlorn looking banker. I almost felt a twinge of sympathy for him. Holmes did not.

"Herr Mundt." Holmes said simply.

He looked up, showing a face of deep sorrow. "I can't tell you how deeply I feel the loss of my dear friend..."

"Don't waste our time, Herr Mundt," Holmes said sharply.

Mundt looked up, seemingly quite surprised at Holmes' tone, although I was not. It was a common interrogation technique of the master detective's to set a criminal back on his heels and run over him before he had a chance to collect his thoughts. I had always found it very effective, even knowing that it was coming.

Though I had seen it many times, each criminal that he had buffaloed only saw it once. The only miscreant who I had ever seen retain his poise in the face of Holmes' onslaught was the devilish Professor Moriarty. Of course he wound up his days of crime dead.

Mundt looked to Holmes curiously and with a growing anger. "Your tone of voice, sir..."

"Will only get worse," Holmes interrupted, "unless you drop your absurd facade of innocence and face the fact that we know everything that you have done."

"How dare you speak to me in such a manner, especially after the devastating loss I have just suffered."

"You have suffered no loss. Your friend, Boelking, if he really was such a thing, has suffered the loss. But he is the second person to die because of your crimes."

"See here Mister Holmes..."

"Let me save you the trouble of any denials. We came here directly from the home of Meyer Friedrich, whom you paid to assassinate Ian Mc Donough. The substantial amount of money you gave him will be found to have your fingerprints all over it. The prints, along with his testimony, would be more than enough to send you to the gallows. Believe me, Herr Mundt, it is over."

We had come so quickly to the critical point. It was a scathing attack on Mundt, but in fact, we had no testimony from Friedrich, who was, of course, quite seriously dead, and we had not recovered any money as yet. Mundt, of course, did not know that. In the first stage of Holmes' assault, he did not break, though he remained on the verge.

"Your only hope for avoiding the gallows," Holmes pressed on, "is to convince us that there are extenuating circumstances. You would be wise to make a complete confession now."

Mundt maintained a stolid countenance, obviously thinking furiously about whether there was any chance for a plausible denial.

Seeking to apply a coup d' grace to any hope Mundt may have of surviving the encounter, Holmes said to Mundt. "Please send your secretary to fetch the gentleman in charge of your safe boxes and tell him to bring his list of subscribers to the boxes, immediately."

Mundt looked as though he had been struck by yet another bolt of lightning. "You have no right to see such a list. How do you dare..."

"Mundt," Schmidt cut him off, "do not make it necessary to chain you to your chair while I fetch a warrant and return within the hour. It will serve you no good purpose."

Mundt had a resigned look on his face, tinged with only the slightest hope that we would find nothing recognizable on the list. At last, he scribbled a note, called for his secretary, and dispatched her to her errand.

For the eight minutes it took to arrange delivery of the document, Holmes stared at Mundt, who tried to meet his gaze, but was unable to maintain it. He lowered his eyes to papers on his desk, probably not even seeing them.

A wiry, timid little man wearing a silver pince nez, came cautiously into the room and approached Mundt's desk. Holmes snatched the sheaf of papers from his hand and told the man to take a seat. He looked over to Mundt, who just nodded.

Holmes took a small scrap of paper from his waistcoat pocket and smoothed it out on the desk. It contained a six digit number. Holmes flipped several pages at a time until he came to the right sheet, then ran his finger down two-thirds of the list and stopped.

He shook his head and smiled mirthlessly. Summoning the pince nez chap, he handed him the scrap of paper with the number on it and ordered him to bring that numbered box to the office immediately.

"I can't do that, sir. Bank rules preclude..."

Schmidt walked to within a foot of him, held his badge six inches from the bewildered man's nose and barked sharply, "Get the box."

He looked to Mundt, who merely gave him a resigned nod.

The pince nez stopped at the door and said, "The box will be of no value without a matching key. It requires two..."

"Get the box and bring the bank's copy." Holmes said brusquely.

Holmes looked back to Mundt. "The noose is tightening, Herr Mundt. You would do well to begin writing your full confession, now."

Mundt continued to stare at the desk, perhaps knowing that he was beaten, but seeking, by mental gyration, some artifice that might yet save the day. None was yet forthcoming.

As Mundt sat impassively, Holmes turned the list of box numbers toward me and placed his finger beside a name. I was stunned to see the name of Garret Dickinson.

We waited in silence as the tension in the room grew. Holmes continued staring at Mundt and finally asked, "What will we find in the box, Herr Mundt."

"I don't have the faintest idea what you will find. I have never seen the inside of a customer's box."

Holmes smiled. "How do you account for the notation on the sheet saying that the box was opened and examined twice at your direction?"

Mundt seemed to turn white, I thought he might be about to convulse. "It says no such thing," he responded weakly.

Holmes snatched up the list and went around to Mundt's side of the desk, holding the sheet before him and pointing to the line he had directed me to. Mundt rolled his eyes in amazement and disgust, then closed them as he shook his head. "That idiot," he muttered.

Ten minutes later, the box was set before Holmes, who took from his waistcoat pocket the key that had been around Ian McDonough's neck, and inserted it into the keyhole. Mundt glared malevolently at his hapless safe box attendant. I pictured Mundt dropping him from the office window if the opportunity arose.

"Put your key in and leave," Holmes told the pince nez. He complied quickly, seeming happy to be out from under the fury of Mundt's glare.

As the man left, Holmes reached forward and turned both keys simultaneously, producing faint clicks. Looking around to each of us in the room, Holmes lifted the top off the deep box, as I gasped involuntarily. It was literally stuffed with high denomination currency from at least three countries that I could recognize at a glance, and what I perceived to be easily negotiable bearer bonds.

Holmes seemed a bit concerned at first, taking several packets of currency out of the box and dropping them on the desk. He rifled around the box, moving the remaining contents, until a Voila! Look crossed his face. He took out a small velvet bag, pulled the strings, and dropped the Green Fire of the Incas onto a soft folder.

No one moved or spoke for a moment, such was our shock. Not Holmes, of course. It seemed that he expected to find it there.

"Gentlemen," said Holmes, "what we see before us is actually two things. One is the Green Fire of the Incas, but it is also the reason that Ferdinand Moran is dead. And to account for that, we look to Karl Mundt who had better be very persuasive about mitigation if he hopes to avoid the gallows."

Mundt collapsed like a house of cards. The notations proved that he knew the emerald was in the box, and his belief that we had captured Meyer Friedrich alive, and that he had not only informed on Mundt, but had produced money with Mundt's fingerprints on it was overwhelming. There was no way out. He shook his head, obviously resigned to his fate

"That idiot Friedrich. If he had not gotten himself caught, you would never have had a way to connect me to anything."

Holmes said, "He was more effective than the one you sent to assassinate Norma Bainsteas."

Mundt shook his head. "Norma Bainsteas? No, she was never the target. For one thing, I did not know whether she was Rene LaDier or not.

"It was always that young swine, Garret Dickinson, or Ian McDonough as you knew him, or Ferdinand something, as you also call him, whoever the devil that is."

Holmes nodded, but seemed surprised. "How did you know who he was, or how he was involved?"

"The merest chance encounter. When Rene LaDier was in the process of bilking me out of three million Francs, she was here to sign some loan papers. Later in the morning, I left to meet some associates for an early lunch and I saw her exiting a shop. She couldn't see me, but as she stood at the curb, a carriage pulled up. A young sandy haired man jumped out to greet her and help her into the cab.

"I assumed it was her husband or a very close friend because they greeted each other warmly. I had a very good look at him because he was facing me, though talking to her. The encounter had no significance because her project still seemed legitimate. Since Rene was such an attractive woman, I couldn't help but look closely at a man who might have been her mate. He has an easy face to remember."

Mundt stopped and shook his head. "When Rene's perfidy became evident, I assumed I'd never see her or him again, but incredibly, I did.

"I know that you are aware that I traveled to London to try to persuade that pigheaded Wainwright to suppress the story detailing my humiliation at the hands of Rene LaDier. I almost wound up buying the magazine to kill that story. I would have sacked that arrogant dolt within minutes after completion of the deal.

"After arguing with Wainwright, as you may recall, I went back to Zurich and was approached by Rene to use my bank as a clearing house for the money she would be getting from the Strand. She knew that she could extort these services from me because there was nothing illegal about it. She didn't want any scrutiny of the transactions. It was a way to get the money legally without having to identify herself or draw any attention to herself.

"Then I came to your rooms on Baker Street to tell you of it and who do I find there, but Wainwright and this young man that I had seen with Rene, although he did not know me, and did not know that I had seen him. He is introduced to me as Ian McDonough, Wainwright's assistant.

"Fortunately, I was able to secure a promise not to publish it. But be all of that as it may, you can imagine my astonishment to see a man who, by then, I thought was involved in stealing a large sum of money from me, now in the employ of the magazine that was preparing to publish the whole story."

Holmes nodded as though he understood, while I sat mesmerized at this banking giant relating his descent into the criminal world. Schmidt was trying to be somewhat unobtrusive, but was writing furiously as though trying to take down every word.

Holmes prodded, to keep him talking, "So when you saw young Ian, you recognized him?"

"Of course. If fifty years passed, I would remember that face."

"But you said nothing."

"Certainly not, and I think for quite obvious reasons. I thought that he could possibly lead me to Rene, at a time and place of my choosing. She was the one I wanted."

Holmes said, "A logical plan, but there is one more major point to clarify."

"There is," Mundt agreed, "the safe box."

He breathed deeply and nestled more comfortably in his chair. "I am a very detailed man in my work. This bank operates so effectively because I know what is going on everywhere. I review long lists of deposits and withdrawals daily.

"I personally approve all substantial loan requests and study the file on them. I must sign for everything over a hundred thousand Francs.

"Also...on a random basis, three or four time a week, I view the activity in the safe box area. Obviously, I can't see the customer when he is in the vault, but I have a vantage point from which I can see those entering the vault.

"In the course of my job as Managing Director, I feel it is important to be on top of everything I possibly can. I saw this young man once with Rene Ladier, then

I saw him at a different time entering the safe boxes. That obviously alerted me.

"Then, to my complete astonishment, I saw him at Wainwright's office as some kind of an assistant. Putting things together, as you certainly have already done, or you wouldn't be here, I realized that this might be much bigger than just what they had stolen from me."

"*And...*" Holmes prodded, to keep him talking.

"*And* I decided that I had to get into that safe box, thinking that it may have my three million Francs in it. If so, I was planning to waylay this Garret Dickinson the next time he came in and threaten to expose him unless he immediately returned my money. I had all sorts of threats prepared, mainly involving the police.

"How did you get into the box itself? Your laws are very strict, as I understand them."

Mundt smiled sardonically. "The laws are very strict to keep outsiders from inquiring too deeply. We in the banking industry forced the enactment of those laws for our own benefit, no one else's. Parliament did exactly as we, collectively, asked them to do. The secrecy is one of the reasons banking is such a profitable industry in Switzerland. Anyone with anything to hide secretes it in one of our numbered accounts.

"Internally, we more or less do as we please. I made up a convincing story for Klaus, the little weasel with the pince nez, about an inquiry from the authorities about Dickinson's safe box. The first time I looked into it, I found a great deal of money, far more than the three million he owed me.

"The second time, to my complete astonishment, I found the emerald. That, as you said earlier, sealed

Dickinson's fate. He had to die, leaving me with the emerald and most of the currency and bearer bonds. After his demise I planned to leave some of the cash and the nonnegotiable bonds, which were of no value to me anyway."

Although I did not normally interrupt when Holmes was interrogating, I sensed that we were drawing to a close and that all the important information had already been gleaned. I asked, "Why didn't you just take the emerald and the money and let Ian, or Dickinson as you know him, alone. How could he possibly get it back from you?"

"That certainly occurred to me, but it was not possible. If he had gotten caught for something or other and revealed the presence of the emerald in my bank, it would have been a world wide story. The emerald would have been useless to me even if I got away with it. The police would be watching me night and day for the rest of my life. I would not even feel safe looking at it in the security of my own cellar, not to mention trying to sell it. No, Doctor, Dickinson had to be removed."

Holmes addressed Mundt. "You came close."

"I did, Mister Holmes," he said ruefully, "I did, but I must say that I find it incredible, Mister Holmes, your reputation notwithstanding, that you have figured all of this out from afar, including the arrest and breaking of Meyer Friedrich, not to mention having the actual number of Dickinson's safe box number. You seem to have everything too nicely sorted out for me to even try to deny it."

Holmes smiled, still not informing Mundt that Friedrich was actually dead, saying simply, "So it would seem."

Holmes rose and looked over to Police Director Schmidt. "I believe that you have all the information you need, sir."

"I do, Mister Holmes."

"That being the case, we will leave you to deal with the arrest of Herr Mundt, while Doctor Watson and I will take our leave. Before we do, though, I have a final request. For the sake of the British museum, and its director, who is a personal friend of the doctor and I, please stress that the emerald was actually stolen in Munich, and not in London."

Schmidt smiled warmly. "With the greatest of pleasure, sir."

EPILOG

I SUPPOSE it would not be unseemly to describe it as a celebratory dinner of victory. More glowing terms than the more understated Holmes would have used, but considering the conviviality of the evening, quite appropriate.

Roger Dalton, Director of the British Museum, had stopped in late in the afternoon to gush his gratitude in the most effusive manner and Holmes had insisted that he stay for dinner. Dalton carried a copy of the London Times, which blazed a headline heralding the recovery of the Green Fire of the Incas.

In only slightly smaller type, the paper announced that the gem had most definitely been stolen from the Munich Museum. While Sherlock Holmes' name got only a passing reference, there was no doubt in Dalton's mind of the source of the clarification. "I knew immediately that you had arranged it, Mister Holmes."

While not denying it, Holmes went on to explain that Inspector Lestrade, who had been lavishly praised in an earlier edition of the times for the brief capture of Ian McDonough, would also be coming to dine.

The other invitees were Nevin Wainwright, Managing Editor of the Strand Magazine and Mycroft Holmes, who adamantly refused to come unless the dinner was held either at the Diogenes Club or his own flat.

There was little doubt that he would, in fact, show up, while showing his displeasure at the indignity being visited upon him. He had last been to our rooms several years earlier as we discussed the conclusion of a major case that I later published as The Insidious Succession.

Lestrade and Wainwright were as ebullient as Mycroft was dour upon their arrivals, but after only a few glasses of his favorite Madeira, Mycroft was in as high a state of elation as everyone else.

We toasted Holmes, the Queen, the Prime Minister, Lestrade, and anyone else that we could think of.

The meal was a tour de force of gustatory elegance from the kitchen of the venerable Mrs. Hudson.

Lestrade babbled excitedly about a medal pinned to his lapel by the Queen herself as a reward for his capture of the killer and the quiet prevention of anything that would mar the special day of her son's wedding.

Mycroft managed not to frown, and even congratulated Lestrade on his good fortune. To further demonstrate his good will, Mycroft even waited until much later in the evening to mention that the Queen would like Holmes to reconsider his decision to decline knighthood. Holmes merely nodded, but there was little doubt that he would decline again.

Wainwright encouraged me to spend as little time as possible on such trivialities as food and sleep until I had finished the complete story of what he would entitle Reports from the Dark Side. He insisted even more vehemently that I spend no time on any other case until this one was published.

I may not have evinced the level of urgency that Wainwright felt, so he blurted out an offer to double my fee if I would guarantee completion by a date certain. That elicited a response more to his liking.

The merriment continued to an hour later than normal, but no one seemed in any hurry to end the evening.

Finally, Mycroft, feigning exasperation, said to Holmes, "Alright, Sherlock, you've waited me out and forced me to bring it up. The final detail."

Lestrade, Wainwright and I went blank-faced in surprise. "The final detail?" I asked.

Holmes smiled broadly. "There *is* a final important detail, but as you know, Mycroft and I do quite a bit of mental jousting. Had he left for the evening without all questions answered, I would have been able to chide him for the next several months about it."

Not wanting to embarrass myself, I left it to Wainwright to ask what the final detail was.

"Rene LaDier, of course. She is still out there. That is what Mycroft is referring to."

Mycroft cracked a smile. "Correct. And how do you intend to capture *her*?"

"It's unlikely that I ever will, gentlemen, although...I do have a letter from her. It arrived in today's mail, sent from somewhere in London."

"Great heaven," I blurted out, "Why didn't you tell us?"

"I was waiting for Mycroft to ask, and since he has, I will read it to you.'

He withdrew a single sheet of paper from an envelope on his desk and leaned toward the lamp.

> *"Mister Holmes, I am deeply saddened by the death of my brother, Ferdinand, but recognize that it was probably inevitable. He simply could never see the justice of daddy's incarceration, or get over the sorrow of his brokenness in his declining years.*
>
> *"You saw Colonel Sebastian Moran as an unredeemable criminal, who had to be put away. Ferdy saw him as a towering intellectual giant who, in his twisted way, was entitled to the riches of the privileged if he was clever enough to steal them away. He worshipped daddy as both hero and father.*
>
> *"I am several years older than Ferdy and able to see daddy as father and criminal, and death or incarceration as his inevitable fate.*
>
> *"I tried over the years to reason it out with Ferdy, but he was obsessed with what he considered righteous vengeance, upon you as the man who captured daddy and upon the Queen and Prime Minister as symbols of the system that crushed his father.*

"I tried to tell him that capturing criminals is what you do. There was no more reason to be mad at you than at a tiger that ate your goat. That's what tigers do. So adamant was Ferdinand that he could not even be moved when I pointed out that daddy was captured in the act of trying to kill you.

"Although he was normally a logical man, this obsession was his undoing.

"Setting all of that aside and looking to the future, let me say this. I have never been knowingly involved in anyone's death, except for the venal swine, Meyer Friedrich, and the world is a better place for his passing.

"The reason I say that is that I am going away and retiring from this life of crime. By the time you receive this letter, I will be out of the United Kingdom altogether. You would be very well advised to spend your time on pursuits other than seeking me because you will not find me.

"Friedrich was retired in Switzerland and I will not be living in the United Kingdom again. Please do not risk your precious life trying to find me in someone else's jurisdiction.

I do not expect our paths to cross again."

⊰ঙ্গৈ⊱

Holmes refolded the letter.

"Gentlemen," he said, "we may never know if she is sincere in her intentions or trying to deceive us once again. But I *am* convinced that she has left, or will leave, Great Britain and is therefore someone else's problem.

"I immediately wrote a letter to Gerhard Schmidt in Zurich and apprised him of the situation. The only country other than England that we know she habituates, *for certain*, is Switzerland and that is also the only place that she has committed a murder that she has confessed to.

"For us, this case that began with a submission to Mister Wainwright so many months ago will be concluded and consigned to our memories as soon as Doctor Watson publishes his account, which I'm sure will be unconscionably embellished, in the Strand."

Wainwright took up his glass and said, "A final toast, then. 'To Sherlock Holmes, and a successful conclusion to Reports from the Dark Side."

Five glasses met between us, tinkled softly, and were enthusiastically emptied.

Printed in the United States
213050BV00001B/5/P

9 781440 120459